# The Marriage Book

Nicky and Sila Lee

Illustrated by Charlie Mackesy

Alpha Resources
Alpha North America

Published in North America by Alpha North America, 74 Trinity Place, New York, NY 10006



This edition issued by special arrangement with Alpha International, Holy Trinity Brompton, Brompton Road, London SW7 1JA, UK

*The Marriage Book*
by Nicky and Sila Lee



First printed by Alpha North America in 2002

Printed in the United States of America



Cover design by Button Design
Illustrations by Charlie Mackesy

ISBN 10: 1-931808-48-1
ISBN 13: 978-1-931808-48-4

4 5 6 7 8 9 10 Printing/Year 11 10 09 08 07

# Contents

# Foreword

Marriage is under attack in our society. Many feel it is an outdated institution. In the UK the number of marriages per year has been falling steadily. Those who do get married find it increasingly difficult to stay married. There has been an alarming rise in the divorce rate. What is the answer to all of this? Why should we get married? How can we stay married?

In this book Nicky and Sila answer these questions, showing us the value and potential of any marriage. They suggest how we can not only stay married, but also make the most of our married lives together.

Nicky has been my closest friend for over thirty years. We were at school together and we shared rooms at university. He has always been one step ahead and I have tried to follow in his footsteps. He became a Christian on February 14, 1974. Forty-eight hours later he led me to Christ. Nicky and Sila married in 1976. Eighteen months later Pippa and I followed suit. Our first three children are approximately the same age. They went on to have a fourth.

After university our paths separated as Nicky went off to teach in Japan and I practiced law. Then Nicky went to theological college, and one year later I followed. Nicky and Sila returned to London to join the staff of Holy Trinity Brompton (HTB). One year later we followed. Nicky and Sila ran Alpha for five years, passing the baton in 1990.

They have taught us many things. In particular, we have learned so much from the example of their marriage and family life. We have observed in their home something to which we can aspire.

Nicky and Sila have run *The Marriage Course* at HTB since 1996 and already many couples have found their marriages enriched by it. For some it has literally saved their marriages from separation or divorce. For others it has turned the water of an ordinary marriage into the wine of a strong marriage, a transformation made possible by the presence of Jesus Christ. For still others, the course has provided a forum to think creatively about making a good and healthy marriage even better.

While reading this book, you may feel that the Lees' marriage is "too good to be true," but having observed it for over twenty-four years, let me assure you that it is entirely true and that it inspires us to aim for the very best.

Our hope and prayer is that through this book, many more people would be able to enjoy the fruit of Nicky and Sila's example and wisdom.

*Nicky Gumbel*

# Preface

We would like to thank the many people who have helped us with this book. Between them they have spent hundreds of hours reading the manuscripts and suggesting changes and additions. The book could not have been written without them. We are particularly grateful to John and Diana Collins and Sandy and Annette Millar who have inspired us through their teaching and their lives. We are also very grateful to those who have told us stories from their own marriages, which have rooted the theory in everyday experience.

We would like to express our enormous gratitude to Philippa Pearson-Miles, Mary Ellis, and Joanna Desmond for typing and retyping endless changes with great speed, skill, and patience and to Charlie Mackesy for the fun he has brought to our family as well as to the book. To Jo Glen, our editor, we want to say a special thank you. Without her compelling enthusiasm, humor, imagination, and new ideas each time we got stuck, this book might never have been finished. We would also like to thank Nicky and Pippa Gumbel not only for their friendship and encouragement over so many years but for persuading us to start this project.

Finally we would like to thank our own parents for their constant love and the model of two long and happy marriages.

*Nicky and Sila Lee*

Love is patient,
love is kind.
It does not envy,
it does not boast,
it is not proud.
It is not rude,
it is not self-seeking,
it is not easily angered,
it keeps no record of wrongs.
Love does not delight in evil
but rejoices with the truth.
It always protects,
always trusts,
always hopes,
always perseveres.
Love never fails.

*1 Corinthians 13:4–8a*

# Introduction

## Nicky's story

I first set eyes on Sila at Swansea Docks. I was en route to southwest Ireland for the summer holidays, having just left school. I was eighteen; she was seventeen. It was love at first sight. We spent two weeks in next-door holiday cottages in one of the most beautiful and unspoiled corners of the British Isles—in southwest Cork. Most of that time I hardly dared believe she might feel anything for me at all. Two days before she left I plucked up courage and told her my feelings and found to my astonishment that she felt the same. I could hardly believe it.

Sila was still at school and had "A" levels to take. I had nine months before starting university and realized she probably wouldn't pass any of them if I stayed in the same country, so I went backpacking in Africa on my own. Africa was unlike anything I had experienced before. I felt in awe of the landscape, people, and culture, but secretly I was longing to be back in England with Sila. I was lonely much of the time and lived for the letters she wrote to the capital cities of the countries I traveled through from Addis Ababa to Cape Town. It worked well until I reached South Africa. There had been a gap of more than six weeks when I arrived in Cape Town, pinning all my hopes on a letter being there, only to find nothing (except one from my mother). I was devastated.

I began to wonder if Sila had cooled off because of the time I had been away. I felt no desire to go back to England if that was the case. After several weeks of checking at the post office every day, I hitchhiked back to Johannesburg as a last resort and was elated to find a letter I had just missed four weeks previously. I took the first flight home.

I immediately went to see Sila at her boarding school which was a cross between a prison, to keep the girls in, and a fortress, to keep the boys out. After three wonderful hours together, we realized too late that she was locked out. She was caught climbing in through a window at midnight and was grounded for her last two weeks of school life.

I went to university and Sila left school and moved to London. At this time I was starting to hear people talk about the Christian faith in a way that was new to me. Increasingly it made sense and caused me to think seriously about the meaning of my life. Yet at the same time I kept it very much at arm's length, as my relationship with Sila was far and away the most important part of my life. I was afraid that if I became a Christian and Sila did not, we might drift apart.

After five months of cautious investigation I realized that I had reached a defining moment. I had to decide one way or the other. I broached the subject with Sila, who responded with her usual enthusiasm. As she heard for herself the claims of Christianity, Sila, like me, felt she had discovered the truth and we both embraced it.

Rather than pushing us apart, our newfound faith seemed to add a new and exciting dimension to our relationship. In fact it opened the door to a perspective on life that I had not known existed before. It seemed as though all the different parts of my life were like the pieces of a jigsaw puzzle: my past, my relationship with Sila, my studying English, my being at university, everything. Suddenly all the pieces fell into place.

In the autumn of 1974, after two years of going out, we both felt, independently, that if we were to know for sure whether we should spend the rest of our lives together, we needed to spend some time apart.

So, early one Monday morning at the beginning of October, I walked with Sila to the station. We agreed that we wouldn't see each other or talk until Christmas.

It was a beautiful autumn morning with a carpet of mist in the faintly orange dawn light. Sila was waving good-bye to me out of the train window, and I wondered if I would ever see her again. I walked back through the still deserted streets of Cambridge feeling as low as I had ever felt in my life. I decided not to go to London at all during that time, as it was too painful to be there without seeing Sila.

However, a week later I was playing football with some friends at my old school. As we set off for the return journey, the friend whose car I was in said, "I hope you don't mind going back via London as I have to pick something up from home." I was horrified, but I did not say anything to him. I just hoped that it wouldn't take him very long. Anyway Sila lived in another part of London.

The friend dropped us in High Street Kensington and said, "I will pick you up here in forty minutes," and then drove off. It was pouring rain, and we stood on the pavement trying to decide what we were going to do. At that moment I looked up, and there, about fifty yards away, walking down the pavement toward me was Sila.

I abandoned my two friends without a word of explanation and ran toward her. Then she saw me. She started running toward me. We flung our arms around each other, and I remember swinging her around and around. I shouted back to my friends not to wait for me.

We went to a café and talked for hours. I discovered that

Sila had been traveling by bus along High Street Kensington, got stuck in heavy traffic, and so had decided to get off the bus and walk the last half-mile to where she was going. That was when she saw me.

Meeting like that was a chance in a million, and we took it as a sign from God. We both felt that if God could cause us to meet in this extraordinary way when we were doing our best to avoid each other, He was more than able to show us over the next three months whether we should spend the rest of our lives together. We agreed again not to see each other until Christmas. This time it felt different. There were still tears, but we believed God would guide us.

Being apart was hard, but by the end of term there was no question in my mind that I wanted to spend the rest of my life with Sila. We resumed going out at the beginning of 1975. I still had another year-and-a-half at university. With Sila coming up for most weekends, it was a time filled with some of the happiest memories of my life.

We were married on July 17, 1976 in Scotland, Sila's home, two weeks after I had graduated from university.

**Sila's story**

I grew up in the highlands of Scotland and my childhood was happy and uneventful. I loved the outdoors, was a tomboy, and thought I lived in the best place in the world. There was only one drawback: a lack of people. So, when my best friend at school, Penny, asked me to spend two weeks of the summer holidays with her in southwest Ireland along with family and friends, I jumped at the opportunity. I was just seventeen and I had no inkling that those two weeks would change my life.

We had to travel by ferry from Swansea to Cork. Swansea docks is the most unpromising place I know, and yet that was where I met him. Nicky drove up behind us in the line of cars, climbed out of an old green mini and smiled. It was love at first sight (or perhaps an overpowering attraction at first sight to be accurate). He wore a large black felt hat (it *was* the '70s), jeans, and a white shirt, and he had a great tan. He was eighteen and I thought, "He's gorgeous!"

We spent two idyllic weeks with a large group of friends. We sailed and swam, fished for mackerel, rowed out to islands for midnight barbecues, and sat under the stars talking into the early hours. All the time I was falling madly and deeply in love. I didn't breathe a word about my feelings to Penny and had no idea whether the feelings were mutual.

Forty-eight hours before returning home to Scotland I discovered that they were, and Nicky kissed me for the first time. Even then, though I was only seventeen (and he wasn't the only boy I'd kissed), I remember lying awake that night thinking that I was going to marry him. I'd been with him every day for two weeks, and I felt as if I couldn't live another day of my life without him.

He then went to Africa for six months, which was agonizing as we were only just getting to know each other. All my friends at school told me not to pin my hopes on the relationship: Africa was far away, six months was a long time, and he was sure to meet someone else during his travels. But our relationship strengthened as we wrote long and increasingly intimate letters, discovering more about each other with thousands of miles between us than we might have done if we'd been together.

The moment I heard his voice on the telephone saying he was back, my heart seemed to stop. The strength of my feelings was almost overwhelming. We parted after that evening of reunion both reassured that our love had only grown during our months apart.

In the autumn of 1973 Nicky went to university and I went to London. I was learning to type in the daytime and taking classes in painting at night, building a portfolio to apply for art college. But the lure of university life and my longing to be with Nicky meant that I spent more time at his university than I did on either of my own courses. Our relationship became close and intense—in some ways too intense for our own good.

Learning about God as I grew up, I never doubted His existence, but this belief had no effect on my lifestyle, except that Nicky and I would occasionally go to the college chapel on Sunday for the early Communion service. I had a vague sense that one day, when I was grown up enough, I would earn my way into heaven if I said a few more prayers, went to a few more services, and did a few more good things in my life. For the moment I didn't need anything. I had Nicky.

By the New Year I had been accepted by Chelsea Art College for the following September. Life seemed to hold new possibilities around every corner. So when Nicky came to London to see me one evening in February of 1974, and started talking to me about Christianity, I was as enthusiastic about that as I was about most other things he suggested. But I had no real understanding of what he was talking about and no idea of the implications.

When I went to see Nicky that weekend, he took me straight to hear a Christian speaker named David MacInnes. I was amazed by what I heard. What had happened for Nicky over a period of about five months took place for me in the space of twenty-four hours.

I was fascinated by what David said. Never before had I heard anybody talk about Jesus Christ like this. Nobody had ever told me I could have a relationship with God. For me relationships were everything. That Friday we talked long into the night with Nicky's best friend, Nicky Gumbel, who at that stage was extremely suspicious about what was happening to us.

On Saturday we went to hear David MacInnes again. He talked about the cross. It was a revelation to me. I kept saying to myself, "Why did nobody ever tell me before *why* Jesus died on the cross?"[1] It was as if everything I had ever known fit together, not just intellectually, but also emotionally and spiritually. Everything made sense when the cross was explained. It was as if my life up to that point had been like a black-and-white still photograph, and suddenly it started to move, first in a sort of blurred slow motion, and then faster and faster until it was in sharp focus and beautiful color. Life became very real in a way I'd never known it before. It was a radical change of perspective, and it was the start of a new freedom in our relationship that I hadn't imagined possible.

Living life with a new faith was exciting. Nicky and I were even more deeply involved with each other. But eight months later we both sensed God leading us to distinguish between our faith and our love for one another. This was one of the most testing times of my life—even more difficult than when Nicky went to Africa. Learning to trust that God had the best plan for us was very hard.

It was a remarkable experience to see God intervening in our lives, as it seemed to us, in a way that could only have been Him. On High Street Kensington when we ran into each other's arms and I shouted "Nicky" at the top of my voice, I was thinking, "God, I will never doubt You again." I knew with great conviction that I could trust Him with everything, even the most precious part of my life—my relationship with Nicky. I believe that God showed me that day that, however much I loved Nicky, it was my love for God and His love for me that were most important in my life.

During those three months apart we each grew in our relationship with God. When we resumed seeing each other, it was with a different foundation to our lives, a foundation of personal faith which has strengthened us in our relationship with each other ever since.

Nicky proposed to me in February of 1976 and we got married in July. I was twenty-one and he was twenty-two.

We write from the vantage point of twenty-four years of marriage. During these years, we have lived in Japan, the northeast of England, and central London. We have experienced together the birth of four children and approximately 1,528 sleep-deprived nights. We have known the strain and joy of having four children under the age of eight, as well as the turbulence and complexity of parenting teenagers. We have been through illness and financial hardship together.

Our experience has not been dissimilar to that of many other couples. We must have driven over 200,000 miles together, talked for 10,000 hours and slept 8,000 nights in the same bed. We have worked together and played together. We have laughed and cried. We have been frustrated, irritated, mystified, and entranced by each other. And we still feel passionately about each other and passionately about marriage.

We are not suggesting for a moment that our own marriage is more special than any other. Indeed, there is no textbook marriage: no blueprint or faultless prototype. Each couple is unique and has its own story to tell. But do those who reach the heights get there by luck? And is it true that those who feel let down by their marriage have simply married the wrong person? Our own experience has shown us that we need certain tools to build a strong, happy marriage. We have had to find out about communication and ways of making each other feel loved. We have had to learn to resolve conflict and to practice forgiveness. We have discovered that the joy of sexual intimacy cannot be taken for granted.

For the past fifteen years we have been increasingly involved in seeking to help other marriages. We have seen hundreds of couples and have faced with them a range of diverse and difficult issues. From all of them, and from our own marriage, we have learned that the marriage relationship is not always easy, but it is highly rewarding. These experiences, combined with our own research and plenty of advice from others in the field, enabled us to develop a five-week *Marriage Preparation Course* for engaged couples and another seven-week *Marriage Course* for couples at any stage of their marriage. Hundreds of couples have been on these courses, and we now run each of them three times a year.

*The Marriage Course*, on which this book is based, is designed to help any couple invest in their marriage and to make it stronger and better. We have written the book out of our desire to pass on what has caused us to be more in love now than when we were first married. Our Christian faith has had an enormous impact on the way we seek to love each other, and we try to explain in various places the difference it has made to our marriage. However, you do not need to be a Christian to benefit from this book. Most of the advice given could be described as practical guidelines for making a relationship not only work, but flourish.

We have included many stories from our own marriage and from others. Some examples may seem trivial, but it is the little things that can make or break a marriage. The other couples whose stories we tell have been kind enough to share their experiences in the hope that they might inspire others to persevere and discover for themselves what a dynamic partnership marriage can be. (In the majority of cases, we have changed the names to maintain confidentiality.)

The *marriage wheel* on the next page encapsulates what we believe any marriage needs to hold it together for the duration of the journey. Each section of the book (and each week of *The Marriage*

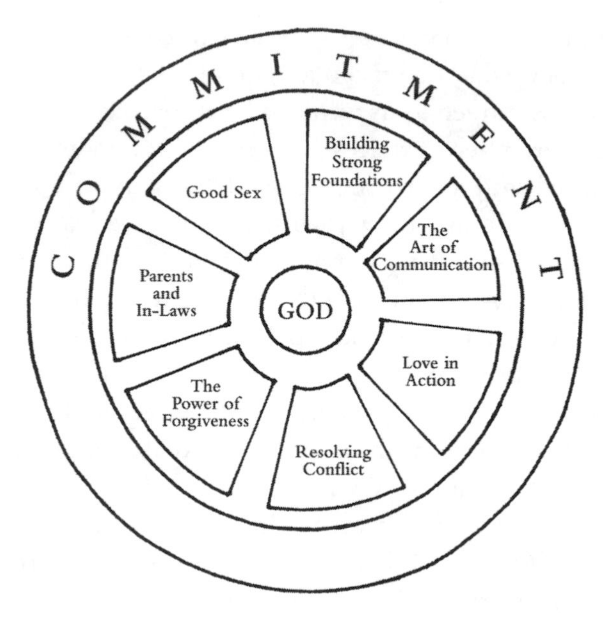


*Course*) represents one section of the wheel. Our experience has shown us that every part is needed if the marriage wheel is not to bump and jar, especially when the road gets rough. In chapter 10 we will explain further why having God at the center of a marriage can, like a well-oiled hub, make such a difference.

The rim of the wheel, which represents commitment, holds the relationship together. Some argue that the ideal of a lifelong marriage should be abandoned today in favor of an arrangement that makes "coupling and uncoupling" as easy as possible. Is there still a case for the traditional view of marriage? We would answer with a resounding yes.

Our view is that marriage remains of vital importance, not only to us as individuals, but as the foundation of any society. Marriage is the ideal God-given basis for family life, particularly because children best learn what committed, loving relationships are all about through their experience of the commitment between their mother and father. Nothing is more important in a child's education.

Children, like adults, always learn far more from what they see than from what they are told. One father said to us recently, "I have realized that the best way to love my children is by loving my wife."

But marriage is not just for the benefit of children. There is a desire deep within us all for someone with whom we can be totally open and honest emotionally, spiritually, and physically. Such intimacy is only possible where there is commitment. We will only dare to expose our innermost selves if we know for sure that we are not going to be let down.

Marriage is designed by God to be a relationship in which a man and a woman give themselves to each other in radical and total abandonment. In the wedding service, the minister, priest, or pastor may bless the couple, pray for them, declare that in the eyes of God and the people they are married, but it is the promises that the man and woman make to each other which establish the marriage, and every phrase of the vows underlines this lifelong commitment:

*Groom:* I, N, take you, N,
to be my wife,
to have and to hold
from this day forward;
for better, for worse,
for richer, for poorer,
in sickness and in health,
to love and to cherish,
till death do us part,
according to God's holy law,
and this is my solemn vow.

*Bride:* I, N, take you, N,
to be my husband
to have and to hold
from this day forward;
for better, for worse,
for richer, for poorer,
in sickness and in health,
to love and to cherish,
till death do us part,
according to God's holy law,
and this is my solemn vow.[2]

The marriage relationship is designed by God to be an adventure of love that lasts a lifetime. The Bible contains much practical advice about how to make such an intimate relationship work. And Jesus Christ says that anyone who hears His words and puts them into practice is like a wise man who digs down deep and builds his house on a secure foundation. When the storms come and the wind beats against it, as they will in any marriage, the house stands firm.

# Section 1 — Building Strong Foundations

# 1

## Taking a Long View

*There is a woman in bed beside me. Right this moment I could reach out my hand and touch her, as easily as I touch myself, and as I think about this, it is more staggering than any mountain or moon. It is even more staggering, I think, than if this woman happened instead to be an angel (which, come to think of it, she might well be). There are only two factors which prevent this situation from being so overpoweringly awesome that my heart would explode just trying to take it in: one is that I have woken up just like this, with this same woman beside me, hundreds of times before; and the other is that millions of other men and women are waking up beside each other, just like this, each and every day all around the world, and have been for thousands of years.*

MIKE MASON[1]

Marriage is a unique opportunity. We have the chance to share every aspect of our lives with another human being. We have promised to stick together through the highs and lows, and out of the security of our mutual promise, we dare to reveal everything about ourselves.

We relate to each other in our common humanity, feeling each other's pain and covering each other's weaknesses. We rejoice in each other's strengths and delight in each other's successes. We are given a counselor, a companion, a best friend—in short, a partner

through life. And if we are patient enough, kind enough, and unselfish enough, we shall discover that each of us is inexhaustibly rich.

Marriage has brought untold joy to millions and has throughout history been celebrated around the world in ceremony, poetry, prose, and song.

## What is marriage?

> "For this reason a man will leave his father and mother and be united to his wife and the two will become one flesh" (Genesis 2:24).

Marriage is about two people being joined together to become one, and is therefore the closest, most intimate relationship of which human beings are capable. Some might object that the parent-child relationship is closer, given that the child's life begins within the mother. However, a healthy parent-child relationship is to be one of increasing separation and growing *independence* with each child leaving the parental nest to make a home of his or her own. The marriage relationship is altogether the opposite. Two people, at one time strangers to each other, meet and subsequently get married. They enter into a relationship marked, at its best, by an increasing *interdependence*.

John Bayley writes about his fifty years of marriage to his late wife in *A Memoir of Iris Murdoch*. Toward the end she suffered from Alzheimer's disease through which he nursed her himself:

> Looking back, I separate us with difficulty. We seem always to have been together... But where Iris is concerned my own memory, like a snug-fitting garment, seems to have zipped itself up to the present second. As I work in bed early in the morning, typing on my old portable with Iris quietly asleep beside me, her presence as she now is seems as it always was, and as it always should be. I know she must once have been different, but I have no true memory of a different person.[2]

This process of growing together is not automatic. Most couples

come into marriage with big expectations. As they leave their wedding through a shower of confetti and meander off into the sunset, they cannot imagine ever not wanting to be together. The long-term reality is different and, potentially, far better.

Both husband and wife must be ready to build the marriage. Each stage of the process brings its own challenges and opportunities. In the early days we may be shocked by the things that we discover about each other which were not apparent during the heady days of courtship and engagement.

For ourselves, even though we had known each other for four years prior to getting married, we both had to make adjustments in the light of what married life revealed: irritating habits, unexpected behavior, values which differed from our own.

The first lesson of marriage is to accept our husband or wife as they are, rather than trying to make them into the person we had hoped they would be. This mutual acceptance must continue as the passing years will inevitably bring change. As Shakespeare mused:

> ...Love is not love
> Which alters when it alteration finds,
> Or bends with the remover to remove.
> ... Love's not time's fool, though rosy lips and cheeks
> Within his bending sickle's compass come;
> Love alters not with his brief hours and weeks ... [3]

Despite our best efforts, we cannot stay the same. Not only will our appearance change, but our thinking will mature, our character will develop, and our circumstances will alter. Perhaps the greatest change comes with the arrival of children, though equally challenging is the distressing and traumatic circumstance of infertility. Difficulties in conceiving can put great stress on a marriage and will call for much patience, loving support, and a refusal to blame.

The birth of a baby brings supreme joy but is often accompanied by physical exhaustion. Later on the teenage years can be immense fun and can provide opportunities for growing friendship with our children but are usually an emotionally exhausting roller coaster ride. When eventually they move out, we may find ourselves grieving their absence, the expression used by one mother whose children were gradually leaving home in their early twenties.

Through these years of bringing up children, when there is so much to think about at home and at work, it is all too easy to neglect our marriages. Undoubtedly children need to be nurtured, but so do marriages. When spouses have continued to invest in their relationship and have supported each other through the varying pressures of family life, the final twenty-five years can be the most rewarding.

A friend of ours was questioning her parents recently about their marriage. Her father turned to her mother and said, "I think we've had a great marriage, but there have been difficult bits and wonderful bits." Both agreed that the hardest phase was in their thirties when they had young children, not much money, and tough demands at work. But as the children became increasingly independent (though still very much part of their lives), the pressures eased, and they had the time and opportunity to rediscover each other in new ways.

Frank Muir described in his autobiography what this stage of his long marriage to Polly meant to him:

> When brother Chas and I were teenagers our granny decided to give us signet rings. I hated the idea of wearing jewelery and so she gave me something else.
>
> It was coming up to our forty-seventh wedding anniversary and Polly asked me if there was something I would like to have as a keepsake, and suddenly I knew exactly what I wanted. I said, "Please may I have a wedding ring?"
>
> Polly was very surprised. She said, "Tell me why you suddenly want a wedding ring after all these years and you shall have one."

"Well, I wanted to be sure first," I said, the sort of slick half-joke inappropriate for a rather emotional moment, but it gave me time to think....

I find it quite impossible to visualize what life without Polly would have been like. Finding Polly was like a fifth rib replacement, or "the other half" we search for to make us complete in the process which Plato called "the desire and pursuit of the whole". It was a wonderfully successful process in my case.

I asked for a wedding ring so that I could wear it as a symbol of the happiness my marriage to Pol has brought. Now that I work at home it is so good just to know that Pol is somewhere around, even though invisible, perhaps bending down picking white currants in the fruit cage and swearing gently, or upstairs shortening a skirt for a granddaughter.

The happy thing is to know that Pol is near.[4]

## Why do some marriages stop working?

Tragically we hear of many marriages today that fail to experience this type of togetherness. For some, after the initial few years, a creeping separation causes them to become disconnected. This may happen when children are young and exhausting or when they leave home. In the latter case a couple may discover that they have nothing to say to each other and they divorce, assuming that they should never have gotten married in the first place.

We grow up believing in a romantic myth: If Cinderella happens to meet her Prince Charming, they will live happily ever after. Should friction arise and we fall out of love, then, the myth states, we have married the wrong person, and we are destined to live unhappily ever after or get divorced. This message is reinforced for adults through love songs, books, and films. Underlying this pervasive and dangerous myth is the belief that real love is something that happens *to* us, over which we have little or no control.

This view is sometimes reported in the press as though it is beyond dispute. A recent article in *The Guardian* stated that some "lucky souls" keep an intimate marriage relationship going for twenty years or more, but the natural time limit is closer to four years. Once you've lost it, "nothing on earth will bring back that magic spark...You either feel it or you don't, and that's the end of the matter." In apparent consolation the article ended, "It can always be rekindled for somebody new."[5]

But anyone who has been in a stable marriage for more than a few years will say that a relationship has to be worked at. It has taken more than romantic feelings to keep a couple together. It has taken a daily choice, on some occasions having to talk through sensitive issues, on others having to control an attraction to another man or woman, and, if the romantic feelings left for a while, in time they returned at a deeper and richer level. Couples who get married thinking that the line in their vows, "for better or for worse," will not really apply to them are in for a shock or a failed marriage.

Marriages that break down are usually the result of a process of growing apart over many years, as this anonymous poem entitled *The Wall* describes.

Their wedding picture mocked them from the table
These two whose lives no longer touched each other.
They loved with such a heavy barricade between them
That neither battering ram of words
Nor artilleries of touch could break it down.

Somewhere between the oldest child's first tooth
And youngest daughter's graduation
They lost each other.

Throughout the years each slowly unravelled
That tangled ball of string called self

And as they tugged at stubborn knots
Each hid their searching from the other.

Sometimes she cried at night and begged
The whispering darkness to tell her who she was
While he lay beside her snoring like a
Hibernating bear unaware of her winter.

Once after they had made love he wanted to tell her
How afraid he was of dying
But fearing to show his naked soul he spoke instead
About the beauty of her breasts.

She took a course in modern art trying to find herself
In colors splashed upon a canvas
And complaining to other women about men
Who were insensitive.

He climbed into a tomb called the office
Wrapped his mind in a shroud of paper figures
And buried himself in customers.

Slowly the wall between them rose cemented
By the mortar of indifference.
One day reaching out to touch each other
They found a barrier they could not penetrate
And recoiling from the coldness of the stone
Each retreated from the stranger on the other side.

For when love dies it is not in a moment of angry battle
Nor when fiery bodies lose their heat.
It lies panting exhausted expiring
At the bottom of a wall it could not scale.[6]

Many marriages break down, not because of incompatibility, but because the husband and wife have never known what it takes to make their relationship work. In our society, fewer and fewer people grow up seeing a strong relationship modeled between their own parents.

We live in a consumerist age in which people are not used to fixing things. If something doesn't work, it is easier and cheaper to buy a new one. Powerful advertising encourages us to focus on wanting what we do not have rather than being grateful for what we do have. It increases the expectation that we should have our desires fulfilled quickly—as in the slogan for the credit card that promised "to take the waiting out of wanting." We are encouraged to believe that fulfillment comes through what we can acquire with as little effort as possible rather than through working at something.

Alvin Toffler, the sociologist and best-selling author, wrote that people today have a "throw-away mentality." They not only have throw-away products, but they make throw-away friends, and it is this mentality which produces throw-away marriages.[7]

Marriage is viewed by many today as a temporary contract between a couple for as long as their love lasts. Our culture stresses the freedom of the individual. If the relationship is not personally fulfilling, then it is better to get out. If there is no more love in a marriage, it is better to finish it.

But we are discovering as a society that the consequences are not so easily discarded. The oneness of the marriage bond means that the two people cannot be neatly and painlessly divided. It is like taking two sheets of paper and gluing them together. They become one, and they cannot be separated without causing damage to both.

In a recent interview the actor, Michael Caine, spoke of the break-up of his first marriage. He was desperately short of money and his wife, Patricia, tried to persuade him to give up the theatre: "...rather than relinquish his dreams, he walked away from his marriage." Now he says, if he'd known the anguish involved, "I would have stayed at all costs. If I'd been as strong as Pat I think we could have made it ..."[8] Michael Caine is right. A marriage can be made to work but it takes deliberate and determined action.

For the last two years our family has lived ten feet away from one of London's largest residential developments. In the midst of the din and the dust we have experienced a bird's-eye view of each stage of the building from our bedroom window. We saw for ourselves the depth and thoroughness of the work beneath ground level. Over several months, four pile drivers created more than two hundred concrete-filled holes to provide secure foundations. Then, and only then, did the present impressive structure start to go up.

If we want to build a strong marriage, we need to lay deep foundations. To do so takes time and may well produce dust and noise. Progress, at times, will seem painfully slow. New ways of communicating may have to be developed. Sensitive or contentious issues may require discussion. Forgiveness will need to become a habit.

For those who have been married for many years, some underpinning of the foundations may be urgently required. We heard recently of some alterations being made to an Edwardian house in north London. After two weeks one of the builders, alone in the house, felt a shudder go through the ground floor. He ran out of the back door, and as he did so the whole house collapsed in ruins. There are marriages around us which have already collapsed. But we know of others brought back from the brink of disaster to a new experience of love and commitment.

Marriage, like a home, requires maintenance and the occasional minor (or even major) repair, but within both homes and marriages there are endless opportunities to be creative, to do something different, to move things around a bit. A marriage can become static and cause a couple to feel trapped and bored. Marriages thrive on creativity and new initiatives.

For any of us to grow closer as a couple we must be *proactive* within our marriage. All too often we are only *reactive*. We react negatively to each other's behavior or comments, blaming each other when things go wrong and retaliating when we are hurt.

This book is intended as a toolkit for building a strong marriage. Each chapter provides a different tool with which you can shape, fix, maintain, or repair your relationship. We believe that by using even one of these tools, you will begin to see improvements.

We hope that as you read and discuss the following chapters you will find it easier to talk together about your marriage. Some will discover wonderful things about their husband or wife that have never been disclosed. Others will recognize areas of their marriages that need attention. Some of the practical application may at first seem contrived, but we know from our own experience that by persevering it becomes a normal and natural part of our relationship.

The advice columnist Claire Rayner said about her marriage to her husband Desmond:

> We'll have been married forty-three years this year. It wasn't an accident. It wasn't luck. The harder you work at your marriage, the luckier you get. We have become a couple, not two individuals. We have fun together, more fun that we have apart. I still fancy him and, thank God, he still seems to fancy me.[9]

# 2

## Planning to Succeed

*But meanwhile time is flying, irretrievable time is flying.*
VIRGIL[1]

*We must use time as a tool, not as a couch.*
JOHN FITZGERALD KENNEDY[2]

We can clearly remember the first time a couple asked us for advice about their relationship. They had been married for sixteen years and had two children. The husband, a successful businessman at the height of his career, phoned in desperation to say that his wife was about to leave him. They arrived together at our house looking slightly awkward. We opened the door feeling equally awkward and wondering if we had anything to say that could help.

We started by asking where things had gone wrong. They were both highly articulate in describing their version of the events of the preceding months and years. Neither allowed the other to finish a sentence. After ten minutes it became clear that they were more interested in attacking each other than in answering our question. Their marriage looked like a ball of string so tangled that it would be easier to throw it away and buy some more than patiently to undo each knot. Thankfully they were prepared to make an effort to stay together.

We saw two changes that had to happen if their marriage was to stand a chance. First, they needed to spend much more time together. Second, they needed to use that time effectively. And so very tentatively we suggested that every day they set aside thirty minutes to talk together. Each would allow the other to speak about his or her feelings for at least five minutes without interrupting. We also encouraged them to plan an evening once a week to go out as a couple in the way they had before they were married.

Two weeks later, we opened the door to two different people. They had made a start along the road of understanding each other. We were excited to see how a marriage could be transformed when a couple moved from being reactive to being proactive, and when they were willing to make time available exclusively for each other.

## Time together

To deprive a marriage of time spent together is the equivalent of depriving a person of air or a plant of water. Some plants can survive longer than others, but eventually they wilt and die.

Rob Parsons, the executive director of *CARE for the Family*, describes what he calls "the great illusion":

> You can run several agendas in life, but you cannot run them all at a hundred percent without somebody paying a price... We have so many excuses. The main one is that we convince ourselves a slower day is coming. We say to ourselves, "When the house is decorated, when I get my promotion, when I pass those exams—then I'll have more time." Every time we have to say, "Not now, darling..." we tell ourselves it's okay because that slower day is getting nearer. It's as well that we realize, here and now, that the slower day is an illusion—it never comes. Whatever our situation, we all have the potential to fill our time. That's why we need to make time for the things that we believe are important—and we need to make it now.[3]

Anna Murdoch attributed the breakdown of her marriage to Rupert to a lack of time kept for each other. In an interview that she gave in 1988 when her second novel *Family Business* was published, she said of her writing, "I needed something to do with my time. I have a preoccupied husband and my children don't need me so much any more. I do it to fill in the loneliness."[4] A friend of the Murdochs commented, "My belief is that Anna has had enough of him working so hard and she is saying this isn't how I want to spend the rest of our marriage. I think she is trying to get him to slow down... Rupert is completely devoted to work. If you are dealing with the U.S., U.K., Far East, and Australia, it means you are on the phone all the time."[5]

Rupert Murdoch himself, in an interview with his biographer William Showcross in 1999, gave similar reasons when asked why his marriage split up:

> I was traveling a lot and was very obsessed with business and perhaps more than normally inconsiderate, at a time when our children were grown up and home was suddenly an empty nest. The family home suddenly becomes a home for two people without their central shared interest, which has dispersed around the world. Those are the underlying reasons we drifted apart[6]

In total contrast, the former Beatle, Paul McCartney, and his late wife Linda were very particular about making time to be together, despite the pressures of fame. Hunter Davies, their friend and biographer, recalled that Paul had decided that there were two things that were most important to him: being with his family and playing music.

> He was willing to go backward, to start where he had begun, playing in local halls, college campuses. It struck me as so mature, so clever, so adult, to realize that and act upon it. And so Wings was born, putting his two passions in life together. He would take Linda and the children on tour with him all around the country, sleeping

> in caravans if need be.
>
> Naturally the critics were horrible to Linda, criticizing her musical skills or lack of them, and were snide about Paul, saying how stupid to drag her round. Wings weren't all that brilliant at first, but they got better, learned and improved together. Just as they did in their marriage.[7]

Time together with the people who matter most does not just happen. It requires a deliberate and determined decision. Before they get married, most husbands and wives contrive to spend every available minute together. Gary Chapman, a marriage counselor, describes it well:

> At its peak, the "in love" experience is euphoric. We are emotionally obsessed with each other. We go to sleep thinking of one another. When we rise that person is the first thought on our minds. We long to be together… When we hold hands, it seems as if our blood flows together... Our mistake was in thinking it would last forever.[8]

We have been led to believe that if we are really in love such emotions will never fade. Psychologists' research, however, indicates that this state only lasts an average of two years. After that a couple can no longer rely solely upon their feelings. They must *choose* to love each other.

Once married, time together can quickly cease to be a priority. As we are living under the same roof, we all too easily think that we no longer need to coordinate our schedules; we can begin to take each other for granted. We are convinced that *married* couples need to continue planning special times for each other. The effort that went into meeting when we first fell in love, the anticipation, the excitement, the variety of times and places all added to the pleasure. If in marriage we continue to make time for each other, the romance will be kept alive, we shall have the chance to communicate effectively, and our understanding of each other will deepen. The regularity and nature of this time together will create the fabric of our relationship over a lifetime.

In our own marriage we have sought to set a pattern of fixed times for one another. What is possible and workable will vary for each couple, but we know that without such a pattern, we would have failed to spend enough time together. When people ask us for one thing that a couple could do to keep their marriage alive and their love growing over the years, our answer would be this:

> *Plan a regular time every week of at least two hours to spend alone together.*

As we do not have an equivalent word or phrase for a "date" in the U.K., we use the rather prosaic term *marriage time* when we refer to it on *The Marriage Course*. This time is intended to be different from the other hours spent together during the rest of the week. An evening at home can so easily become just another night when the bills are paid, the broken door handle is fixed, or the ironing is done. These dull domestic necessities are an inevitable part of married life, but if we *only* meet around the bank statement or the toolbox, meaningful communication will be stifled and our love will struggle.

Carefully planned time together rekindles romance in a marriage. Exhausting organization is not required: candles on the table, music in the background, ordering take-out food (to give the cook a break), and putting on the answering machine are all that is necessary. These times should be fun and memorable. We could go to the movies or out for a meal. It is time to hold hands, time to laugh, time to enjoy doing things together, and above all, time to talk. This is the time to share our hopes and fears, excitements and worries, struggles and achievements. Such sharing builds intimacy. It's simple but very powerful.

But keeping this time for each other is not easy. There are obstacles that get in our way: schedules at work over which we have little control, transporting children from one activity to the next, or a self-inflicted pressure that "there is always something else that needs to be done." Many of us are overcome with exhaustion at the end of the day, and the easiest option is to sit in front of the television physically together but mentally apart.

Experience has shown us that keeping our weekly time together requires the following three commitments. The first is to *plan it.* Both husband and wife must look at their schedules to find the best time each week. This will depend on whether we have children; how old they are; whether our work is at home or some distance away. We need to consider what suits us best. Now that our own children are older, and because of our particular jobs, we have discovered that a two-hour lunch is usually the best time for us. We put it in our planners, once a week, and we give it as high a commitment as an invitation we have accepted or an appointment we have made. Because our lives are busy, we usually plan our weekly time for three months ahead, putting each other's name in our planners once a week like any other appointment.

This idea of planning time together with our husband or wife may seem contrived. However, it is the first thing that can slip quietly out of a loving relationship. We don't set out to neglect one another. Rather the routines of daily life steal the time we once spent with each other.

The second commitment is to make this time together a *priority*. This means recognizing the importance of it over and above the many other good things that we could be doing with our spare time, such as seeing family, entertaining at home, going to a party, watching a football game with friends, or going to church meetings. Making our time together a top priority is a powerful indication of our love.

When we were first married, we often failed in this. When other people invited us to do something with them, it seemed unfriendly to say we were keeping the evening for ourselves. So now, instead of telling them, "We are having an evening in," we say, "I am so sorry but we are busy," without saying *what* we are doing. If we receive an exciting invitation which clashes with our marriage time, we have an agreement not to accept it without consulting the other, and we will usually only make a change if we can find an alternative time that week.

The third commitment is to *protect it*. Interruptions can destroy our time together. The telephone can hold us for ransom. Some of us cannot resist answering it; others find it hard not to talk for hours. If we fall into either of these categories, we should think about buying an answering machine or unplugging the telephone.

For others the television is the prime intruder. Television can so easily claim many hours each week, some of which could otherwise be spent in conversation. Alan Storkey in his book *Marriage and its*

*Modern Crisis* writes, "...the power of television as a *retreat* from relationships in the home must be great, and its impact on marital sharing devastating. Television grows from and promotes a culture of individual gratification."[9] If the television is a problem, do something. Banish it from the sitting room—or make the house a television-free zone.

We try to arrange our weekly time at a place where we are not going to bump into people that we know. The needs of family and friends are important, but none of them is as important as the need to invest time in our marriage.

The busier we are, the more important and the more inconvenient this time together becomes. On occasions, one or both of us have been distracted by other pressing demands, but the temptation to cancel our time together is far easier to resist when we are convinced of its long-term benefits. Of course, there have been weeks when it has been impossible, but we have discovered that two weeks without the opportunity to relax together and communicate properly is a long time in a marriage. We soon find that we are out of touch with each other and often out of sorts too. When we have had time together, we experience a sense of well-being: the week feels more balanced, we are less stressed about the demands of life, and we relate better to each other and to our children.

*A day together*

Every four to six months we plan a day away by ourselves. This is a time to talk over those things that in everyday life we have neither the time nor the energy to discuss. It is a time of looking back to see what is working well and what needs attention, to consider our finances, to look forward to our goals for the future, and to dream up new ideas for our marriage and family life.

Setting aside time every few months helps to prevent a backlog on these bigger issues. These days have become special and fun for us. Because we live in the city, we try to get out to the country. We go for a walk and have lunch together, giving ourselves plenty of time to talk. We have sometimes written down plans and goals to review in the months to come.

*Vacations*

We have discovered the need to consider carefully how and where to spend our vacations, taking into account our different needs and preferences. It is all too easy to think we will just "go with the flow," see what comes up, or accept the first invitation to go away with other people. We have been on vacations which we failed to think through, and on our return realized that we needed a vacation in order to recover. The main purpose of a vacation is to have fun and time together away from our usual routine. We have found vacations with lots of other friends, friends' children, or family are wonderful for *some* of the time, but not all of it.

*Mini-honeymoons*

Two or three days away as a couple once a year, without our children, have had an amazingly revitalizing effect on our relationship. For couples with young children, it can be difficult to organize, but it is well worth persevering. If you do not have family who could look after the children, what about the possibility of swapping with friends who have children the same age?

If going away is too expensive, you could stay at home (but without your children) and do something completely different. Alternatively, swap houses with friends or family who live in another part of the country. We see this time as a mini-honeymoon every year. The benefits more than repay the effort it takes to organize it.

## TIME APART

While stressing the need to spend time together, most husbands and wives will spend a certain amount of time apart. Some friends of ours, who have been happily married for several years, recalled that he, the husband, had to go away for a week only three weeks after the wedding. Everyone felt sympathy for the poor abandoned wife. She, however, was delighted. She could now sleep properly again. The complexities of sharing a bed with extra limbs kicking around, plus other nocturnal activity, had totally exhausted her. A week's recovery was exactly what she needed.

Where time apart is not available out of necessity, it will need to be obtained with the genuine and freely given agreement of both husband and wife. An overdose of "guys' weekends" or "girls' nights out" will not be helpful to a marriage, and any invitation of this kind needs to be considered carefully and jointly. It is better to disappoint a friend than to harm a marriage.

Some friendships from our single days may deepen when the relationship is enjoyed by both husband and wife. But it will not be possible to maintain every friendship. Those that are in any way a threat to the marriage must be allowed to die, particularly if there is a danger of physical infatuation. In this way we shall be faithful to our marriage vows: "forsaking all others, be faithful to him or her as long as you both shall live." This is part of the new start that marriage involves.

That is not to say that we must do everything together. We are not to try and force our partner to become like us in every way. There may be social occasions, church activities, events in the community, work, or leisure-related invitations that we feel differently about. This may have much to do with our personality type or our ability in a certain area or our level of self-confidence. Of course, our priority is to find activities we both enjoy, but there will be some interests couples do not share.

> Many couples have trouble with this aspect of marriage. They feel abandoned when their spouse wants time apart. In reality, spouses need time apart, which makes them realize the need to be back together. Spouses in healthy relationships cherish each other's

space and are champions of each other's causes.[10]

There are four questions to consider, particularly if you have young children.

1. Are both husband and wife being given some opportunities to develop their individual interests?
2. Are your separate interests causing mutual resentment or are you genuinely pleased to give each other this time?
3. Are you both seeking first to release the other rather than to grasp time for yourself?
4. Are you willing to give up your separate interest if family circumstances require it?

If the attitude of both husband and wife is right, pursuing interests separately can prevent a relationship from becoming one-dimensional or claustrophobic, bringing refreshment, stimulation, new thoughts, and stories into the marriage. Some interests, however, will need to be curtailed or dropped if they cause a distance to come between us or put a strain on our marriage.

**Sila** One of Nicky's passions is sailing. When we first met in southwest Ireland I soon realized this, and I was always the first to volunteer to crew for him during the two weeks of racing in August. Some years later we discovered that dinghy sailing and small babies are totally incompatible. After much tension, occasional resentment, and some agonizing, we decided that taking our family vacation with four children under the age of eight during the two weeks of racing was going to cause more conflict than it was worth.

As a result, for many years we overlapped our vacation with three or four days of racing to give Nicky the chance to compete in a few races and then to have the rest of the time free to spend all together. Now they are all avid sailors, and

I find myself vying with them to be Nicky's crew.

## STAYING IN TOUCH

The process of blending two lives into one can only happen as we develop a regular pattern of disclosing to one another our separate worlds. This may at times take great effort but our different contributions over a lifetime establish a reservoir of shared experiences and a level of mutual understanding that draw us closer.

Normally we start each day by talking about our plans as well as any potential areas of stress or anxiety, and we then pray for each other before we part. (We describe in more detail how we do this in Appendix 4.) These few minutes have had to be fitted into the changing pattern of family life. When our children were young, we would (with some difficulty!) talk and pray before getting up. Now that our children are older, we do so as soon as they have left for school.

There are huge long-term benefits if we stay in contact about the daily minutiae of our lives. When we are spending one or more nights apart, we still try to keep in touch by phoning each other at least once a day. This enables us to be a part of each other's world and has a profound effect on our understanding of one another. It also helps us to reacclimatize ourselves to each other when we are back together.

In the evening, the day can easily grind gradually and separately to a halt: one of us falls asleep on the sofa and the other crawls into bed alone. For the sake of our relationship, and despite our tiredness, we generally try to connect with each other at the end of the day as we are getting ready for bed or as one of us is soaking in the bath. One wife after twenty-five years of marriage described the late evening in these words, "This is the cream of our marriage: this nightly turning out and sharing of the day's pocketful of memories."

# Section 1 – Building Strong Foundations

## Conclusion

At the heart of a strong marriage is a strong friendship. Even good friendships drift apart unless positively fed and held together. A pattern of regular time spent together daily, weekly, and annually is the first investment needed to keep our friendship growing, and it will provide a firm foundation for a strong marriage.

Our weekly marriage time has been for us a wonderful investment and has become the single most important means of staying closely connected with each other and keeping the romance alive. Time planned, prioritized and protected, counters the illusion that "the slower day" is coming. We often remember Rob Parson's words: "...we need to make time for the things that we believe are important—and we need to make it now."[11]

## First Golden Rule of Marriage

Be sure to make time for each other
and have fun together.

# Section 2 — The Art of Communication

# 3

## How to Talk More Effectively

*The only real essential is to carry on the conversation you started.*
LIBBY PURVES[1]

In December of 1986, Anna left her husband James after three years of marriage and set up housekeeping with another man. She wanted a divorce and had begun proceedings. James began to pray for a reconciliation, though she refused even to see him.

After two-and-a-half years the *decree nisi* (the first stage of the divorce) had come through. In July, 1989, he sent Anna and her new partner two tickets to hear Billy Graham. She sent them back. As it happened Billy Graham decided to stay on for an extra night, to speak at Wembley Stadium. James sent her two more tickets. Anna phoned and said that her partner did not want to go, but that she would like to if James went too.

She wrote later, "Everything Billy Graham said seemed to hit my heart. My job was going well; I had another relationship but still wasn't happy. Billy Graham said a lot about making a clean start. In my mind I thought, 'Get the divorce out of the way and start again with my partner or on my own.'"

At the end of the talk, Anna went down front to give her life to Christ. "Through the tears I felt an incredible sense of God's love and a reordering of all the priorities in my life. I believed that God was giving me a clean start, but I also clearly felt Him saying, 'Now I am going to rebuild your marriage.' At that moment I realized that my marriage was very precious to God, and that He was going to do something extraordinary. He reassured me—somehow—that He wasn't just going to patch up my marriage but totally renew it."

A counselor from the Billy Graham organization approached her and asked if she had come with anyone. Through her tears Anna said, "Yes." The counselor asked whether the person was a Christian. Again she said, "Yes." The counselor suggested she get the person. Anna replied, "But it's my husband." The counsellor said, "That's great!" To which Anna replied, "But you don't understand; this is the first time I've seen him for two-and-a-half years." At this point the counselor herself started crying.

Anna knew that she needed to return to her husband. She and James had to go to court to get the *decree nisi* set aside. The judge was delighted, and the usher wept for joy. Now, ten years later, they have two children and are deeply committed to one another.

Recently, we asked them to reflect on what had gone wrong before they separated. Both agreed that it was the result of a breakdown in communication. Anna wrote, "Our marriage collapsed because we failed to share our real feelings with one another. I began to confide in my sisters and close friends rather than in my husband. This began—subtly at first—to drive a wedge between us. When we were back together, I resolved not to have a thought-life which was secret from James. In the past, I used to dwell on the negative aspects of our relationship but rarely voiced my feelings. I was effectively setting up a case against him without allowing him to defend himself.

"We have become much better at recognizing when one of us is brooding over something and we persistently ask questions to get things out into the open. I tend to have more dramatic mood swings than James and, if I am rather low, I find conversation difficult because I tend to shut down emotionally. We have to work much harder during these times to keep real communication going."

James wrote, "If I had to identify one reason for our separation, it would be ineffective communication. I remember so well the ease with which it is possible to settle downward into a norm in which the air is filled with words but nothing is really said. All current wisdom on this subject stresses the importance of quality time being carved out of hectic schedules. But this, in my experience, only marks out the space. Effective communication must mean revealing all parts of our lives, in my case the parts which I am well practiced at keeping hidden. For me, at least, it requires more than time; it requires courage.

"As well as needing to know that Anna has accepted me unconditionally, I need courage beyond my natural resources. I have found that this sort of courage only comes using God's resources. Without Him I was, and would have remained, a hopeless case. My best intentions to change would have come to nothing. The most common phrase used about me by all the women I knew prior to becoming a Christian was: 'We never know what you are feeling.' I actually thought I was emotionally retarded and that one chunk of me had somehow remained deep-frozen. It was like walking around with a hidden handicap, hidden that is, until I attempted to get close to anyone.

"In the last twelve years I have come to see that with God's grace it really is possible to grow together—to have a relationship that gets better with the passing of years. I have experienced this myself and have seen it again and again in other Christian couples. It is what I always wanted but had thought, previously, was the stuff of romantic movies and mushy novels."

---

What was true about James and Anna's difficulties in communicating is true in many marriages. To communicate is not just to exchange information but means literally to make common our thoughts and feelings. In this way we make ourselves known to each other.

Even though Winston and Clementine Churchill spent much of their fifty-six years of marriage apart through the demands of politics and two World Wars, they constantly communicated by letters, notes, telegrams, and memoranda, of which over 1,700 still exist.[2] They maintained the habit of making common with each other all that they were thinking and feeling. This constant communication must help to account for their lifelong love for each other.

In the best marriages there are no secrets between husband and wife. In a recent television drama about Queen Victoria there was a conversation between the queen and her prime minister, Lord Melbourne. The queen was seeking advice as to whether she should talk to her new husband, Prince Albert, about affairs of state with which he, as a German, might disagree. Lord Melbourne's reply was very wise, "In marriage, disagreements are not nearly as dangerous as secrets. Secrets breed mistrust."

Of course we may need to learn *how* to communicate with one another. An article in *The Mail on Sunday*, describing the break-up of a celebrity marriage, quoted the husband as saying, "When we went to marriage guidance counseling, I was shocked to find we had never really talked. I heard my wife telling a complete stranger about feelings I never knew existed. And I heard myself doing the same. We could only communicate through a stranger."[3]

Professor John Gottman, who runs the Family Research Laboratory at the University of Washington and has been analyzing marriage relationships for more than twenty years, has observed:

> What typically happens is that one person reaches out to the other to get the partner's interest and it falls flat. The basic problem is emotional connectedness... people are asking their partner to "show me you love me." Many people live in an emotional desert. That's why they are so needy.[4]

Some of us fail in our ability to listen well. Others of us fail in our ability to express our feelings, as James described earlier. We need to become good at both talking and listening.

## TALKING

*The importance of conversation*

Robert Louis Stevenson described marriage thus:

> Marriage is one long conversation, checkered by disputes. Two persons more and more adapt their notions one to suit the other and in process of time, without sound of trumpet, they conduct each other into new worlds of thought.[5]

Some years ago, when our children were young, we left them with their grandparents for three days so that we could spend some time on our own. We went to stay in a small hotel in the highlands of Scotland and had been greatly looking forward to this break, not least because we would have an extended opportunity to talk. We arrived at the hotel in the evening, unpacked, and went down to the dining room.

It was full of other couples, most of whom looked as though they had been married for twenty-five years or more. However, apart from the sound of knives and forks on plates, there was total silence. We were given a table in the middle of the room and sat as close as possible, talking in whispers so as not to be overheard by everyone else.

We are sure that, if those same couples had been out with friends or even if they had been at a party with complete strangers, they would not have sat in silence throughout the evening. They would have made an effort to initiate conversation. The tragedy for many husbands and wives is that they fail to recognize that their *greatest effort* should be made with each other.

Of course, unless we plan time for each other, we usually meet at our worst moments: first thing in the morning when we are barely awake or last thing at night when we are exhausted. Television or newspapers take the place of talking. What conversation there is consists of little more than functional requests: "Please could you take my coat to the drycleaners?" or "Could you mail this for me?" or a simple exchange of facts: "Robert's been promoted" or "The woman across the street has had her baby."

*Making an effort*

If, when we first went out with our husband or wife, we had never bothered to talk to them, we would probably not be married now. Relationships grow when we make an effort. One woman who was on the point of being drawn into an affair told us why she was so attracted to another man: "He seemed to be interested in me—asking me questions and so on."

We won't discover how interesting someone is unless we make the effort to be interested in that person. A great secret in marriage is to ask questions about the day, about each other's activities, concerns, interests, worries, hopes, and plans. We can discover one another's opinions on everyday matters as well as how we view issues of wider significance.

Many couples spend their days in different ways. Recently we were talking to a businessman from Australia. He has a stressful job and spends most of his time on his mobile phone. The phone rings as he gets into his car in the morning and does not stop ringing all day until he turns it off in the driveway of his home when he returns.

His wife, who used to have a similarly demanding working schedule, is now at home full time looking after three children under the age of five. As she hears the door open, she is desperate to talk to an adult and longs for stimulating conversation over dinner. As he enters the sanctuary of his home, all *he* wants is to unwind on his own. Both know they have to make a supreme effort to be sensitive to each other's needs.

Another couple we know has devised a strategy to deal with this situation. As soon as the husband leaves work, he considers the time to belong to his wife. So, during his journey home, he starts thinking about her and how she has spent her day, thus preparing himself for seeing her again and for their evening together. She does the same as she anticipates his arrival. Such mutual effort leads easily into conversation and can scarcely fail to draw a couple closer together and deepen their friendship.

Other situations require a similar degree of effort. Consider the nurse in a cancer ward who is married to a banker; each will have to try hard to understand the other's pressures and to respect the other's job. The husband or wife of a schoolteacher may need to be extremely patient as the term ends, since a considerable part of each evening is spent preparing lessons and marking books with less time for conversation and relaxation together. The pressures will be weighted differently during the holidays as the teacher enjoys sleeping in late while the partner struggles off to work each day.

*Increasing our topics of conversation*

Some couples find themselves short of topics of conversation. In this case they may need to increase their number of *joint* interests. Shared experiences lead naturally to stimulating conversation. A friend of ours told us of the interests her parents have come to share over the last forty years:

> When Mum met Dad, she had never held a pair of binoculars to her eyes and her knowledge of birds did not extend past a sparrow. It is quite touching to see her incredible ornithological knowledge at the age of sixty-five. She got interested because she loved Dad and this was his passion. They have walked thousands of miles together in pursuit of birds over their forty-plus years of marriage.
>
> Similarly, Dad is not remotely arty, and an evening at the opera or theatre would not have been his choice as a young man. This is Mum's kind of thing. Over the years, he has chosen to go

> with her and tried his best to be interested. On occasions, he comes home having genuinely loved a play or an opera, but he sometimes falls asleep, often can't remember either the title or anything that happened upon his return, and has mainly spent the evening working out the mechanics of the scenery.

It will sometimes require a conscious decision to show an interest in what your husband or wife already enjoys. This may mean doing again what you did together when you first met; or you may need to find a new activity that attracts both of you. The list of possibilities is endless and could include: taking up a new sport; starting photography and keeping a record of family life; fixing up the house; gardening; going to flea-markets or garage sales (as sellers or customers); visiting unfamiliar places (with a guidebook of the area); watching sports, perhaps supporting a local team; going to the theater or movies; reading poetry; going for walks; listening to music.

Then we can discuss our different reactions. We must draw out of the other his or her thoughts and feelings: likes and dislikes, what he or she wants to do next time and so on.

*Making use of mealtimes*

The original meaning of the word *companionship* is *taking bread together*. The comedian and travel-writer, Michael Palin, commented after his journey around the world:

> In almost every country I visited on Pole-to-Pole, the sharing of food was an important social activity, which is as it should be. A shared meal is the best forum for the airing of grievances and celebration of pleasures that has yet been devised.

In biblical times, meals were an opportunity for developing friendships. Perhaps this lies behind Jesus' choice of words when He describes His desire for a relationship with us: "I stand at the door and knock. If anyone hears My voice and opens the door, I will come in and eat with them, and they with me" (Revelation 3:20).

Eating together has always been valued as a means of drawing a family together, and only in the second half of the twentieth century in the West has this been neglected. The danger of convenience foods and microwaves is that they allow people to eat quickly and separately. In parts of America, this has gone so far that some houses are being designed with no place for communal eating, but with a place for a television in every room. This is a great loss. One couple commented to us, "We find mealtimes one of the most important occasions for conversation. No matter how convenient the food, setting the table, and sitting down to eat together without interruptions or distractions is always beneficial."

*Talking about our feelings*

Many years ago we received a sad letter from a woman who had been married less than a year. She wrote, "To all the world we look like a happy newly married couple. He puts on a veneer when we are with others. But a few weeks after we were married I felt so disappointed.

I thought we would be able to talk about everything, but he never tells me about his feelings."

Men in our culture typically have a harder time than women when it comes to showing emotion. Certainly in the past, and to some extent today, men have been expected to keep their feelings to themselves and women encouraged to share theirs with their friends and family. As Anna said of the breakdown of her marriage to James, "I began to confide in my sisters and close friends rather than in my husband."

Some people think of themselves as "not the emotional type." But emotions are a fundamental part of being human, and we must learn to talk about our feelings if we are to communicate effectively in our marriage. A woman who took *The Marriage Course* recently, when asked what she had most enjoyed about the course, wrote, "My husband *had* to communicate with me his thoughts and feelings. There are many lovely things he thinks but never puts into words." To ask your husband or wife at appropriate moments, "What are you feeling?" can help them to talk more freely. If we learn to express our feelings when we are feeling fine, then there is a much greater chance we will be able to do the same when we are under pressure.

In the course of a marriage, we are all likely to go through difficult times such as financial hardship, serious illness, a car accident, problems with a teenage child, a miscarriage, bereavement. The handling of a crisis can make or break a marriage. The death of a child in particular puts an enormous strain on a relationship, and the divorce rate among such couples is significantly higher than average. In times of bereavement or sadness we easily slip into denying our feelings, withdrawing from each other, or disappearing into our work. But an essential part of coping with these experiences as a couple is to voice our feelings, however painful that might be, to allow each other to respond differently, and to work through the grief together.

In a magazine article entitled "Do men understand intimacy?" a wife named Alison is quoted as saying, "James relies on me to do all the feeling in our relationship... He is English and very remote—he was sent away to boarding school when he was eight years old. When that happens to a little boy, he soon learns that having emotions will just make life a lot harder."

After Alison suffered a miscarriage, the couple began to grow apart. Alison continued, "I found it helpful to talk about the tragedy, but James suppressed his feelings. He dealt with it by becoming highly critical of me and angry over the smallest things. Then one night in bed, I realized that he had been feeling depressed for weeks too. 'Why didn't you tell me you were feeling this way?' I asked him."[6]

Deep communication requires us to be open about our inner selves and to make ourselves vulnerable to each other. If we fail to communicate painful and complex emotions and try to cope on our own, we drift apart. For those of us who feel unable to *recognize*, let alone *talk about*, our feelings, change is possible. A good way to start is to write down three or four things (of minor or major significance) that have happened to us over the course of a normal day. Against each of these events, record what you felt about them. For example:

> Caught the train—felt bored/alert/tired; made a telephone call—felt angry/hopeful/anxious; went to the bank—felt ashamed/calm/annoyed; met husband or wife—felt happy/tense/excited.

It will require courage to begin to articulate these emotions if you are not used to doing so. As you are likely to feel exposed and vulnerable, you must be sure that your husband or wife is not going to reject you, get angry, or blame you for what you reveal.

*Choosing the right moment*

While it is important not to keep secrets from each other and to be able to express our feelings, it is not always right to say immediately what we think. We need to consider the effect of our words carefully. There is a proverb in the Bible which says, "The right word at the right time is like a custom-made piece of jewelery" (Proverbs 25:11).[7] Restraining ourselves until a more suitable moment is part of the costliness of love. This may require waiting until neither of us is overtired or preoccupied, and we have time to talk the matter through.

One couple described what they do when they have been irritated by the other's behavior and know that it is likely to be a sensitive issue. Rather than raising it at once they first talk to God about it, asking Him to cause the subject to be brought up at the right moment. They have been amazed how often the other has then taken the initiative in introducing the topic.

*Expressing affection*

While we are wise to delay raising sensitive issues, there are no right or wrong moments to talk about our *positive* feelings toward each other. And to do so frequently has a powerful effect upon a marriage, as Frank Muir relates:

> As far as Pol and I are concerned, being in love certainly developed into something more lasting: love. And love is altogether a much deeper, give-and-take, *affectionate* relationship than being "in" love.
>
> Polly and I confirm our feelings towards each other every night along with prayers for the rest of the family and Sal's Dalmatian Dotty, and our cat Cinto (named after the tallest mountain in Corsica, such a sensible name for an Abyssinian cat), so should a journalist from a women's page telephone me today and ask me how often I have told my wife that I love her, I will reply (after a quick arpeggio on the calculator to check), roughly 16,822 times. And I spoke the truth every time.[8]

# 4

## How to Listen More Effectively

*Two may talk together under the same roof for many years,*
*yet never really meet.*
MARY CATTERWOOD[1]

Our husband or wife is talking to us about their day. We go on looking at the television or reading the newspaper, making the occasional grunt. The phone rings. It is one of our friends. We put down the newspaper and listen to every word he or she says. Our partner hears us responding animatedly, showing avid interest, deep sympathy, or robust enjoyment during the conversation. There are long silences as we take in exactly what our friend is saying. We motion to our husband or wife to turn the television down and we sit on a chair with our back turned giving the telephone our full attention.

Most of us are perfectly capable of listening, but we often neglect to do so with the person we see most and whose voice we hear most. It is easy to think that the most important part of communication is *talking*: being articulate, a good storyteller, having knowledge to divulge and opinions to proclaim. The Bible strongly challenges this view, placing much greater emphasis on the need to listen.

We are told in the Book of Proverbs, "To answer before listening—that is folly and shame" (Proverbs 18:13). But how many of us do just that? The Apostle James in the New Testament urges us similarly, "My dear brothers and sisters, take note of this: Everyone should be quick to listen, slow to speak and slow to become angry" (James 1:19). Perhaps that is why God created us with two ears and one mouth—that we might learn to listen twice as much as we speak. When we live by James' advice, all our relationships function better.

As human beings one of our greatest longings is to be listened to and understood. It meets the fundamental need we all have: not to be alone. The Samaritans once launched an advertising campaign with a poster of a huge ear and a caption under it saying "Open 24 hours a day." The organization exists to give support through listening to anyone at any time. Some people visit counselors or therapists simply to ensure that at least someone will listen to them for an hour or so. But surely we should not need to pay for this.

In marriage the danger is that we don't bother to listen, either out of laziness, or because we think we already know what is going to be said. We easily fall into bad habits such as interrupting, switching off, or finishing each other's sentences. In the words of one counselor:

> The gift of being a good listener, a gift which requires constant practice, is perhaps the most healing gift anyone can possess; for it allows the other to be, enfolds them in a safe place, does not judge or advise them, and communicates support at a level deeper than words.[2]

Listening is a powerful way of showing that we value each other, but it is also costly. It takes effort to listen to a husband or wife pouring out feelings or expressing opinions.

Many of us are not the listeners we might be. Yet to improve our listening is to improve our marriages. We have found the following five profiles helpful in recognizing where we fall short.[3] (One of us was able to identify with all five!)

### FIVE PROFILES OF A POOR LISTENER

*The Advice Giver*

Instead of aiming to empathize with a husband or wife, the *advice giver* wants to sort out the problem, quickly suggesting, "This is what you need to do." Carried to an extreme and unchecked, this can destroy a marriage:

> I met Patrick when he was forty-three and had been married for seventeen years. I remember him because his first words were so dramatic. He sat in the leather chair in my office and after briefly introducing himself, he leaned forward and said with great emotion, "Dr. Chapman, I have been a fool, a real fool."
>
> "What has led you to that conclusion?" I asked.
>
> "I've been married for seventeen years," he said, "and my wife

has left me. Now I realize what a fool I've been."

I repeated my original question, "In what way have you been a fool?"

"My wife would come home from work and tell me about the problems in her office. I would listen to her and then tell her what I thought she should do. I always gave her advice. I told her she had to confront the problem. 'Problems don't go away. You have to talk with the people involved or your supervisor. You have to deal with problems.'

"The next day she would come home from work and tell me about the same problems. I would ask her if she had done what I had suggested the day before. She would shake her head and say no. So I'd repeat my advice. I told her that was the way to deal with the situation. She would come home the next day and tell me about the same problems. Again I would ask her if she had done what I had suggested. She would shake her head and say no.

"After three or four nights of that, I would get angry. I would tell her not to expect any sympathy from me if she wasn't willing to take the advice I was giving her....

"I would withdraw and go about my business. What a fool I was," he said. "What a fool! Now I realize that she didn't want advice when she told me about her struggles at work. She wanted sympathy. She wanted me to listen, to give her attention, to let her know that I could understand the hurt, the stress, the pressure. She wanted to know that I loved her and that I was with her. She didn't want advice; she just wanted to know that I understood. But I never tried to understand. I was too busy giving advice."[4]

*The Interrupter*

Instead of listening when someone else is speaking, we can easily be working out what we are going to say next. Best-selling author Stephen Covey writes:

> Most people do not listen with the intent to understand; they listen with the intent to reply. They're either speaking or preparing to speak.

They're... reading their autobiography into other people's lives.[5]

A few years ago on vacation our children had been water-skiing and were talking excitedly about their achievements. A man standing nearby joined in the conversation. No sooner was he aware of the subject matter than he started to regale them with tales of his own prowess at water-skiing, his children's water-skiing, the speed of his boat, the price of his wetsuit, and so on. Our children, even though they were quite young at the time, have not forgotten him. He spoiled a very happy afternoon through his inability to listen and his tendency to interrupt with his own autobiography.

An individual listens on average for 17 seconds before interrupting. This has sometimes become such a habit that husbands and wives are not even aware that they are doing it to each other. It will be a particular danger to the one who is more articulate than his or her partner. Some tend to work out what they think as they speak while their partner's way is to sort out their thoughts first and then speak. In these cases it can take great restraint not to finish our husband or wife's sentences or respond to what we think they are going to say. We need to learn to wait and listen as the *interrupter* can discourage his or her partner from any self-expression at all, beyond the minimum reporting of facts required for daily living.

*The Reassurer*

The *reassurer* is the person who jumps in prematurely, before a sentence is finished, with comments such as, "It probably isn't as bad as you think," or, "I'm sure it will work out all right," or, "You'll feel much better tomorrow." Reassurers prohibit any real expression of feelings, whether of anxiety, disappointment, or hurt, often because they themselves need the reassurance that there is no major problem and that their own lives can go on uninterrupted.

*The Rationalizer*

The *rationalizer*, rather than seeking to listen, focuses on explaining

*why* we feel as we do. In response to, "I've had a terrible day," he or she might reply, "That no doubt is the result of a combination of factors: the weather has been oppressive, you are under pressure at work, and you are probably worried about our finances."

*The Deflector*

Some people, instead of commenting on the issue raised, take the conversation off on a tangent, usually into an event that interests them. They say, "That reminds me of when ..." and away they go.

We can all become good listeners but we need to be willing to recognize where we fail and then to learn new skills. The following guidelines may appear artificial at first, but they are essential for good listening, and they have helped us improve our communication over the years.

## LEARNING TO LISTEN

*Giving our full attention*

We watched a film recently about a teenage daughter who rebels against her parents' values. In an early scene the daughter wants to talk to her father about some issues that are worrying her. He is desperate to finish a piece of writing, and he continues to work at his computer, while she tries to summon up the courage to voice her concerns. His eyes never leave the computer screen, and after a few minutes she decides not to say anything. The father's failure to listen has disastrous consequences in his daughter's life.

By contrast, a woman wrote of her father:

> I had been so proud of him, with his high posts in the Indian government. I could still see him, impeccably dressed, adjusting his turban at the mirror before leaving for his office. The friendly eyes under bushy brows, the gentle smile, the chiseled features and aquiline nose. One of my cherished memories was seeing him at work in the study. Often, as a little girl, I would have a question to ask him and I would peek at him from around the door of his office, hesitant to interrupt. Then his eye would catch mine.
>
> Putting down his pen, he would lean back in his chair and call out, "Keecha?" Slowly, I would walk into the study, my head down. He would smile and pat the chair next to his. "Come, my darling, sit here." Then, placing his arm around me, he would draw me to him. "Now, my little Keecha," he would ask gently, "what can I do for you?" It was always the same with Father. He didn't mind if I bothered him. Whenever I had a question or problem, no matter how busy he was, he would put aside his work to devote his full attention just to me.[6]

One father showed that he was listening. The other failed to do so. In marriage, as with parenting, giving our full attention communicates love.

Studies in communication reveal that less than 10 percent of what we want to communicate involves the words we use. The tone of voice with which we say it accounts for approximately 40 percent and our body language for the remaining 50 percent. This is as significant for listening as it is for talking.

Physical proximity aids communication; shouting our conversations from one room to another is not very effective. If your husband or wife needs to tell you something that has upset them, sitting close, putting an arm around him or her, and most of all looking at your spouse will show that you are concerned. Eye contact conveys the message: "I am interested in what you are saying and I am giving you my undivided attention."

*Coping with distractions*

**Sila** I find it difficult to give my full attention to Nicky if there are practical jobs that need doing. Nicky can happily sit among the chaos or be clearing up and holding an in-depth conversation at the same time. All I can think about is getting the debris from breakfast cleared, the house tidied, or the dirty clothes put into the washing machine. I know that I am not concentrating on what Nicky is saying, and therefore it is better for me to ask, "Can you give me ten minutes to tidy up?" Sometimes, however, there is no time for that and it takes a great effort for me to stop what I am doing, look at him, and give him my full attention.

It is also very hard to listen to someone when there is a lot of background noise.

**Nicky** If there is a television on in the room, I find it practically impossible to concentrate on what someone is saying to me. Equally I am easily distracted by another conversation in the same room or a newspaper with an interesting headline.

But a still greater hindrance to listening than the television or a newspaper is that, unconsciously, we often spend time in conversation listening to *ourselves*. It is as though there is a television switched on inside us which constantly distracts our attention. The other person's words trigger thoughts and memories of our own.

If the husband says, "I was talking to Chris today; he's just lost his mother," a wife might immediately start thinking about what it felt like when one of her own parents died. If a wife says, "As I was driving home the blossoms looked amazing..." a husband's mind fills with gloomy thoughts of how much needs to be done in the garden. Thus our own thoughts and memories obstruct our listening, and our next remark may have little to do with our partner's conversation.

It can be hard not to hold a separate conversation in your own head, especially if you are busy and your mind is full. Your aim should be to put your own views and agenda aside and try to grasp what your partner is saying. Steven Covey underlines the impact this has:

> If I were to summarize in one sentence the single most important principle I have learned in the field of interpersonal relations, it would be this: Seek first to understand, then to be understood.[7]

Significantly the Chinese character for hearing includes symbols for the eyes, the heart, and the mind as well as for the ear.

*Showing an interest*

If we are determined to be interested in what another person is saying, we listen carefully; otherwise we can easily switch off. A woman told us about her visits to her mother. She wanted to use the opportunity to talk about important issues, the meaning of life, and so on. Her mother, however, enjoyed discussing more mundane matters such as the price of potatoes, the neighbor's dog, or a recent television program. The daughter quickly stopped listening, thinking what a boring life her mother led.

Then one day she suddenly saw that this *was* her mother's life. This brought her up short. She recalls, "I said to myself, 'My mother is always interested in everything I do,' and I suddenly realized I had not been very generous toward her. So I made a conscious effort to be interested and to listen, and this has made a huge difference to our relationship."

Inevitably, people have different interests. Making an effort to listen to what others find interesting is a compelling way of showing our love. Author and speaker, Dale Carnegie, writes of the skill of being a good conversationalist:

> To be interesting, be interested. Ask questions that other persons will enjoy answering.[8]

*Listening intelligently*

To relive and describe in detail some hurt or long-standing problem can be costly. It is easier to skirt around the subject or allude to it through humor. It is sometimes necessary to listen *behind* each other's words to detect a hidden agenda. A good listener will have the courage to draw the other out by probing with gentle questions at the right moment.

We must give each other enough time to talk because often we are only half aware of why we feel as we do. Articulating our pain enables us to begin to see things in perspective. Do not be afraid of silences. For some people silence allows them to organize their thoughts and waiting quietly shows our concern.

*Listening uncritically*

Communication flourishes with acceptance of each other and is crushed by criticism. We need to be able to listen without becoming defensive and without butting in. If we can fathom what a spouse is feeling, we shall be at least halfway to resolving a difficult situation.

We often talk to a spouse when we feel raw emotionally. Our words may seem confused and contradictory. We may change our minds about what we feel in the course of expressing ourselves. The listener fails totally (and cruelly) if they start to pick holes in the spouse's case or logic.

*Acknowledging our partner's feelings*

To repeat in your own words what your partner has been telling you is very helpful, particularly when deep feelings are being expressed. This enables your husband or wife to know that you are on the same wavelength and that you have properly understood them.

For example, a wife says, "The children have been driving me mad. They haven't stopped crying and arguing all day." Rather than immediately suggesting a solution, her husband might acknowledge her feelings with, "That must have been really hard for you."

Or a husband says, "I can't see how we are going to make ends meet. I can't earn any more. I'm really worried about it." His wife can show she has listened to his feelings by saying, "I'm really sorry you've been so worried. Let's talk about it."

Or a wife says, "It really upset me when you suddenly told me about the possibility of a new job. If we have to move away, I hate the thought of losing contact with our friends." Again, her husband needs to show he has heard and understood what she is feeling, perhaps by replying, "I didn't realize that you'd be worried about losing contact with our friends'" Using their exact words at least indicates that we have been listening.

Acknowledging feelings in this way may seem unnatural and contrived at first but it is a powerful tool in learning to listen and in building emotional intimacy.

**Nicky** A few months ago a leader dropped out of one of our courses. Although my diary was already crowded with evening commitments, I saw no alternative but to agree to lead the group myself for four evenings. When I told Sila, I expected sympathy from her for the extra commitment of time and work. Instead Sila was cross and unreasonable, or so it seemed to me.

A few weeks later she started to tell me how upset she was that I had given away some of our free evenings without

> discussing it with her. Feeling full of self-pity, I immediately defended my decision. I realized later that the real need was to listen to Sila and understand her feelings. She was hurt. She felt that the people on the course were more important to me than our family.

In situations like this the aim of listening is to understand and accept our partner's feelings, not to judge whether they are right or wrong.

*Giving advice only if asked*

We need to guard against the desire to *fix* the situation. Giving advice is often counterproductive because finding a quick solution is not what is required. Advice can appear to diminish the importance of what we feel. The process of exploring our feelings and meeting with acceptance and empathy *is* the solution. Our husband or wife will usually ask us for advice if that is what they are seeking.

Learning to listen to each other can transform your whole marriage. Many couples on *The Marriage Course* have commented on the difference it has made:

- "We listen much better and we don't feel we have to blame one another."
- "I learned to listen to what my wife's needs really are."
- "It has helped us to listen to each other with compassionate ears."
- "Listening has improved for both of us. We allow each other to have a say."
- "I have learned to listen with new ears; the small things *are* important."

# Section 2 – The Art of Communication

## CONCLUSION

Diane Vaughan, a sociologist working at Oxford University, spent 10 years researching reasons for the failure of marriages. As part of her conclusion she wrote:

> It starts with the partner who first feels discontented. At first, he or she will try to hide the discontent, pretend it doesn't exist, or that it will go away. Instead it grows stronger and after some time the initiator will attempt to convey the discontent to the other partner usually with vague hints or complaints *that are almost always ignored or unnoticed* (italics ours).[9]

In other words her 10 years of research revealed that, in almost every marriage that breaks down, there is a failure of communication.

There is no substitute in marriage for effective talking and effective listening. Two individuals with separate thoughts and separate feelings come together as one. Communication is the bridge which connects one to the other, for we cannot read each other's minds nor see into each other's hearts. If we fail to communicate, we draw up the bridge and retreat to our lonely castle. As we choose to communicate, we let down the drawbridge and invite each other in. We allow each other access to the secret places.

## Second Golden Rule of Marriage

Keep talking and keep listening to each other.

# Section 3 — Love in Action

# 5

## The Five Expressions of Love

*It is possible to give without loving,*
*but it is impossible to love without giving.*
ANONYMOUS

A group of children were asked their opinion as to why people fall in love. One nine-year-old replied, "No one is sure why it happens, but I heard it has something to do with how you smell. That's why perfume and deodorant are so popular." An eight-year-old boy had a different theory: "I think you're supposed to get shot with an arrow or something, but the rest of it isn't supposed to be so painful." Gary, age seven, was convinced it had to do with more than your appearance: "It isn't always just how you look. Look at me. I'm handsome like anything and I haven't got anybody to marry me yet."

Some adults are equally in the dark about the real nature of love. They have been brought up to believe that love is principally an emotion over which we have little control, a belief that is reinforced by the lyrics of many popular songs. Our children recently discovered (to their great amusement) some of our records from the '60s with phrases such as:

Before the dance was through
I knew I was in love with you
and

I didn't know just what to do
So I whispered, "I love you."

Infatuation, which can be triggered as easily by physical appearance as by any real knowledge of the other person, and which is likely to go as quickly and mysteriously as it came, is often portrayed as the sum total of love. The popular understanding of love has largely been reduced to *feelings*.

But there is another kind of love which is deliberate and which is cultivated over a period of time. In Louis de Bernière's novel, *Captain Correlli's Mandolin*, Dr. Iannis describes to his daughter the type of love that lasts:

> Love is not breathlessness, it is not excitement, it is not the promulgation of promises of eternal passion, it is not the desire to mate every second minute of the day, it is not lying awake at night imagining that he is kissing every cranny of your body. No, don't blush, I am telling you some truths. That is just being "in love," which any fool can do. Love itself is what is left over when being in love has burned away... Your mother and I had it, we had roots that grew towards each other underground, and when all the pretty blossoms had fallen from our branches, we found that we were one tree and not two.[1]

Some people get married on the basis of infatuation. They think that their strong feelings of mutual attraction will be enough for their marriages to survive. Eventually and inevitably, however, infatuation wears off and then, if there is no understanding of how to create a love that develops with time, their roots will fail to entwine, and their marriage will wither.

Christian love, as the New Testament describes it, is not so much an abstract noun as an active verb. Love involves doing. It means reaching out to meet the needs of another often at a cost to oneself.

In marriage, it may mean doing the dishes out of love for your partner when you would rather be watching television. It may mean sitting down to talk with your husband or wife when you would rather get started on some work. It may mean hugging your partner when you know that they have had a hard day. Only *this* sort of love is able to sustain a marriage relationship over many years, causing it to mature and to deepen.



In practice there are five ways through which we can actively show love to our husband or wife:

1. Loving words
2. Kind actions
3. Quality time
4. Thoughtful presents
5. Physical affection

These ways of putting love into action are called *The Five Love Languages* in Gary Chapman's excellent book in which he uses the metaphor of language to examine the different ways in which we communicate and understand love.[2] His work as a marriage counselor over many years has revealed that, just as we all have a native language which we find easy to speak and comprehend, so each of us has a first *love language* through which we most easily understand love.

All five are important ways of showing love, but which is primary? A husband may shower his wife with *presents*, but she may first and foremost need to hear him say kind *words* in order to feel loved. A wife may work hard in the home for her husband, but he may need regular *physical affection* in order to feel her love for him.

The greatest need we all share is to know we are loved, that we matter to another, that we are special to them. We must therefore ask ourselves, "What is it that makes my husband or wife feel most loved?" We can find this out through conversation and through deliberate and careful observation. A friend of ours who has been married for many years claims that in order to have a happy marriage, a husband and a wife must "study each other." In doing so we discover important and sometimes unexpected information.

While there may be plenty of romantic ways on a honeymoon to demonstrate love with the minimum of words, daily life would be near impossible without being able to speak the same language. Daily love will be impossible if we never find out and learn our husband's or wife's first love language (and quite possibly their second and third too).

**Nicky** I have come to realize that time and touch convey love most powerfully for Sila while words and actions are most important for me. It would therefore be disastrous for our relationship if I only gave time and touch to my computer but not to Sila, or if she showed love through her words and actions to our children but not to me.

Having found out what makes a partner feel loved, we must then decide to act on our discovery. It may seem unnatural at first and, as with learning a foreign language, it will require time, determination, and a great deal of practice. Some have grown up in homes where

there has been little or no physical affection, and they will not naturally and spontaneously give this to their partner. But this expression of love can be learned. And it will be essential to do so if this is the way your husband or wife feels loved. Others have not heard loving affirming words being spoken during their upbringing. In which case, if this is particularly important to your partner, you will need to practice this way of showing love. As you do so, you will become increasingly fluent.

We write in detail about these five expressions of love, because we know from our own experience that in its simplicity it is a profound and far-reaching principle which any couple can utilize for the strengthening and well-being of their relationship. Numerous couples we know are still very much "in love" many years after the initial infatuation has worn off because each has a thousand times each year shown love to a spouse in the way that he or she understands it best.

Some couples never discover what makes their partners feel loved. They may study each other but with the wrong intention; they are looking to criticize rather than to find out each other's needs. In a short story, *The Eyes of Love*, we read about an American couple, Kenneth and Shannon, who are in their car driving home after a family party.

> Before he can suppress it, anger rises like a kind of heat in the bones of his face. "Okay, what is it?" he says…
>
> She doesn't answer right away. "I'm tired," she tells him without quite turning to look at him.
>
> "No really," he says. "I want to hear it. Come on, let it out."
>
> Now she does turn. "I told you this morning. I just don't like hearing the same stories all the time."
>
> "They aren't all the same," he says, feeling unreasonably angry.
>
> "Oh, of course they are….Your mother deserves a medal."
>
> "I like them. Mom likes them. Everybody likes them. Your father and your sisters like them."
>
> "Over and over," she mutters, looking away again. "I just want to go to sleep."
>
> "You know what your problem is?" he says, "You're a critic. That's what your problem is. Everything is something for you to evaluate and decide on. Even me. Especially me."
>
> "You," she says.
>
> "Yes," he says. "Me. Because this isn't about my father at all. It's about us."

According to Kenneth, she has looked upon the evening and his father's storytelling as she looks upon him, as a critic. The conversation continues:

> He's quiet a moment, but the anger is still working in him. "You know the trouble with you?" he says. "You don't see anything with love. You only see it with your brain."
>
> "Whatever you say," she tells him.
>
> "Everything's locked up in your head,'" he says, taking a long drag of the cigarette and then putting it out in the ashtray.
>
> He starts the car. "You know those people that live behind us?" he says. The moment has become almost philosophical to him.
>
> She stares at him with her wet eyes, and just now he feels quite

powerful and happy.

"Do you?" he demands.

"Of course I do."

"Well, I was watching them the other day. The way he is with the yard – right? We've been making such fun of him all summer. We've been so smart about his obsession with weeds and trimming and the grass."

"I guess it's really important that we talk about these people now," she says.

"I'm telling you something you need to hear," Kenneth says.

"I don't want to hear it now," she says. "I've been listening to talk all day. I'm tired of talk."

And Kenneth is shouting at her. "I'll just say this and then I'll shut up for the rest of the year if that's what you want!"

She says nothing.

"I'm telling you about these people. The man was walking around with a little plastic baggie on one hand, picking up the dog's droppings. Okay? And his wife was trimming one of her shrubs. She was trimming one of the shrubs and I thought for a second I could feel what she was thinking. There wasn't anything in her face, but I was so smart, like we are, you know, Shannon. I was so smart about it that I knew what she was thinking. I was so perceptive about these people we don't even know. These people we're too snobbish to speak to."

"You're the one who makes fun of them," Shannon says.

"Let me finish," he says. "I saw the guy's wife look at him from the other side of the yard, and it was like I could hear the words in her mind: 'He's picking up the dog droppings again. I can't stand it another minute.' You know? But that wasn't what she was thinking. Because she walked over in a little while and helped him—actually pointed out a couple of places he'd missed. And then the two of them walked into their house arm in arm with their dog droppings. You see what I'm saying, Shannon? That woman was looking at him with love. She didn't see what I saw—there wasn't any criticism in it."

Finally, Kenneth and Shannon stop arguing.

> The fight's over. They've made up. She reaches across and gives his forearm a little affectionate squeeze. He takes her hand and squeezes back. Then he has both hands on the wheel again. Their apartment house is in sight now, down the street to the left. He turns to look at her, his wife, here in the shadowed and watery light, and then he quickly looks back at the road. It comes to him like a kind of fright that in the little idle moment of his gaze some part of him was marking the unpleasant downturn of her mouth, the chiseled, too sharp curve of her jaw—the whole disheveled, vaguely tattered look of her—as though he were a stranger, someone unable to imagine what anyone, another man, other men, someone like himself, could see in her to love[3]

As the story ends, we realize that, unlike the husband and the wife who live behind their house, Kenneth and Shannon have become each other's critics. We reap what we sow. "You don't see anything with love," Kenneth said. But neither does he look at her with love. In a world full of critics, we are called as husband and wife to study each other, not with critical eyes, but with the eyes of love, searching for what our partner needs to feel loved and special.

Over the next two chapters we will describe each of the five expressions of love. As we do so, ask yourself the following three questions:

1. Do I regularly express love in this way?
2. How important is this expression of love for my husband or wife to feel loved?
3. How important is this expression of love for me?

It is easy to expect your husband or wife to know instinctively about your needs, and then to get hurt when they fail to meet them. We all tend to express love in the way that we like to receive it. Despite your good intentions, this will not work if your spouse has different needs from your own.

We can let our marriages fall apart. Or we each can take the opportunity to have the best possible marriage. If we are to have a real sense of intimacy and a true enjoyment of each other, we must study one another with the eyes of love and then use our lives appropriately—our words, our actions, our time, our money, and our bodies—to communicate love effectively.

# 6

## Words and Actions

*Pleasant words are a honeycomb,*
*sweet to the soul and healing to the bones.*
PROVERBS 16:24

*Where love is lacking, sow love and you will soon gather love.*
ST. JOHN OF THE CROSS

### LOVING WORDS

The playground rhyme, "Sticks and stones may break my bones but words can never hurt me," is only true in a physical sense. The Bible often reminds us of the power of our words: "The tongue has the power of life and death" (Proverbs 18:21).

Studies have shown that words can affect behavior and ability to an extraordinary degree. If children are told that they are useless at math, they are likely to do very badly in that subject. Conversely if they are told their creative writing is wonderful, they are likely to become aspiring novelists overnight. People will live up to the reputation they are given.

This has enormous implications for the way we speak to each other in marriage. We need to maintain love, gentleness, and respect in our tone and to avoid getting into the habit of putting each other down. We need to build up our husband or wife both at home and in public; it is highly destructive for them to be made the butt of our jokes.

The way to make each other feel loved through our speech is by affirming each other. This will include how we give compliments, how we say thank you, how we encourage, how we show kindness, and how we make requests. The failure to do these things skillfully and graciously leaves our marriage partner open to temptation from outside. The following extract from a poem, written over a hundred years ago by Ella Wheeler Wilcox, is a wife's explanation (though not her excuse) for having an affair:

> Each day,
> Our lives that had been one life at the start,
> Farther and farther seemed to drift apart.
> Dead was the old romance of man and maid.
> Your talk was all of politics and trade.
> Your work, your club, the mad pursuit of gold
> Absorbed your thoughts. Your duty kiss felt cold
> Upon my lips. Life lost its zest, its thrill

Until
One fateful day when earth seemed very dull
It suddenly grew bright and beautiful.
I spoke a little, and he listened much;
There was attention in his eyes, and such
A note of comradeship in his low tone
I felt no more alone.
There was a kindly interest in his air;
He spoke about the way I dressed my hair.
And praised the gown I wore.
It seemed a thousand, thousand years and more,
Since I had been so noticed. Had mine ear
Been used to compliments year after year,
If I had heard you speak
As this man spoke, I had not been so weak.[1]

There are many different ways of using words to convey love to one another.

*Paying compliments*

People who have not been used to hearing compliments during their upbringing may not easily accept them, let alone give them. But we can learn. Compliments draw attention to what we admire and appreciate in a husband or wife. Many of us keep such thoughts locked up in our minds, thinking they are too trivial to verbalize or superfluous because our partner already knows that we love him or her. Yet the marriage service speaks of *cherishing* one another. Paying compliments is an excellent way of cherishing each other, and all of us can learn to do it. Try something as simple and direct as:

"You look really great in that suit."
"You handled that meeting brilliantly."
"I love the way you always think of the right thing to say."

*Offering thanks*
Gratitude confers value and worth upon someone. When we live together day by day, we all too easily overlook the many things our partners do for us. Some are small and regular; others show great care and require a lot of effort.

"Thank you for taking out the garbage" or "Thank you for taking my suits to the cleaners" sound mundane, but it is important to give recognition for small acts of love. "I'm so grateful you remembered my mother's birthday" gives appreciation for what could easily be taken for granted. "Thank you for being so helpful at Tom's birthday party; I couldn't have handled it without you," shows gratitude for the other's involvement.

*Being encouraging*
Another way we can use words positively is by encouraging, that is, inspiring *courage* in each other. All of us have areas of our lives where we feel insecure: we lack courage. It is within our power to give the encouragement which will enable our husbands or wives to reach their potential. Conversely, if we criticize, our words have the power gradually to rob our partner of their self-worth and self-confidence. When we encourage, we are saying to each other, "I believe in you."

**Sila** There have been many areas in my life since we've been married where Nicky's encouragement has spurred me on to do things that I might otherwise not have done. His words have often made all the difference to me, a full-time mother, giving me confidence and self-esteem, particularly as the role of motherhood is largely undervalued today.

*Being thoughtful*
Thoughtful words build someone up whereas untimely, thoughtless words cause much hurt in a relationship.

**Sila** In our own marriage, I have had to learn to be careful with my words. I like to discuss things immediately after an event and, when we were first married, I had little concept that I might need to choose a better time to voice my opinion to Nicky, particularly when he had made himself vulnerable.

It took me some time to realize that Sunday lunch is not the right moment to give my analysis of his sermon or the church service he has just led. I have discovered that it is better to wait until at least the next day, when he is more able to be objective.

Even then I have to choose my words carefully. I am not advocating false flattery but it can require a conscious effort to make sure that our words are encouraging, kind, and affirming and that they will build our partner up. I have come to realize over the years how important these words are for Nicky. For him affirming words are the key way in which he feels my love, and it gives him a foundation of confidence which affects all other aspects of his life.

*Making requests*

There is the world of difference in a marriage between making demands and making requests. When we make requests of our spouses, we are affirming their worth and their abilities. If we make demands, we become intolerant and tyrannical in our own homes, often without realizing it. That kind of person is not easy or pleasant to live with. We can become demanding when we start to take our partners (and their gifts and abilities) for granted.

**Sila** Nicky is very practical and capable of turning his hand to anything that needs fixing in our home. Yet there are times when I can be complacent about that. I've heard myself say, "You haven't fixed that flat tire yet, have you? I need my bike by tomorrow." A better way of saying it would be, "Nicky, would you be able to fix the flat on my bike before tomorrow?" A request like that creates the possibility for him to express his love for me by responding to it. Demands exclude that possibility.

If verbal affirmation is deeply important to your spouse and he/she has not received any for some time, he/she will probably be feeling low. To hear positive words from you again will be like reaching an oasis in the desert. As we learn to build our partner up with words, we will reach a new level of love and intimacy in our marriage. The words we use have the power to renew love daily. Criticism and self-pity are powerful separators. Words of affirmation are powerful uniters.

## Kind actions

The Apostle Paul describes kindness as love's second characteristic. We show kindness to our husband or wife when we serve each other in practical ways. Within a marriage this can take many different forms: making a cup of coffee, taking out the trash, cleaning the windshield of the car, cooking a favorite cake, ironing a shirt. Of course routine activities may be taken for granted, but, when done willingly, constantly express love. However, it is the nonroutine, practical acts of service that communicate love most powerfully to those for whom this is one of the ways they feel loved.

**Nicky** I can recall many occasions when Sila has done things for me which I was not expecting. She has packed for me when I have had to go away overnight and have been under pressure. She has brought tea and toast to my study when I have been struggling to prepare a talk. Often the crisis has been self-inflicted through taking on too many commitments and I have felt much loved by Sila's thoughtfulness.

After many years of marriage, I continue to be amazed and delighted by all that Sila does for me, routine and non-routine. I sometimes catch myself wondering why she does it. And the only answer I can come up with every time is that she loves me!

In *Captain Corelli's Mandolin*, Dr. Iannis succeeds in curing an old man called Stamatis of deafness by removing a dried pea that has been in his ear since childhood. Stamatis returns to the doctor to ask him to reinsert the pea as he cannot stand his wife's constant nagging. Dr. Iannis refuses but suggests an alternative. He recommends a cure for his wife's nagging:

> "My advice is to be nice to her."
>
> Stamatis was shocked. It was a course of action so inconceivable that he had never even conceived of conceiving it. "Iatre..." he protested, but could find no other words.
>
> "Just bring in the wood before she asks for it, and bring her a flower every time you come back from the field. If it's cold put a shawl around her shoulders and if it's hot bring her a glass of water. It's simple..."
>
> "Then you won't put back the...the, er...disputatious and pugnacious extraordinary embodiment?" [referring to the dried pea]

"Certainly not. It would be against the Hippocratic oath. I can't allow that. It was Hippocrates, incidentally, who said that 'extreme remedies are most appropriate for extreme disease.'"

Stamatis appeared downcast: "Hippocrates says so? So I've got to be nice to her?'

The doctor nodded paternally, and Stamatis replaced his hat. He watched the old man from his window. Stamatis went out into the road and began to walk away. He paused and looked down at a small purple flower in the embankment. He leaned down to pick it, but immediately straightened up. He peered about himself to ensure that no one was watching. He pulled at his belt in the manner of girding up his loins, glared at the flower, and turned on his heel. He began to stroll away, but then stopped. Like a little boy involved in a petty theft he darted back, snapped the stem of the flower, concealed it within his coat, and sauntered away with an exaggeratedly insouciant and casual air. The doctor leaned out of the window and called after him, "Bravo Stamatis," just for the simple but malicious pleasure of witnessing his embarrassment and shame.[2]

A strong marriage consists of both husband and wife finding opportunities to serve each other and to express their appreciation for what the other does. When life is hectic for us both, we instinctively think, ""Why isn't he or she helping me?" But when instead our partner asks, "What can I do to help you?" or spontaneously does the job that we most dislike, this is unmistakably "love in action."

A friend describes the effect upon her of such acts of sacrificial love:

My husband often has to leave for work very early in the morning, before the children and I are even awake. Quite often, when we come downstairs, the dishwasher has been emptied, the table is set for breakfast, and he has left some little surprise for each of the children—nothing too dramatic—a jelly baby in an egg cup or a custard cream. When this happens, I can almost feel my heart physically warm as I enter the kitchen, and all three of us seem to start the day with a skip in our step (occasionally the mood lasts all through breakfast). The next challenge I face is to feel cheerful when it doesn't happen. How quickly we take each other for granted!

# 7

## Time, Presents, and Touch

*You know very well that love is, above all, the gift of oneself.*
JEAN ANOUILH[1]

### QUALITY TIME

A couple who took *The Marriage Course* two years ago were recently traveling back to London from Australia. Their flight had been delayed enroute, and consequently they spent four hours together in Hong Kong airport reading newspapers and magazines and entertaining their young daughter. They then spent a further twelve hours sitting side by side on the airplane.

On their way home from the airport, the husband said to his wife, "I've missed having our marriage time recently. We must book it in." His wife was astonished. "What do you mean?" she asked, "We've just been together for the past sixteen hours!" But her husband needed more. He needed a time and a place in which he and his wife could give their total attention to each other without all the distractions and without worrying when the plane would leave or what time they would get home.

Every couple needs to spend time together regularly, as we discussed in chapter 2, but for some, this quality time is their primary *love language*. If so, the longed for togetherness is more than physical proximity; there is a need, indeed a hunger, for total, focused attention.

**Nicky** For Sila the surroundings and the activity take second place to my spending time with her, talking and listening, discussing ideas and sharing our hopes and fears. Such regular times together enable her to face the pressures in her life because she is confident of the love in our marriage. I have found that the value of our weekly time together is more than doubled if I manage to arrange for us to go somewhere where we are unlikely to see anyone we know.

We wrote in chapter 2 of our plan each year to go away by ourselves for two or three nights. For the last two years we have gone to Paris. We have spent our time exploring the city, visiting art galleries, and eating in little cafés. These two or three days have been very romantic and great fun. But for Sila, they have a disproportionate effect on her feeling of being loved. For days after our return, nothing has been able to diminish her sense of joy and well-being. I have realized increasingly that these breaks are one of the best investments I could make in our marriage.

The Bible tells us to "live a life of love" following the example of Jesus who "gave Himself up for us" (Ephesians 5:2). Most of us will not be called to give up our lives for each other, but we can demonstrate our love for our husband or wife by regularly giving up our time for them.

This may mean sitting down together after work for half an hour to hear how the day has gone. It may mean getting up earlier to spend time together in the morning. It may involve going out of our way to have lunch together. It may mean making arrangements for the children so that we have our marriage time alone. Love in action requires effort and sacrifice but the rewards far outweigh the cost.

## Thoughtful presents

Giving presents is a fundamental expression of love that transcends all cultural barriers. They are visual symbols, which have a powerful emotional value. For some of us these symbols are so important that without them we will question whether we are loved at all. A person who is good at *giving* presents probably loves *receiving* them. If this is true of our husband or wife, we will need to practice this art.

This is the easiest of the five expressions of love to learn. However, we may need to change our attitude toward money. If we are naturally *spenders*, it will not be difficult for us. But if we are naturally *savers*, we may well struggle against the idea of spending money as an expression of love. We are not talking here about the difference between being generous and being mean.

**Sila** Nicky is one of the most generous people I know but he is a natural saver. Because he does not easily spend money on non-essentials for himself, I know he finds it difficult to buy such things for me. However, he has discovered that presents are another form of investment. For me presents are not the most important expression of love, but when Nicky quite spontaneously (without it being my birthday or our anniversary) comes home with flowers or chocolates, it makes me aware again that he loves me and has been thinking about me.

A few guidelines about present-buying are worth considering:

*Presents can be inexpensive*, but have a high value. For example, one flower picked from the garden and given with a note can express love as powerfully as a bunch from a store.

*Don't wait for special occasions.* Spontaneous and unexpected presents bring a huge amount of joy and a great sense of being special and loved to the recipient. A present can cheer someone up during difficult times, such as when one of you is unwell, under pressure, or having a hard time at work. Conversely, if your husband or wife has done something that particularly helped you, a present can show that this has not been taken for granted.

*Find out what your partner particularly likes to receive.* It is worth noticing which presents your husband or wife has especially liked receiving over the years either from you or from others. If you are out together, you could make a mental note of something your spouse points out in a shop window.

**Sila** Over the years, we have collected blue and white china of all different sorts and patterns. Nicky once gave me a pair of large breakfast cups in blue and white which have become very special. I associate them with a long leisurely breakfast on a Saturday morning. Each time we use them, I am reminded of Nicky's care and thoughtfulness in choosing them for me.

There are endless possibilities. The key to being a good present giver is this: the present must be something that the other person will enjoy, not what we ourselves would like to have!

It is easy to dismiss this expression of love as materialistic or shallow. But we are all different. One husband for whom presents mean little only recognized several years into marriage how important they are for his wife to feel appreciated and loved. Initially he paid little, if any, attention to how they were wrapped or presented. Now he realizes the thought and care he puts into the presentation is as important to his wife as the present itself.

If a husband or wife demanded a diamond ring or a sports car every week, we would probably be right to question their motives. Nor should we pay our partner off with presents as a substitute for spending time together or discussing difficulties. The time and thought which go into choosing a present make it truly a gift. Given appropriately, the value of a present far exceeds its cost.

## Physical affection

> Many couples who fervently desire a long hug or a romp in bed have to make do with a new kitchen or another holiday in the Bahamas.[2]

Being shown love through touch is a basic need for every person. Babies need to be shown physical affection to develop healthily. Pictures of orphanages in Romania and China provide plenty of tragic evidence that this is so. Mother Teresa clearly understood the importance of touch. Whenever she was with people, whether they were babies, children, or old people dying of incurable diseases, she would hold them, stroke them, caress them. She knew that touch can often communicate love more effectively than words.

Physical affection is a powerful communicator in marital love and not just as a prelude to making love. As one writer put it, "To touch my body is to touch me. To withdraw from my body is to distance yourself from me emotionally."[3] For those who feel loved through touch , hugs can sort out all the problems of the week while a lack of them causes isolation, emptiness, and a deep sense of rejection. If we have grown up in a family where physical affection was lacking, the practice of showing love in this way will almost certainly need to be learned. And it is important to understand that if one of us has been denied physical affection while the other has not, it may cause some initial awkwardness. But persevere!

In marriage, the touch of love can take many forms: holding hands, an arm around the shoulder or waist, a kiss, a hug, a brush of the body as you pass, a back massage, as well as the variety and richness of arousing each other as a prelude to making love.

**Sila** I love holding hands with Nicky when we are walking together. Although I know there are certain situations when he would not do that naturally, he has learned that some embarrassment on his part is worth it to have a wife who feels loved.

He also knows from years of experience that if I'm anxious or worried, the best thing he can do is to take me in his arms, hug me, hold me, and kiss me tenderly, at which point my worries evaporate!

Both sexual and nonsexual touch have their place but we should recognize that men and women generally function quite differently in this area. For most women, much of their desire for physical touch stems from their need for affection rather than for sex. By contrast, men often see physical touch as part of sexual foreplay and are quickly aroused by it.

These different ways of responding can become a vicious circle. If a wife does not get enough affection, she will often shut out her husband sexually. And if a husband does not get enough sex, the last thing he feels like is being affectionate. All too often the result is a stalemate. This is often where the sexual relationship starts to wane. We need to recognize what is happening, talk about it, and then agree how to help each other break this dangerous pattern. For some people there is a fine line between their desire for sex and their longing for physical affection. The two cannot be easily separated.

Matt and Penny, a couple on *The Marriage Course*, were experiencing great tension after the birth of their second child. Penny was not interested in sex while Matt became frustrated and tried to persuade her. She stopped touching him at all in case he took it as an encouragement to make love. The more he wanted sex, the less she did and the less she did, the more he did. And so they spiraled down in misery. Matt was confused, not understanding why his wife didn't want him. As touch is his primary way of feeling loved, he felt undervalued and unloved.

Meanwhile Penny felt hurt and angry and interpreted his persistence as insensitivity, thinking he was ignoring her emotional turmoil. The result was that they were locked into a cycle of hurting and blaming each other and had no physical contact at all.

Eventually, on the advice of friends, Matt apologized to Penny for putting his needs above hers, and she forgave him. He then backed off sexually for a period of about two months. This was an important sign to Penny that he meant his apology, and it allowed time for the hurt to heal. As a result she began to open up to him again. With the lines of communication cleared, they could draw close and start to touch each other again without fear of misunderstanding. Soon Penny was able to accept Matt's advances and even make a few of her own.

If physical affection is your husband's or wife's most important expression of love, at a time of crisis, holding, and hugging him or her will communicate how much you care. Those gentle, tender touches will be remembered long after the crisis has passed.

# Section 3 – Love in Action

## Conclusion

There are few things more important in marriage than discovering what makes our husband or wife feel loved and then making the effort to love them in this way, remembering that their needs may well alter over time and under different circumstances. Rather than trying to change our partner we must accept their needs and learn to communicate love accordingly.

It is worth noting that in the Gospels Jesus showed love in all five ways: through words, actions, time, presents, and touch. He spoke *words* of affirmation to His disciples, saying, "I have called you friends...You did not choose Me, but I chose you." He served them with practical *deeds*, washing their feet when no one else was prepared to do this menial and unpleasant job. He spent *time* with them, taking them to quiet places away from the crowds. He gave them *gifts*, supremely the gift of His Holy Spirit. And He showed His love to many through *touch*, taking the children in His arms, putting His hands upon the leper and allowing the prostitute to dry His feet with her hair. At the Last Supper, Jesus said to His disciples, "Love each other as I have loved you" (John 15:12). We must fulfill this command first and foremost with our husband or wife, showing love in the way that will assure them that they matter and are special to us.

Do you know which is your partner's first *love language*? How about your own? The starting point is to talk together about what each of us does or fails to do that makes the other feel most loved or most neglected.

Don't put it off! It may lead to a surprising discovery about your husband or wife.

## Third Golden Rule of Marriage

Study the ways your partner feels loved.

# Section 4 — Resolving Conflict

# 8

## Appreciating Our Differences

*Pol and I are on paper reasonably incompatible, so important an ingredient in a good partnership.*
FRANK MUIR[1]

*Change is not made without inconvenience even from worse to better.*
RICHARD HOOKER[2]

**Nicky** I remember vividly as a seven-year-old practicing the three-legged race for our school sports day. For several weeks before the event I went around with my left leg tied with a red handkerchief to my friend's right leg. To start with it was agony. Our strides were different lengths; we kept forgetting which leg we had agreed to start with; we fell over on the tarmac; the handkerchief chafed our ankles, and we had several heated arguments. However, by sports day we could run almost as fast tied together as we could on our own. And we won the race!

Marriage is a bit like doing the three-legged race, and it would be surprising if at times we would not prefer to be running on our own. According to Paul Tournier, author of *Marriage Difficulties*, "Disagreements are entirely normal. As a matter of fact, they are a good thing. Those who make a success of their marriage are those

who tackle their problems together and who overcome them."[3]

A survey in 1998 of the principal causes for arguments between British couples revealed that money came top, followed by personal habits (particularly untidiness), children, housework, sex, parents, and friends. *The Times* newspaper, reporting on the survey two days before Valentine's Day, said, "The most common form of argument is a blazing argument followed by a total lack of communication." In one marriage counselor's view: "The way a couple handles its arguments is the single most important key indicator of whether their relationship will succeed or not."[4]

Marriage involves two people with different backgrounds, personalities, desires, views, and priorities being joined together in the most intimate relationship possible for the rest of their lives. Added to this is the inherent selfishness of human nature: the desire to have it *my* way, to maintain *my* rights, to endorse *my* opinions, to pursue *my* interests.

One woman who had been married for six months commented that she had been more surprised in her marriage by the things she had learned about herself than about her husband: "It was like having a mirror held up in front of my face and I saw how selfish I really was." For all the joys of marital intimacy, our freedom to do just what we want is seriously curtailed.

**Sila** I vividly recall one argument between us. Our first child was six months old, we were living in Japan and a bachelor friend who lived two hundred miles away invited us to stay for the weekend.

He was a great entertainer with boundless energy, and whenever we went to stay for the weekend he would arrange breakfast parties, invite friends over for mid-morning coffee, and then host lunch, tea, and dinner parties!

On the Wednesday before we were due to go, I expressed my anxiety about the weekend because I felt exhausted from looking after a six-month-old, and anticipated that a weekend socializing with our daughter on display might finish me off. Nicky was adamant. Having accepted the invitation and knowing that a number of parties would have been arranged around us, we had to go.

We both felt our particular point of view very strongly. When I had failed to convince Nicky with my words, and he did not seem to appreciate how tired I was, I saw red.

Unfortunately for Nicky it happened to be the Japanese

season for apples, and we had just bought a large box of them. They were arranged in a pyramid in a basket and, starting at the top, I proceeded to hurl these apples at him one by one across the room.

He managed to escape serious injury by ducking down behind the sofa until the basket was empty. I'm glad to say these are the only objects I have ever thrown at Nicky, though I can all too easily hurl words at him when I get angry. The conclusion to the story follows later in the section.

Disagreement and conflict either build or destroy a marriage. When a husband and wife are determined to get their own way and to do all they can to change the other to their way of thinking, the result is usually a type of trench warfare. We dig in to defend our own positions, protecting ourselves by keeping the other at bay and occasionally launching an offensive. One of us may seem to win the odd skirmish, but really we have both lost as there is a hundred yards of no man's land between us, full of barbed wire, and barbed comments, unexploded bombs and unresolved issues. Conflict has destroyed our intimacy.

Disagreements can, however, lead to growth when both partners are prepared to tackle them together. The resolution may of course require us to change profoundly. The three-legged race means both partners adapting their strides to the other. The church reformer, Martin Luther, observed that there were two ways of becoming less selfish and more like Jesus Christ. The first was to enter a monastery; the second to embark upon marriage!

What follows is the first step toward resolving conflict effectively.

### RECOGNIZING OUR DIFFERENCES

Uniqueness makes for conflict but it also makes for excitement and color. If we had the same views on everything, marriage would

be dull. It is about teamwork. And in the most effective teams, people contribute their different gifts, temperaments and insights for the benefit of everybody. A football team is ineffective if all the players are defenders. A business will not operate successfully if every member is a visionary and nobody is interested in working out the details.

In the last section we looked at one common difference: the way each of us feels loved. There will be many other differences in our approach to life, particularly as opposites are often attracted to each other. Unconsciously we are drawn toward someone who makes us feel complete—who has the qualities we lack.

Typically at the start of our relationship we accommodate ourselves to each other. Many couples are not even aware of their fundamental differences. Infatuation causes us to be highly tolerant and to adapt our behavior to fit in with each other. Then, when the honeymoon phase has worn off, those very differences that attracted us can become the irritants that cause conflict.

At this stage mutual accommodation is replaced by attempts to eliminate the differences. We try to force our partner to think and behave as we do. If we like planning ahead, we expect our spouse to like planning ahead. If we put our clothes in the wardrobe each night, we expect our spouse to do the same. If we squeeze the toothpaste from the bottom of the tube, we expect our spouse to follow suit. We make demands; we manipulate; we become irritated; and we voice our dissatisfaction. All of this inevitably extinguishes intimacy. Sadly many couples then conclude that they are not compatible. But this is not so. Differences can be complementary and made to work to our advantage. We need to move on from attempted elimination to deliberate appreciation of our diversity.

*Our different personalities*

What follows is a description of five categories of differing personality types. In each category we have preferences which may be mild or may be extreme. Where the trait is extreme we shall find it easy to see ourselves; where mild we may only recognize it in contrast to our husband or wife. As you look at the five categories, ask yourself to which personality type you and your partner belong. Where we differ, we need to consider whether these differences cause conflict or a greater appreciation of each other.

*Category one: extrovert or introvert*

This first category relates to our energy source. Extroverts derive energy from their interaction with people. They want to spend much of their time with others and come alive at a party. Talking is important as it enables them to organize and clarify their thoughts. In fact, much of their speaking is thinking out loud. Extroverts enjoy solitude now and then but too much of it drains them emotionally. They need to be stimulated by the outside world to recharge their batteries.

Introverts by contrast derive energy from quiet reflection. Their natural focus is on the inner world of thoughts and ideas. They may be warm, friendly, and caring, but too much social interaction drains them and they need time on their own to recover. They usually prefer a few close friends to many acquaintances and often opt for a night at home in preference to a party. They tend to be quieter and to organize their thoughts before they speak.

The introvert may value the extrovert's ease of relating to many different people, while the extrovert may value the introvert's quiet thoughtfulness.

*Category two: logical or intuitive*

This category involves the way in which we view the world around us. Those with a preference for logic use their five senses to gather information. They want facts. They look to the past and learn through experience. They feel an urge for clarity and prefer matters of practical importance to conjecture. They are interested in detail and solve problems through a careful analysis of the facts. Others would describe them as methodical, pragmatic, and focused on the here and now.

Those who are intuitive prefer ideas to facts. They are more innovative than practical. They look at the big picture rather than the detail. They love to speculate about what could be and are likely to concentrate on the future. They often solve problems through hunches and will easily skip from one activity to the next. They are seen by others as imaginative and unconventional.

The first type could be seen as a "stickler for detail" while the second might be described as having his or her "head in the clouds." But any project requires both personalities. The more intuitive person is drawn to vision, ideas, and goals; the more logical focuses on practicalities, detail, and a plan of action.

*Category three: task-oriented or people-oriented*

This category determines the way in which we make decisions based on the information we receive. Those who are more task-oriented are clear about their goals. They are motivated by efficiency, justice, and truth. In business, productivity and profit have the highest priority. Given a clear objective, the task-oriented person moves quickly and in an orderly way to the destination.

In those who are more people-oriented, the heart rules over the head, and relationships rule over goals. They themselves feel deeply and empathize easily with the feelings of others. Their decisions are based on how their choices affect others. They tend to excuse rather than blame and will often see gray where the task-oriented person sees black and white.

Those who are more people-oriented may admire the more task-oriented person's single-minded pursuit of a vision, while the latter may value the former's ability to create an atmosphere of tolerance, encouragement, and care of others. An effective team requires both personalities.

*Category four: structured or flexible*

This category is concerned with whether we like plans to be drawn up in advance or whether we tend to be spontaneous. Those who prefer a structured life decide easily on their course of action and then follow it through. Those who prefer to remain flexible like to keep their options open for as long as possible in case they receive new information, a better offer, or a cheaper deal.

Those who enjoy structure are good at setting priorities. They tend to be well organized. They gain satisfaction from beating a deadline but are not so good at handling the unexpected.

Those who prefer to remain flexible tend to go with the flow. They like freedom and spontaneity and hesitate to finalize plans. They appear laid-back and are unconcerned with the exact timing of events as they are confident that things will probably turn out for the best. They sometimes miss an opportunity through delaying a decision. However, they are good at adjusting to the unforeseen and will sometimes find success where others see failure.

*Category five: initiator or supporter*

This category reflects whether naturally we prefer to lead or to follow. Initiators enjoy coming up with new ideas, make decisions easily, and are not afraid of change. They like to take charge and make good leaders. Supporters like others to take the initiative. They listen carefully and hesitate to express their opinions. They prefer to avoid confrontation and are prepared to adapt their own preferences to maintain harmony.

In order to obtain the right balance of leadership and support, there are two dangers to avoid. Initiators can fail to consult their partner. Supporters may defer all responsibility for joint decisions to their husband or wife. Neither tendency is healthy in a marriage as each partner should be included in all decisions which affect them as a couple. It is worth remembering that "leadership" does not mean dominating, controlling, or imposing our own agenda. Nor does "supporting" mean following passively or remaining unheard. In order to work effectively as a team the initiator suggests and implements while the supporter encourages and assists.

Marriages work best when each partner initiates in some areas and supports their husband or wife in others.

## Making the most of our differences

To put ourselves into these categories is not to deny our uniqueness. Each different personality type contains enormous variety. Our typical responses do not mean we cannot develop characteristics from the opposite end of the spectrum. These traits do not suggest that the task-oriented person is not interested in relationships or that the people-oriented person has no goals, nor does it conclude that the introvert cannot enjoy a party or the extrovert a solitary walk in the countryside. The preferences are, however, fundamental for our different approaches to life.

The first step is to recognize our differences. The second is to accept that there is no right or wrong way. Our instinctive way of thinking is not better or worse than our partner's. It is just different. Each preference makes a valuable contribution, yet is limited on its own. If we regard our own way of behaving as "normal" and the behavior of others as "defective," we are unlikely to build an intimate marriage.

The third step is to believe that our different approaches can be complementary. A marriage is strengthened immeasurably when we concentrate on what we admire in each other's personality rather than what irritates us.

For Bill and Lynne Hybels, leaders of one of the largest churches in America, discerning the differences in their personalities transformed their relationship from one of irritation and frustration to one of understanding and appreciation. Bill writes of Lynne:

> Lynne was more structured and organized than me. For myself I preferred a more spontaneous approach to life, a make-it-up-as-you-go kind of approach. I found her penchant for planning rather charming… but several years into our marriage, the fascination turned to frustration. I began to resent some of the very qualities that had attracted me to her initially...There was the structure issue. She simply could not live with question marks. She always wanted to know the plan—like where we were going on vacation, when we were leaving, and when we were coming home—in advance! ...Now I have come back full circle to a deep appreciation of the differences between us.
>
> Because Lynne is an introvert our home is a safe and tranquil place. It is a refuge. My life is crowded to overflowing with people... I need a wife who knows how to keep life in order. Thanks to Lynne's preference for structure, we have an organized home. We have clean clothes. We have a healthy diet. We have a budget that works. We have two children who know how to sit down and finish their homework. And I have to admit that some of our adventures have actually been enhanced by her thoughtful planning.
>
> Many times I was tempted to take out a hammer and chisel and reshape Lynne into a replica of me. I even tried a little now and then. Thank God I didn't succeed. I realize now that one of me is plenty in our home.[5]

Lynne tells part of the same story from her side:

> I have learned from Bill to loosen up a little in regard to structure. I still generally prefer to plan ahead and maintain an orderly routine, but I have discovered that splashing the routine with a little spontaneity now and then can add fun to life and enhance relationships. This is particularly true in parenting. Some of the best times I have shared with my kids were spur-of-the-moment events I probably would have missed had I not been influenced by Bill's make-it-up-as-you-go approach to life.[6]

In the table at the end of the chapter, we have listed some of the areas where a husband and a wife can have very different approaches. With each issue, decide how far along the line each of you falls. Then see where you differ and ask yourselves whether this causes conflict. At the end of the table there is space to write in other areas where there are differences between you.

### DISCUSSING DIFFERENCES OVER MONEY

With each issue on the table it is easy to assume that *my* way is the *better* way and to criticize my husband or wife for thinking differently. Nowhere is this clearer than with the issue of money. The natural saver usually blames the natural spender and assumes that all the virtue lies on their side.

**Nicky** Sila and I embarked upon marriage with very different attitudes toward money. This reflected our personalities, although our parents probably helped to shape our views.

There are three choices with money: save it, spend it, or give it away. We have had no problem agreeing on how much and when we should give. With the other two options we are poles apart. Sila is better at spending while

I prefer saving. (As a child I remember saving the old silver sixpences. Eventually I discovered that the coins were no longer legal tender and my full money box was worthless!)

When we were first married, I was employed while Sila was still a student. Each month I would give Sila a portion of the money I earned for the household expenses. I hoped that she would avoid being overdrawn. I hoped in vain. I always kept enough back to pay it off but I felt resentful of Sila's apparent inability to control how much she spent, while she felt guilty about the whole subject. We both thought that I was better than Sila with money because I did not spend it as easily as she did.

It suddenly came home to me after fifteen years of married life that I was quite wrong. I realized that we are better at different things. Sila is better at spending: she is good at working out what is needed each week, as well as buying occasional treats and surprises for the family and presents for others. I on the other hand am better at saving. I do not mind working out how much we have (or haven't) got. I manage our saving and make sure the bills can be paid.

Ever since we realized that our different tendencies are complementary, I have stopped feeling resentful and money has ceased to be a source of tension. By talking through how much we should allocate for different needs each month, we have been able to identify the areas where each of us could help the other. Sila has helped me not to be overly cautious and to use money more freely for the benefit of others and ourselves. For their weekly pocket money, our children used to have 1 pence for each year of their age: 6p when they were six, 8p when they were eight and so on. I saw no problem in this until Sila pointed out that 10 pence was not really going to teach our ten-year-old daughter to handle money sensibly.

I am so glad now that Sila, with the strong support of the children, persuaded me to change my mind!

On the other hand, I like to think I have helped Sila to keep track of her spending and to stay within our budget. Now, instead of keeping some money back each month in the vain hope that we can save it for emergencies, I give Sila everything we have agreed to spend that month and she uses it for what she feels we need.

**Sila** The discipline of budgeting does not come naturally to me. The fact that I am not good with figures certainly has something to do with it. I would not describe myself as extravagant and I do not enjoy shopping much. However, I buy most of what we need as a family to live on and anything extra for entertaining or presents. On the whole, I do most of the spending while Nicky does most of the saving. This happened without us planning it.

Each month I would feel guilty about the overdraft (although I was convinced I couldn't manage on less) and Nicky felt frustrated that I couldn't do anything about it. As Nicky was extremely forgiving, we didn't face our differences until quite a few years into our marriage.

Eventually we had an honest discussion about our feelings and what to do about the situation. Our roles have remained much the same since then, but with Nicky's help I've started to plan ahead and more importantly to tell him when I think I might have overspent. I realize now that it's better to bring this out in the open rather than hope that the problem will somehow resolve itself.

In the past I didn't understand money, was fearful of it, and reluctant to discuss it. Recognizing my weaknesses and being able to talk the situation through has made a huge difference to how I feel.

As finances are the greatest source of tension in most marriages, every couple will need to discuss how they use their money. This sounds absurdly obvious but it is extraordinary how few of us actually do it.

Often couples have different spending priorities so planning ahead and agreeing to allocate a certain amount to each area is important. Keeping the money in different accounts can help: a joint account for housekeeping, bills, and necessities, and separate accounts to buy presents for each other and other non-necessities. In this way each partner has some room for making his or her own decisions.

If you find it hard not to overspend, you should use cash and avoid credit cards. (Where one partner has serious problems or you are heavily in debt, seek help. We have recommended three helpful resources at the back of this book.) If on the other hand you recognize that you are overly cautious with money, then you will benefit from agreeing to allocate a certain amount for leisure, presents, entertainment, charity, and so on.

When one partner works while the other is at home, it is easy for the earner to feel, "I work myself into the ground making money and all you do is spend it." Of course the "unpaid" partner may also be working himself or herself into the ground. In this scenario there can easily be misunderstanding about each other's day-to-day lives. "All you do is sit at home all day," may be countered with, "All you do is go out for nice lunches."

Marriage must be based on the understanding that everything we have, including our wages or salary, belongs to both of us. Both husband and wife should be aware of their true financial position. If one partner is kept in the dark about the couple's joint level of income or the value of their savings or the extent of their debts, it can cause serious problems—not only with regard to spending but through feelings of deception and betrayal. We need to work out *together* how we are going to use our money. It may be worth setting a limit on how much each of us can spend on any one item or activity without consulting the other.

A couple on The Marriage Course told us that they argued regularly about how their money was spent. The wife did not know how much money they had, yet the husband regularly chided her for overspending. Two years ago they worked out a detailed budget, deciding together how they should spend their money and making sure their expenditures matched their income. Whereas previously he had kept track of their accounts (in a somewhat haphazard manner), they agreed that she was better suited for this role. Since that time they have not had a single quarrel about money.

Discussion about finances can draw us closer together, but left undiscussed, misunderstanding and resentment will push us apart. To help make informed decisions, we have included an appendix on how to work out a budget. The very process of doing it together will enable couples to discuss any fears and frustrations regarding money. And it will help each to recognize his or her respective strengths and weaknesses.

### MAINTAINING A SENSE OF HUMOR

Differences between us make for either conflict or color. Appreciating our differences means continuing to enjoy each other's uniqueness. For most couples when they first start going out together laughter will be a part, and often an important part, of their relationship. They are amused by those aspects of each other's personality and behavior that are different from their own, and, as their relationship develops, they will often start to laugh at these individual traits of character. Such "teasin'" further enhances their enjoyment and appreciation of each other.

This is the opposite of cruel teasing, which seeks to expose and humiliate. It is a gentle, affectionate teasing which expresses a deepening intimacy in a marriage: our mutual laughter marks out the exclusive territory of our relationship—a place of private jokes, shared funny memories, and a lifetime of reciprocal humor. All of this stops us taking ourselves too seriously and prevents our relationship from becoming intense and heavy.

In her research surveying fifty happily married couples and seeking to discover the common factors that make marriages last, Judith Wallerstein identifies humor as a key ingredient:

> Over and over again, the couples in these happy marriages said that their laughter was one of the most important bonds between them. Many used the word "funny" to describe a spouse. But by humor and "fun" these couples meant something deeper than the latest jokes making the rounds. They were referring to an intimate way of relating to each other, a low key, spontaneous bantering that kept them connected.[7]

Continuing to enjoy our differences and to tease each other kindly and gently will keep laughter and humor alive in our marriage. It is the opposite of taking each other for granted and will put many of the little annoyances of life in perspective. Joan Erikson, when asked what she considered the most important factor in maintaining her marriage of sixty years to psychoanalyst Erik Erikson, replied without hesitation: "A sense of humor. Without humor, what have you got? Humor is what keeps everything in place."[8]

### BEING PREPARED TO CHANGE

While we *cannot change* our own or each other's basic personalities, we *can change* our habits and behavior. Indeed marriage requires us to do so in order that our strides match. It is no good saying, "That's just the way I am." In working through our differences there is a simple but important principle for a happy marriage:

> We can change ourselves; we cannot change each other.

The adjustments need to continue throughout a marriage. Richard Selzer, a surgeon, describes the following incident:

> I stand by the bed where a young woman lies, her face post-operative, her mouth twisted in palsy, clownish. A tiny twig of the facial nerve, the one to the muscles of her mouth, has been severed. She will be thus from now on. The surgeon has followed with religious fervor the curve of her flesh, I promise you that. Nevertheless, to remove the tumor in her cheek, I have cut a little nerve.
>
> Her young husband is in the room. He stands on the opposite side of the bed and together they seem to dwell in the evening lamplight, isolated from me, private. "Who are they?" I ask myself. "He and this wry mouth that I have made, who gaze at and touch each other so greedily."
>
> The young woman speaks. "Will my mouth always be like this?" she asks. "Yes it will," I say. "It is because the nerve was cut." She nods and is silent, but the young man smiles. "I like it," he says. "It's kind of cute." And all at once I know who he is and I lower my gaze. One is not bold in an encounter with a god. And unmindful I see he bends to kiss her crooked mouth, and I, so close, can see how he twists his own lips to accommodate hers, to show the kiss still works. And I remember that the gods appeared in ancient times as mortals and I hold my breath, and let the wonder in.[9]

When either husband or wife is willing to embrace the inconvenience of change, the marriage has a chance to move forward. When both choose to embrace it together, a marriage that is static and stuck finds a new and enticing horizon.

Nancy, whose marriage to Ric was rescued from the brink of disaster, described the most important insight she gained from the experience:

> ...a relationship won't work if you try to make someone fit into your way of thinking. Making a marriage work is not about tolerating your partner's differences; it's about treasuring them.[10]

Mark with your initial where on the line your different preferences lie. For example: (N=Nicky; S=Sila)

| | | | |
|---|---|---|---|
| ***Money*** | *Spend* | *S N* | *Save* |
| ***Punctuality*** | *Have time in hand* | *S N* | *Cut it close* |

| **ISSUE:** | | | |
|---|---|---|---|
| **Clothes** | Casual | ____ | Formal |
| **Disagreements** | Fight it out | ____ | Keep the peace |
| **Holidays** | Seek adventure | ____ | Seek rest |
| **Money** | Spend | ____ | Save |
| **People** | Spend time with others | ____ | Spend time alone |
| **Planning** | Make plans and stick to them | ____ | Be spontaneous and go with the flow |
| **Punctuality** | Have time in hand | ____ | Cut it close |
| **Relaxation** | Get out | ____ | Stay in |
| **Sleeping** | Go to bed early | ____ | Go to bed late |
| **Sport** | Enthusiast | ____ | Uninterested |
| **Telephone** | Talk at length | ____ | Make arrangements only |
| **Tidiness** | Keep everything tidy and under control | ____ | Be relaxed and live in a mess |
| **T.V.** | Keep it on | ____ | Throw it out |

**OTHER ISSUES:**

# 9

## Focusing on the Issue

*Speak when you are angry and you will make*
*the best speech you will ever regret.*
ANON

In *Love in the Time of Cholera,* Gabriel García Márquez portrays a marriage that disintegrates over a bar of soap. The husband feels that his wife has failed him supremely in forgetting to replace the soap and comments, somewhat accusingly, "I've been bathing for almost a week without any soap." She vigorously denies the error, so for the next seven months they sleep in separate rooms and eat in silence.

> "Even when they were old and placid," writes Márquez, "they were very careful about bringing it up, for the barely healed wounds could begin to bleed again as if they had been inflicted only yesterday."[1]

When conflict arises, it is all too easy to retreat into sulks and silence, building a wall that grows thicker by the hour, day, week, month, or even year. Alternatively, we start to attack on all fronts—by sea, land, and air—attempting to weaken our partner's position and persuade them to surrender. This can lead to verbal or even physical abuse as we try to force our partner to embrace our point of view. Whatever our tendency, the following advice has helped us to

face our point of conflict by focusing on the issue rather than attacking each other. The aim is to prevent specific areas of disagreement affecting our whole relationship.

## Negotiating our differences

There will be times in every marriage when our different approaches require discussion.

**Nicky** One of the differences between Sila and myself is the time we allow when catching a train or a plane. Sila left to herself would be likely to arrive in time to catch the previous flight or train. I on the other hand prefer to give the train or plane a "sporting chance" and arrive as close as possible to the actual departure time. Otherwise I feel that I am wasting valuable time that could be used productively on something else. For Sila, time spent waiting at a station or an airport can be used enjoyably talking, people-watching, or reading a magazine.

For many years we did not discuss the reasons for our different preferences but were aware that journeys were always preceded by some of the most stressful moments in our marriage. We clearly needed to make some changes.

When our behavior is incompatible, what do we do? There are four main options: attack, surrender, bargain, or negotiate. Some people attack, trying to force their partner to accept their way of thinking. That will not work. The most common reactions to attempts at coercion are either to become defensive and dig our heels in or to cooperate outwardly but seethe inwardly.

"But - it leaves at midday tomorrow Sila"

Others surrender: they let their husband or wife have it all their own way and never express a view. That is not healthy either and will not produce a dynamic partnership.

Still others bargain, working on the basis of meeting halfway: "I'll give a bit on the understanding that you also give a bit." The difficulty with this is that our behavior becomes conditional on our partner's response. When we regard marriage as "give and take" in equal proportions, we easily focus on what we are giving and what our husband or wife is taking. We each have our own perception of where halfway lies. If we feel our partner is not doing their part, we stop doing ours.

The fourth and best way is negotiation about our differences. This requires both of us to be prepared to move toward each other. Unlike attack, which is "me-centered," or surrender, which is unhealthily "you-centered," or bargaining, which is also "me-centered," negotiation is "us-centered." We are both asking, "What is the best solution for us together?" Sometimes a husband will say, "I need to change." Sometimes a wife will say, "I need to do things differently." Usually both need to make adjustments.

**Nicky** We sometimes manage to reduce the tension prior to journeys by having a discussion well in advance about what time we ought to leave, allowing a reasonable amount of leeway to avoid a rush. I usually have to fight my instinct that I am wasting time by arriving early, and Sila sometimes has to adjust her overcompensation so that we do not have an excessive period of waiting.

Negotiation is a skill that can be practiced and learned by choosing to adhere to some basic principles.

### FINDING THE BEST TIME

A survey by *Relate* revealed that "Half of all arguments between couples take place in the evenings and a quarter of those surveyed admitted to arguing in the stressful moments leading up to a special occasion."[2] Some close friends told us of a simple but highly effective rule they imposed on their marriage. They call it *the ten o'clock rule*. The rule states that if after 10 p.m. a disagreement has erupted between them and strong feelings are being expressed, either one of them is able to postpone further discussion until a more suitable occasion.

We soon adopted a similar rule. We recognized that the majority of our heated arguments happened late in the evening when tiredness distorted our perspective. At such times we find it harder to listen and see each other's point of view. The ten o'clock rule demands great restraint, but can prevent many disagreements developing into hurtful and futile arguments.

There is (usually) no perfect time to air grievances or differences of opinion, but it is well worth working out together the moments to avoid. These are likely to include the few hectic minutes before leaving for work or getting ready to go out. Time constraints usually cause a greater sense of urgency to persuade each other of our point of view and a commensurate unwillingness to listen to each other.

We have tried to avoid using our weekly marriage time as the opportunity to bring up contentious issues. We heard of two husbands who had come to dread a "date night" as they found themselves waiting in trepidation to discover what they'd done wrong *that* week! The benefit of this weekly time together will be lost if it is not enjoyable to both of us.

## BEING READY TO LISTEN

Rather than seeing a disagreement as our husband or wife's problem, we need to see it as our joint problem for which we need to work out a solution together. Reaching an agreement may require some hard talking but, rather than fighting against each other, we are on the same side as we attack a difficulty that we both have. It is often helpful to make a list of all the possible solutions and then to weigh up together the pros and cons of each one.

Listening is vital. In the heat of a disagreement we instinctively want to make sure our partner has really grasped our point, but we don't feel quite so passionately about understanding theirs. Taking turns to talk will help us to negotiate effectively. As we listen to each other's perspective, we shall often see a way forward that is neither my way nor your way but a new way.

### Being prepared to express our views

While conflict causes some people to become loud and argumentative, others become quiet and withdrawn. The latter may keep the

peace but this response does not build intimacy in a marriage. While extroverts often need to learn to control the expression of their feelings and to take time to listen, introverts need to be prepared to express their views and to learn to be open about their feelings.

A woman called Jane gained the confidence to do so when she and her husband Rick became Christians:

> For the first few years of our marriage I was very passive and compliant; I would rarely put forward my own opinions. Through my relationship with God I've gained a new self-confidence, which allows me to express myself more freely. Also, I don't fear that Rick might leave if the relationship gets difficult, as I sometimes used to. I know that we can work through our differences and that gives me the freedom to disagree with him. I am more assertive but less judgmental. The way we handle conflict has changed … I no longer let things fester, our relationship is more honest and differences can be aired.[3]

### Avoiding accusations

A few weeks before our wedding, the clergyman who married us gave us some valuable advice. Twenty-four years later we can still remember it:

In marriage, there are two phrases you must avoid at all costs: "you always" and "you never."

The wisdom that lay behind that simple rule escaped us at the time, but we came to see how in the heat of battle those two phrases can easily be used to label and denigrate each other:

"You never lift a finger to help."
"You always come home late."
"You never think of anybody except yourself."
"You're always talking on the telephone."

If we catch ourselves saying "never" or "always" at times of conflict, we have probably stopped focusing on the issue and started attacking each other's character. The use of *you* with "never" or "always" is generally an explosive combination.

Sentences that use *I* and *me* and which express our own feelings are more productive than accusing our partner. The sentences above could be rephrased thus:

"I am exhausted and would really appreciate your help in the house."
"I feel lonely and I miss you when you come home late in the evening."

> "I feel upset because you don't seem to be interested in me when we are together."
> "I feel hurt when you spend so much of the evening on the phone rather than talking to me."

Speaking in this way demonstrates gentleness, a vital component of love; for disagreements can easily become like a sword fight except that unkind words leave deeper wounds which take longer to heal than physical cuts. The journalist, radio broadcaster, and author, Libby Purves, makes the point powerfully, quoting a young wife she knows named Maureen:

> "My husband once told me I was a selfish, stupid, fat, frigid bitch. Admittedly I had just called him worse things, but when he said that about being frigid, I couldn't forget it. Whenever we make love now, I keep thinking that's what he thinks about me. I sort of stopped trusting him." She is also dieting obsessively, slim though she is, because of the "fat" bit of the insult. Saying "I didn't mean it" is all very well, but in that case, broods the victim, what made you say it? The old line that angry people "always say things they don't mean" is counterbalanced by the equally old line that only when you are angry do you dare say what you really mean. Most of us have a fairly total recall of things said to us in anger.[4]

We must be careful not to drag up past incidents or to make cruel personal comments. Even if our partner's words have hurt us, we must resist the temptation to retaliate. Restraint is part of the cost of true love. No single contentious issue, however strongly we may feel about it, is more important than our marriage relationship. The Bible emphasises the potential of our words to hurt or to heal:

> Be gracious with your speech. The goal is to bring out the best in others in a conversation, not put them down, not cut them out (Colossians 4:6).

> Make it as clear as you can that you're on their side, working with them and not against them (Philippians 4:5).[5]

Nowhere is this more relevant than within marriage.

### Being prepared to back down

There are few things we find harder than to admit that we are wrong. We desperately want to justify ourselves, to show we are right and to be vindicated. Rob Parsons describes the process:

> We each have what I call an "inner advocate," a hidden lawyer within, who springs to our defense whenever we enter a conflict situation. This eloquent speaker is determined to present to our mind the best possible case in our favor...We are portrayed as sensible, logical and gracious—the other party as raving and unreasonable...By the time this inner lawyer takes his seat, we are totally vindicated; the jury has brought in a verdict: "Innocent!" And all would be well, save for the fact that at that very moment, not very far away, the other person's lawyer is making his closing speech and, incredibly, getting the same verdict.[6]

Winning an argument can be counterproductive. For those who are good with words, who can make others feel small or stupid, the ability to win will prove a disability in the long term.

We so often feel that admitting we are wrong puts us in a weak position. But when we decide that we don't always have to win and try instead to see the issue from our partner's point of view, they will no longer feel the need to defend their corner. As the Book of Proverbs says, "Starting a quarrel is like breaching a dam; so drop the matter before a dispute breaks out" (Proverbs 17:14). Backing down and, if necessary, saying sorry may cost us some pride but we shall gain a happier marriage. If we find it difficult to lose an argument, we should try it and see what happens.

## Facing the issue together

Martin's parents separated when he was a child. His father lived abroad and his mother became an alcoholic. Martin was sent to boarding school from the age of seven. His parents often forgot his birthday and at Christmas he was lucky to get a present. Occasionally there was some token, but it was certainly never wrapped. With the adaptability which is so admirable in children, Martin accepted his circumstances and threw himself into school life.

As an adult, he found it difficult to form lasting relationships. But eventually he fell madly in love and got married, dreaming that his marriage and family life would somehow redeem and heal the miseries and failures of the past.

His wife Lucy came from a close-knit family and idolized her parents. She particularly loved the way they had always celebrated birthdays and Christmas with so much plotting and fun: the surprises, presents, silliness, and secrecy.

Her birthday came a few months into marriage. Martin asked her what she wanted. She made some suggestions, hoping he would also think of some surprises. He bought two items from the list and left them unwrapped on top of the fridge sticking out of the carrier bags. He felt that he was making a real fuss over her—no one had ever bought him two expensive presents for his birthday. Three days before her birthday she saw the two items on the fridge, unwrapped, and felt confused and unloved, but she kept her thoughts to herself. What could she say?

On her birthday, they woke up; there was no card, no breakfast in bed, no flowers. Then, just before they left for work, Martin took the two items off the fridge (still in their carrier bags) and gave them to her, smiling. She burst into tears and rushed out of the house.

Their relationship never really recovered from the events of that morning. It was never discussed. Lucy presumed that either he did not love her or that he was by nature mean and thoughtless, possibly both. Martin noticed that Lucy had turned cold and assumed that she had simply stopped loving him. The pattern of rejection was well established in his life. For Martin and Lucy years of misery with similar silent misunderstandings followed until they finally divorced.

What a tragedy that on that fateful day (Lucy's birthday), they did not see the need to focus on the issue. They could have listened to each other's childhood experiences of birthdays. They could have expressed their views, feelings, expectations, and disappointments. They would have seen that there was only one issue causing conflict in their marriage that day. They could have resolved it so easily. Instead, it was the first dark blot on their relationship, which then spread, like ink on blotting paper, until it had darkened and destroyed their marriage.

If there is unresolved conflict in your marriage, discuss the following questions:

1. What is the main issue causing the conflict?

2. When would be the best time to discuss it?

3. Have we listened to each other's perspective?

4. What possible solutions can we think of?

5. Which solution should we try first?

# 10

## Centering Our Lives

*Matrimony: an absurd invention that could only exist by the infinite grace of God.*
GABRIEL GARCÍA MÁRQUEZ[1]

*Dear God, I bet it is very hard for you to love all of everybody in the world. There are only four people in our family and I can never do it.*
DAN[2]

Dan has a point. Conflict is inevitable with those closest to us and it is not always easy to find the love we need. Most marriages have their times in the desert. In our own marriage we have discovered that the presence of God is a fountain of life. When both husband and wife put their lives into God's hands and ask Him to be at the center of their marriage, their relationship is watered from within and fed by a source from without.

For some, the presence of God in a marriage allows trust to be re-established; for others, loving concern will replace selfishness; for others, destructive patterns of behavior will be transformed.

David and Anne met when they were both fifteen years old and started going out at the age of eighteen. After seventeen years of marriage and with two teenage children, Anne was on the point of giving up. David, who had come from a difficult home background, turned to drink for help with the pressures of his job. In his own words: "I had nothing else to fall back on. There were weaknesses in me I was not able to cope with. They seemed more manageable after a drink or two."

Their marriage spiraled downward. David's unpredictable moods and quick temper frequently led to criticism being hurled back and forth. Anne defended her corner, but his ridicule left her totally undermined in her role as wife and mother. Their respect for each other had gone. Both felt isolated.

In April 1996, David was invited to attend an Alpha course—a ten-week course designed as a practical introduction to the Christian faith.[3] He had recently started a new job but knew that he would fail the physical and lose his job if he did not curb his drinking. On the third week of the course his desperation made him tell some of the course leaders. They offered to pray with him, and that evening David put his future into God's hands, asking for His help.

He was not prepared for the difference and was surprised that by lunchtime the following day he had felt no urge to have a drink. Normally, he would have been craving one by 11:30 a.m. and would have needed several at lunch time to get him through the day. Miraculously, his addiction disappeared, leaving no physical side effects.

David started to pray for Anne and for his marriage to be healed. Though Anne was suspicious of David's involvement with the church and poked fun at him about it, she and the children noticed the difference. David didn't fire back when she was critical of him, and she felt that he had begun to care about her again. Anne went on the next Alpha course mainly to investigate what had happened to David. As she continued to witness the profound change in him, her understanding of Christianity increased and her trust in him was rebuilt. Anne recalls that, "There was total, unspoken forgiveness between us."

During the course, instead of attacking each other, they began to discuss the issues that were raised week by week. They would telephone each other during the day to tell each other about a new idea that had occurred to one of them.

Love was returning to their marriage, increasingly affecting their home and their children. "David courted me all over again," said Anne, "and the second honeymoon was even better than the first." For David, "Our love was more soundly based. I didn't slip back and the newness and freshness didn't wear off in the same way."

There are still times when David and Anne are irritated by each other, but there is no longer the old destructive pattern of trying to get even, to score a hit. They now have someone to fall back on. David sums up the difference: "We are more controlled in trying not to answer back when we think we are being attacked unfairly. I am not always on the defensive. I have started to dare to believe that I am an equal—without the alcohol. Before becoming a Christian, I was like an unguided missile. Now I have this stabilizing influence inside—like a gyroscope."

In Anne's words, "When one of us is out of sorts, we turn to the Bible and pray to put God back at the center. He fills us with love to keep our marriage going."

God is the ultimate healer of conflict. We know many couples like David and Anne and James and Anna (quoted in chapter 3) who would not be together but for God being at the heart of their marriage. Whether we have huge obstacles to face or just the smaller issues of everyday life, having God at the center makes an enormous difference. We shall suggest four reasons why this is so.

## Marriage is a gift from God

When Adam first saw Eve, he said, "This is now bone of my bones and flesh of my flesh" (Genesis 2:23). These beautiful words speak of identification, intimacy, celebration, and a sense of completion.

Often, without realizing it, after several years or even months of marriage we find ourselves focusing on each other's faults and being critical of them. Instead, if we concentrate on how good it is to have one another's companionship and try to see each other's strengths, thanking God for them, our love will be reinforced.

Our thoughts should never dwell on the question: "Why did I marry my husband or my wife rather than...whoever!" Instead, thanking God for our husband or wife on a regular basis will increase our appreciation of each other. Criticism and ingratitude only highlight the other's weaknesses. When we perceive our husband or wife as a gift from God, we remain grateful for each other.

## The Bible requires mutual respect

Jesus' teaching on marriage was given in an age when the wife was considered inferior and a husband expected to impose his will on her. Under Roman law, the husband had total rights over his household—his wife, children, and slaves. His wife had no protection from the abuse which his superior physical strength allowed.

So the teaching of the New Testament was revolutionary: "Husbands, love your wives, just as Christ loved the church and gave Himself up for her," and, "husbands ought to love their wives as their own bodies" (Ephesians 5:25, 28).

Paul's instructions reflected the extraordinary respect and concern that Jesus Himself showed toward women. On one occasion, against the opinion of the crowd, Jesus offered acceptance and forgiveness to a woman arrested for committing adultery (John 8:1-11). On another occasion, we read of Him breaking with social tradition by talking with an unknown woman in public (John 4:4-10). At a dinner party and to the disdain of His host, He allowed a prostitute to anoint His feet with her tears and wipe them with her hair (Luke 7:36-50).

Jesus gave equal value to men and women. This affected the marriage relationship profoundly as Christian belief and teaching spread through Europe. To follow the example of Jesus means to respect each other and to value each other's opinions. It rules out the possibility of either husband or wife expecting to impose their will in decisions that affect them both.

### GOD IS THE SOURCE OF LOVE

Many people marry with unrealistic expectations of their husband or wife: they hope that in each other they will find the answer to all their needs; that their insecurity will be solved through the other's unconditional and unfailing love; that their lives will be given ultimate purpose and significance through their relationship. But experience shows us that another person can never fully meet these needs. Only God can do that.

A couple who marry presuming their husband or wife can meet their deepest needs will end up disappointed. Unrealistic expectations can then lead to a downward spiral of demands followed by blame, as in the diagram below.

The Bible encourages us to look to God with great expectation and to call upon Him for the love, patience, hope, forgiveness, courage, or anything else that we lack. We are to draw on His limit-

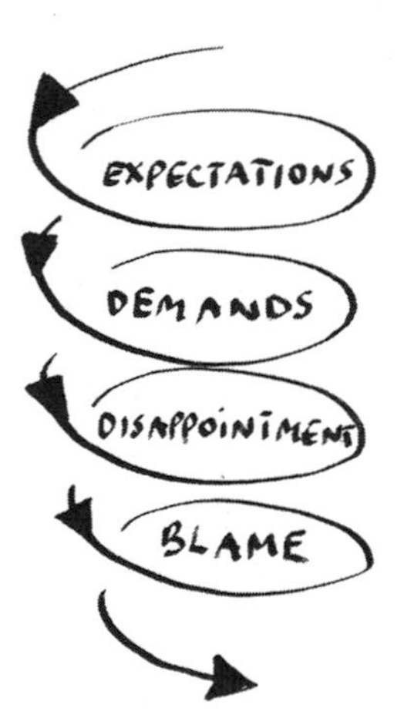

less resources and to find in His unending love the security and significance that we crave. The Christian pattern is to receive love through a close personal relationship with God and then give love to each other.

We heard recently of a couple called Billy and Debbie who live in Northern Ireland. They got married eight years ago and neither of them had any church background. Their marriage was a nightmare. In 1994, Billy's mother died of cancer and his father from an accident. In Billy's own words, "When Dad died, I decided I was never ever going to get hurt like this again and I made a conscious decision to harden myself and not let myself be close to anybody. I got to the stage where I became a really horrible person.... I was bad-tempered and not much fun to be around."

In 1996, Debbie's mother died and Billy was unable and unwilling to help her in her grief: "I thought, 'Debbie wasn't much help to me when my parents died, so why should I be any help to her?' This meant Debbie couldn't share her feelings with me at all. Instead I started blaming her because the whole family was breaking apart."

In 1999, they went to Paris in a vain attempt to restore love to their marriage, but found they couldn't talk to each other any longer. Debbie said, "Our relationship was coming to an end. Everything was just going rapidly downhill and I couldn't fix it and neither could Billy." According to Billy, "I knew I loved Debbie but it was a downward spiral. We were spiraling down, out of control. There was only one outcome—separation."

At that point they met a Christian couple who invited them to attend an Alpha Course in their home. To their surprise, Billy and Debbie found it fascinating and became more and more interested in what they were hearing. Billy describes what happened after the third week of the course, by which time Debbie had already committed her life to Christ: "I told Debbie, 'I want to become a Christian tonight.' So that is what I did.

"I sat on the bed and said, 'Lord, I've lived in this world for thirty-two years without You and I've just heard about You for the first time. I'm so, so sorry for all the things I've done wrong in my life. I need You in my life because I'm going over without You.'

"As the weeks went on, I started to forgive everyone who had ever hurt me and I felt the bitterness being lifted from my heart."

Debbie describes the effect on their relationship: "After that, our marriage began to mend, big time. It felt like we had started all over again and all those years before were just nothing. I felt like I hadn't lived. I felt like I was opening my eyes for the very first time.

"As for Billy, he was like a new person—more loving, more caring. I fell in love with him all over again."

Debbie continues, "Before doing the course, I felt that I'd done without love for so long that I couldn't give love out and I didn't want to receive it from anyone. Afterward I felt I was going to burst if I took in any more love."

Billy concludes, "What God has done in my life is amazing. I was the most ungentle person you've ever met and He's come into my life and turned it around. Patience wasn't a virtue for me—I didn't have it—but now I seem to have it in spades. I find I rarely get angry. I don't raise my voice. I couldn't possibly have made that much of a change in myself on my own. There is only one person responsible: Jesus.

"I always thought Christianity was about what you couldn't do: 'You can't do this' or, 'You can't do that'—but it's not. It's about what you can do."

Calling upon Jesus Christ for His help gives a marriage a strength from a source outside itself. We are free to love out of the knowledge and experience that we ourselves are loved passionately and unconditionally by God. As the Apostle John puts it in his letter, "We love because He [God] first loved us" (1 John 4:19). We are set free to give to each other out of the confidence that God knows all about our own needs and promises to look after us.

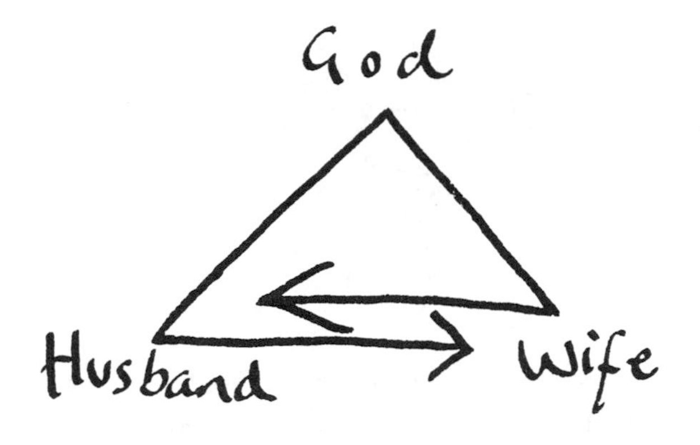


GOD BRINGS HARMONY TO A MARRIAGE

Over the course of our own marriage, we have tried to submit important decisions and disagreements to God and to seek His way forward. Time after time, we have seen that prayer brings great harmony to a marriage.

The Bible assures us of the power of two people praying with or for each other. "Confess your sins to each other and pray for each other so that you may be healed" (James 5:16). This is a promise as much for the healing of our relationships as for physical healing.

There have been times when we have disagreed and there has seemed to be no way forward. Praying about the issue is not designed to enlist divine help for our own particular point of view! To pray with integrity involves asking God to give us His wisdom and to show us *His* way forward.

After praying together (even through gritted teeth) we have often been amazed that we have come to appreciate each other's point of view and have seen a third option of which we had previously been totally unaware. In the process of bringing the issue to God, our feelings of anger and resentment have disappeared and we have ended up closer to one another than before.

**Nicky** To return to the apple-throwing incident described in chapter 8, that evening Sila and I decided we should pray together for God's help and wisdom. We were both still convinced that we were right.

By the time we finished, however, I discovered I had a new perspective. I realized that I had not taken sufficient account of Sila's tiredness, the result of breast-feeding a small baby. I had also become aware that her welfare was more important than my embarrassment over our friend. Meanwhile Sila felt that, if I was aware of her needs, she would be able to cope.

We did go and we had a great weekend, not least because I had realized that my first priority was to support Sila.

Praying at moments of conflict is hard. We are forced to examine our attitudes and the emotions we are harboring. Prayer, rage, and resentment don't go together. We will, of course, only be able to pray in times of disagreement if we pray together at other times. We describe in Appendix D some practical suggestions of how a couple can get started in praying together.[4]

When a marriage seems dry, God can water it. When a marriage is stuck, God can remove the obstacle. When a marriage seems to be dying, God can breathe in new life.

# Section 4 – Resolving Conflict

## Conclusion

Differences and disagreements do not need to destroy a marriage. Indeed it can be their very resolution which strengthens and develops our relationship. Marriage is not about suppressing our personality. Rather, it involves discussing our different points of view, seeking to understand each other, and finding ways of combining our wisdom and gifts. When we do this, we discover that the issue that threatened to divide us has drawn us closer together and caused our marriage to move forward.

To live consciously in the presence of God—in the knowledge of Him around us, in us and with us in our marriage—and to call on Him for His wisdom and love, is not opting out of the hard work of reaching agreement and unity. It is rather affirming our belief that God has brought us together and that there is always a way through.

## Fourth Golden Rule of Marriage

Discuss your differences and pray together.

# Section 5 — The Power of Forgiveness

# 11

## How Can Intimacy Be Lost?

*Do not let the sun go down while you are still angry.*
EPHESIANS 4:26

Two weeks before the wedding, Deborah went to have the final fitting for her dress. "I was going from my office in a taxi at Christmastime, so London was very busy," she explains. "I was in a traffic jam, feeling very excited, when I saw this couple in front walking away from me with their arms around each other and I thought, 'Hey! They look really great together.'

"As the taxi drew nearer to them I was shocked to see that it was Miles—my fiancé—with his arm around another woman. What's more, I knew her and knew that Miles had gone out with her before he went out with me. It was like a horror movie.

"My taxi was going very slowly so I watched them for a bit longer and thought, 'What shall I do? Shall I jump out of the taxi?' My heart was beating like mad. I couldn't believe my eyes. Then I saw them arrive outside her office. They said good-bye and kissed each other. It wasn't a passionate kiss, but it was enough of a kiss. At that moment my taxi suddenly picked up speed and I arrived for my fitting. I was so upset that I couldn't even cry.

"During the fitting, I kept asking them to hurry up. All I wanted to do was to get on the telephone. As soon as I could I rang Miles and said to him, 'Did you have a good lunch?' He replied, 'What do you mean?' I said, 'I saw everything!' He again asked, 'What do you mean?' Again I said, 'I saw everything.' He replied, 'Well, I meant to tell you about it this morning. I tried to get you on the phone to say I was going to meet Anne for lunch.'

"I slammed down the phone and went back to the office bawling my eyes out. Miles tried to call me but I wouldn't talk to him. When the next day I tried to explain to Miles what it was like for me to see all this happening, he didn't understand how I felt.

"Then we got married and, to add insult to injury, this story kept coming up at parties, as a joke. Miles would tell it as his party piece: 'Guess what happened as Deborah was on her way to the wedding dress fitting...'"

*Miles tells his side of the story:*
"I really blew it. I realized that before I got married I needed to apologize to Anne for my failure to end our relationship properly. Anne and I talked and had a great lunch. I was elated that I had gone through with it. I had tried to call Deborah a couple of times in the morning to tell her what I was doing. Unfortunately I had failed to get hold of her.

"Once I had apologized to Anne, it was a great relief for both of us so I put my arm around her and gave her a big kiss before we parted. When I was back at the office, Deborah phoned me and asked, 'How was your lunch?' I told her, 'I tried to call you.' So, as far as I was concerned, I had done what I could and my intentions were honorable. In fact, I was quite defensive. I never said I was sorry to Deborah because I never felt the need to.

"Then, on *The Marriage Course*, when we were asked to write down ways we had hurt each other, we each came up with about four or five. Deborah's were all from well in the past and this was clearly number one. So we talked about it.

"I really tried to see it from her point of view, to sit in a taxi and to see your future husband walking along the road with his arm around another woman. No matter what the reason, just to have experienced that and never to have had the hurt recognized or acknowledged in some way, I realized was the issue. Even then, I found it hard. I said grudgingly, 'Okay, we will deal with it now.'

"It was when I said sorry to God that I realized how much it had hurt Deborah. So I said I was really sorry to her and asked her to forgive me. She did, which was wonderful. It is a very powerful process to go through, step by step, dealing with the emotions that come up, and it has brought us much closer to each other."

*Deborah concludes:* "When I actually started to talk to Miles I realized that I had suppressed how upset I was because the incident had turned into a good story. As a result I had continued to feel hurt. Every time the topic came up it hurt a bit more. But, because I felt Miles wouldn't listen to me, I tried not to let it affect me. During *The Marriage Course* when he really listened to me for the first time, I felt that my emotions were valid and that Miles understood them. That was important for me. I was then able to forgive him and let it go."

---

Dealing with ways we have hurt each other restores trust. Trust is as vital to a marriage as glass to a window. The function of the glass is to allow the light in but to keep wind and rain out. Being one of the hardest materials, it is capable of withstanding the most violent of storms. And yet it can be shattered with a blow from a brick or a hammer.

Trust between a husband and wife, however strong it has grown, is equally fragile. It can be shattered with a single act of adultery, abuse, or violence. Or it can be destroyed by an accumulation of "white" lies, deception, critical comments, or unkindness. These are like the dirt that can accumulate on a window and shut out the light.

Intimate relationships are built on trust and openness. These two qualities belong together and feed each other. Where trust exists, a husband and a wife are able to be open about their deepest feelings, their hopes and fears, their joys and sorrows, their thoughts and dreams. They allow each other into their inner world to know them as they are. This openness then causes trust to grow stronger, allowing for even greater openness.

When we hurt each other, whether intentionally or unintentionally, we damage the trust and become less open. Our tendency when hurt is to close up, sometimes unconsciously, to keep our partner at a distance and to protect ourselves against further hurt. The greater the hurt, the greater the damage.

Often in a marriage it is not one deliberate act that destroys the intimacy between us but the accumulation of smaller hurts that are left undiscussed and unhealed. One husband, whose marriage had failed, wrote a sad and moving account of the situation he and his wife had gotten into:

> After all, our marriage wasn't hellish, it was simply dispiriting. My wife and I didn't hate each other, we simply got on each other's nerves. Over the years we each had accumulated a store of minor unresolved grievances. Our marriage was a mechanism so encrusted with small disappointments and petty grudges that its parts no longer closed.[1]

Hurt occurs every time we act in an unloving way toward each other: when important decisions are made without consultation; when the desire for an intimate conversation is met with coldness; when criticism predominates over encouragement; when our times together are used up by other people or other activities; when no presents are forthcoming on birthdays and anniversaries pass without notice; when selfishness and laziness replace loving deeds; when kindness is met with ingratitude; when an attempt to hug is met with, "Can't you see I'm busy?"

Even within the most loving marriages, there are times when a husband and wife will hurt each other. Occasionally this is deliberate, but usually it is unintentional and we are unaware of the pain we have caused. Hurt like this *must be resolved* if trust and openness are to grow. Indeed, the very process of resolving the hurt builds greater understanding and closeness. But where it does not happen, the walls around the heart get higher and the cement gets harder until there is no intimacy left and, sometimes, no marriage at all.

In this section we want to provide the tools which enable us to resolve past hurt, to dismantle any walls that have been built, and to prevent future hurt having such serious consequences. The process is not complicated but it is challenging and it always involves a choice. The choice is this: whether we are going to let the hurt fester and poison our relationship, or whether we are going to deal with it. The more open we are to resolving it, the easier it becomes. But if we fail to do so, even relatively minor issues can become large mountains which separate us.[2]

## Getting angry

After being hurt, sometimes only a split second later, comes the next emotion: anger. While hurt is what we feel about ourselves, anger is what we instinctively feel toward those who have inflicted the hurt upon us.

It is important to recognize that the *feeling* of anger is not wrong in itself. It is the way in which we deal with it that can cause damage. The behavior of two animals when physically hurt or threatened illustrates two typical human reactions. A rhino acts aggressively and, if provoked, is likely to charge you. By contrast, a hedgehog, when in danger, throws up a protective shield by raising its prickles in an attempt to keep its attacker at bay.

Just as animals respond differently to attack, so people react differently when they are hurt and angry. There are two major patterns of behavior and from a show of hands on *The Marriage Course* it would appear that the population is split roughly fifty-fifty. Half of the population are like the rhino: when they are angry, they let you know it. The other half of the population are like the hedgehog: when they feel angry, they hide their feelings. They become quiet or withdrawn. It is not that they do nothing with their anger. They tend to express it in less obvious ways: they may withhold their affection, suddenly develop selective hearing toward their partner, or run them down in company. This group sometimes regard themselves as more virtuous than the rhinos but their reactions can be just as damaging to a relationship.

Many couples, like ourselves, are made up of one who is liable to respond like the rhino and one more like the hedgehog. The story of the apple-throwing in the earlier chapter illustrates quite graphically into which category Sila falls; the following story shows what Nicky's natural reaction is likely to be.

**Nicky** One of the differences between Sila and myself is that when we go out to a party in the evening we have very different ways of leaving. My way, when we have agreed that it is time to go home, is to say thank you and good-bye to our host and hostess, and then to leave. Sila's way is to start to say good-bye and then get involved in what will usually be her most interesting conversation of the whole evening.

I have discovered over twenty-four years of marriage that if we are to get home by an agreed time, we need to start leaving just as the soup is being served.

Recently we went to a birthday party of a great friend. As the following day was going to be particularly busy, we agreed on the way to the party that we should aim to be home by midnight. To make this possible, I decided to double the time needed to get home and we both started to leave at 11:30 p.m. I duly said good-bye and, to encourage Sila to tear herself away, I went to get the car that we had parked at the other end of the road where they live. I double-parked outside our friends' house in a narrow and crowded London street and waited for Sila to join me.

After fifteen minutes there was no sign of her. I decided to repark the car, a maneuver that had not been easy the first time and proved to be no easier the second. I walked back up the street to our friends' house, rang the bell, and went in to find Sila standing at the bottom of the basement stairs deep in conversation with our hostess.

Keeping a fixed smile on my face so as not spoil the party, I mentioned to her that I had been waiting in the car and that it was now past midnight. Sila replied, "Oh, I didn't even know that you had left." At that point I had to cope not only with my frustration about being late home, but also with the fact that she hadn't even noticed my absence. I went to get the car for the second time and after about ten minutes she joined me.

On the way home we were talking about the party. Sila

was animated about the people she had met and the interesting conversations that she had had. I was keeping up a cheerful exterior while seething inside. It is amazing how our minds can operate on two levels. As well as carrying on the conversation, I was weighing whether to say anything about my frustration and the fact that we were going to be in bed quite a lot later than we had planned. I didn't want to spoil Sila's happy mood; on the other hand, I was finding it hard to be as relaxed as she was.

In the end I struggled through my tendency to hide my feelings and said as casually as I could, "Did you realize I was sitting waiting in the car for fifteen minutes?" Sila stopped dead in her tracks, looked at me, and said in a worried voice, "Oh, no! Were you feeling cross with me?"

When I told her about my true feelings of frustration she immediately said, "I am so sorry. Please forgive me." As soon as it was out in the open, it wasn't difficult to forgive and my feelings of annoyance evaporated even more quickly than they had built up.

My tendency to bury my anger is potentially no less harmful for our relationship than Sila's tendency to vent hers. In order to have a strong marriage, I have had to learn to talk about my feelings as much as Sila has had to learn to control the way she expresses hers.

### Getting even

If the hurt and the ensuing anger remain, our next instinctive reaction is the desire to get even: hurt for hurt, insult for insult, rejection for rejection. We want to retaliate, not least to let our husband or wife know what it feels like to have been hurt in this way. We must get even.

One summer holiday we drove to the southernmost tip of Greece, a part of the Peloponese called The Mani. It was hot and the population sparse, yet there was evidence from a number of deserted and ruined villages that there had once been more people living there. What puzzled us were the remains of many unusually high towers that had been built as part of the houses. We learned that these towers were the result of feuds between families in the same village.

An aggrieved family would build their house higher than the surrounding houses in order to be able to throw rocks or pour hot oil on their opponents. Their neighbors would then build higher still to try to steal the advantage and get revenge.

These feuds eventually led to the collapse of the whole village. There is a similar pattern within marriage when both partners are intent on seeking justice and revenge. This is a pattern which no marriage can survive.

## GIVING IN TO FEAR

A third reaction to hurt is fear: we are afraid of being hurt again and, as a result, we withdraw. This will be particularly true for those who, like the hedgehog, keep others at a distance to protect themselves. We stop being open and close down deep communication.

In the words of C. S. Lewis:

> To love at all is to be vulnerable. Love anything, and your heart will certainly be wrung and possibly be broken. If you want to make sure of keeping it intact, you must give your heart to no one, not even to an animal. Wrap it carefully round with hobbies and little luxuries; avoid all entanglements; lock it up safe in the casket or coffin of your selfishness. But in that casket—safe, dark, motionless, airless—it will change. It will not be broken; it will become unbreakable, impenetrable, irredeemable.[3]

## Carrying guilt

Hurt will never be all one way in a marriage. We give as well as receive. There is great destructive power in the guilt we carry around if we fail to own up to our part in hurting our partner. The self-deception involved in denying our responsibility leads quickly to emotional separation.

---

These four effects of hurt—anger, retaliation, fear, and guilt—can lurk beneath the surface of a marriage. The danger of such unresolved hurt on a domestic level has its counterpart internationally in the dilemma of how to rid old war-zones of landmines, which are hidden from sight but which maim and kill. In a marriage all can look well on the surface, but one or both partners are forced to tread carefully, not knowing when the next explosion will come. There is a loss of trust and openness, which has usually built up gradually over a number of years as the grievances accumulate. Finally intimacy is quenched.

When this happens in a marriage, the symptoms can be a lack of communication, criticism, outbursts of anger, resentment, little interest in one another, a lack of desire to make love, and a preference for doing things separately. There may be other emotional effects such as low self-esteem and depression, and for some, it becomes easier not to allow themselves to feel anything any more, to avoid the pain.

Some who are on the verge of separation say words to this effect, "I don't feel love any more. In fact, I don't feel anything at all. I feel numb." This is hardly surprising. The unhealed hurt which has accumulated inside them needs to be resolved before there can be any space for the return of positive feelings of love, romance, and attraction. It is not so much that there is no possibility of love being restored; it is rather that it has been squeezed out by hurt and anger.

The author Valerie Windsor tells the story of an English woman on holiday in Paris who decides on the spur of the moment to leave her husband. It becomes clear that any intimacy they once had in their marriage has been lost:

> I try to think what it was that made me do it, and I have no idea. I mean what specific thing made me choose that moment rather than any other. It was an odd afternoon. I don't know what was the matter with me. It was windy: either the wind or the noise of the plastic chair scraping the pavement started a strange sensation in the bones of my head. Tony chose the café: one of those salons des glaces where they serve expensive cocktails.
>
> "Will this do?" he said. "Here?" and he flicked at the seat with his handkerchief. "Don't sit down yet," he said. "They haven't been wiped.'" But I deliberately sat down anyway, without looking, even though I was wearing a white skirt. It annoyed me to hear him fussing about such things. A man should not fuss about such things. A man should not even notice them. I didn't. So was he implying that I should; that because I so patently failed to notice them, he was forced into doing it, against his will? The odd sensation in my head turned into a thin, high buzzing as if a wasp were trapped in the hollows of the skull.
>
> "What will you have?" he asked.
>
> It was June, I think. May or June, I forget which. But cold. Warm enough to sit at a pavement cafe but cold enough to want something hot to drink.
>
> "Coffee," I said.
>
> He was reading the menu. Behind him was a bank of potted plants with spiky orange flowers.
>
> "Plastic," said Tony turning to look.
>
> "Are they? I don't think they are." I leaned over to touch one. I wanted it to be real. I wanted it to be alive, and as vicious as it looked. But he was right, of course: it was plastic. The buzzing in my head grew worse.

"What's the matter?" he asked.

I lied. "I think there's a wasp."

"Where?"

"I don't know."

Any kind of uncertainty infuriated him, "Well, either there is or there isn't."

"I don't know what the matter is," I said, pressing my fingers against my temples. And then the waiter came.

"Deux cafés," said Tony, without even glancing at him. I had to do all the smiling for both of us.

The waiter smiled back. "D'accord," he said and wiped the table. Tony leaned back in his chair and breathed out. "Well, this is nice," he said. And that was all. That was the sum of what happened between us. There was no atmosphere. The unpleasantness of the previous day when I had got us lost in Neuilly because of incompetent map reading was forgotten. And by mutual understanding we never allowed the surfaces to be disturbed by any mention of the unsatisfactory nightly rituals which, by some failure of imagination, I could never connect with love.

I sat there with my hands folded in my lap, and the buzzing in my head grew thinner and higher, a whining electrical noise in the bone. I stood up.[4]

She stands up and abandons her marriage.

In real life so many who leave a marriage while still full of unresolved emotions find that they carry them into another relationship. The unhealed hurt can then become the cause of a breakdown in this next one—often more quickly than the first. We see this in those who marry several times and find each successive marriage failing for a similar reason.

No wonder the Bible says, "Do not let the sun go down while you are still angry" (Ephesians 4:26). Anger, whether expressed or suppressed, must be resolved and the underlying hurt healed for the relationship to grow. The wonderful news is that we don't need to let hurt destroy our intimacy. Although the process described in the next chapter may be hard and costly for some, it will set us and our marriage free.

# 12

## How Can Intimacy Be Restored?

*Forgiveness is not just an occasional act: it is a permanent attitude.*
MARTIN LUTHER KING[1]

### GETTING TO THE HEART OF THE PROBLEM

When intimacy has been lost, often we do not look deeply enough for the reasons. We are aware only of the symptoms rather than the underlying cause.

**Nicky** When we first moved to London in 1985, I discovered that working for a church has more facets to it than I was trained for at theological college. In the middle of a torrential downpour the drains from the church restrooms blocked, and the alley next to our house was six inches deep in water. Together with Derek, the youth worker, I managed to open the cover of the drains. The sewer was completely full and the contents rapidly started mixing with the rainwater. At that point the make-up of the flood did not bear thinking about too carefully.

We tried to remove the blockage with drainage rods but soon realized that it was impossible to do so from above. Someone had to go down into the drain, which was thigh-deep, to use the rods at a better angle.

> Before I could offer, Derek, who is one of the most selfless men I have ever had the pleasure to know, was down there, rod in hand, crouching up to his waist in the stinking water. He pushed with the rods as hard as he could and after a few moments there was a melodious gurgling and then a wonderful rushing sound as the blockage cleared and the water was sucked rapidly away. In a short time, the alley was clear. We hosed it (and him) down with fresh water; the smell was gone and the crisis had passed.
>
> It would have been no good if, instead of dealing with the blockage, Derek and I had tried to mop up the surface water. The next time it had rained or someone had flushed a toilet, the alley would have flooded again.

Looking at the ways we have hurt each other can be a painful and messy process and one that we instinctively shy away from. But when both partners summon up the courage to face the past, the results will bring lasting change. When there is a backlog of unresolved hurt and anger, we must unblock the drain by doing the following:

(1) Talking about the hurt.
(2) Being prepared to say sorry.
(3) Choosing to forgive each other.

This process acts like a drain carrying away the hurt so that it does not spoil our relationship. Once we have cleared out days, weeks, months, or even years of unresolved issues, we must both make a choice to resolve every big or small hurt as it happens and never again to allow such an accumulation.

For those who have been married a long time and have never felt able to address and resolve painful issues effectively, this threefold process will take time and may be very testing, although ultimately liberating. The positive emotions may not return immediately. But as we persist, this process of healing hurt will become an ingrained habit and our marriage will change for the better.

### Talking about the hurt

**Sila** After Nicky and I had been married for about nine months, we were invited to go to stay with a friend to celebrate her twenty-first birthday. We were excited at the prospect of an idyllic weekend ahead. However, on the journey there Nicky did or said something—I cannot remember what it was now—which really hurt and upset me. Even though I felt very resentful, when we got there I thought, "I am not going to let this spoil the weekend." I wanted to convince myself that it was okay, it did not matter, we were going to have a great weekend.

I tried to forget it. I tried to push it down and pretend it would go away but in fact it got worse and the emotions inside me were boiling over. I found that I could not excuse Nicky by saying to myself, "I love him very much so I will ignore it when he hurts me." I could not help myself reliving the incident over and over again. The resentment built rather than lessened.

Eventually I could bear it no longer and I knew I had to let Nicky know how I was feeling. I probably chose the worst moment just before the party started. We went through the whole process of my telling him how he had hurt me, Nicky apologizing, and my forgiving him. It was a revelation in our marriage and a lesson in realizing that forgiveness is not saying, "It doesn't matter." The hurt did matter and it needed to be faced.

This part of the process is like making the decision to get into the drain. It is no good pretending that all is well. Hurts act like those big plastic beach balls that you play with in the sea. You can with some difficulty push the ball down under the water for a while but then it suddenly comes shooting back up again with a whoosh when you don't expect it.

We must tell our husband or wife when and how they have hurt us. We do not need to do it in a way that is harsh or judgmental. Indeed, we must do so gently, making it as easy as possible for them to apologize. It is worth rehearsing again the advice in chapter 9 about using "I" statements. Rather than general criticism or an attack on our partner's character, we are seeking to make our husband or wife aware of how we felt over a particular incident, as when Deborah told Miles how painful it was for her to hear him tell the story about his lunch with Anne (in chapter 11).

So for example:

"I felt hurt and rejected when you pulled away from me in bed the other night," is much more helpful than, "You never show me any physical affection."

"I felt unsupported and unappreciated when you didn't notice the hard work I put into decorating the house for Christmas," is much better than, "You never show any gratitude for what I do."

"I haven't got over the fact that you weren't truthful to me about that letter," is easier to respond to than, "You're a liar and I can't trust you."

"It upset me a lot when you went out to the pub the first night we got back from our honeymoon," is more helpful than, "Your friends are more important to you than me."

"I felt hurt and humiliated this evening when you said I was 'so slow' in front of our friends," is more gentle than, "You really stuck the knife in tonight."

We may feel that our partner is like a rhino, thick-skinned and shortsighted, charging around causing a lot of damage, in which case it will not be obvious to them that they have hurt us. What matters in identifying hurt is not whether our husband or wife intended to wound us. As one marriage counselor put it, "We don't deal with many people with a premeditated plan of 'How I am going to destroy this marriage.'"

We need regular, private opportunities to deal with ways we have hurt each other, whether in big or small ways, so as not to "let the sun go down" while we are still angry. Hopefully, the need will not arise often, particularly in the early days of our marriage, but it is important to have a framework in place for dealing with hurtful incidents. Sooner or later it will be necessary, even in the most harmonious relationship.

## BEING PREPARED TO SAY SORRY

The 1970s film *Love Story* was advertised with the slogan: "Love means never having to say you are sorry." It could not be more wrong. In a truly loving marriage we often have to apologize to each other, perhaps even daily.

Most of us do not like to take responsibility for our mistakes. Parents will see this in young children who often only say sorry through gritted teeth to avoid more unpleasant consequences. It is easier to rationalize what we have done and to blame everybody else. Some people excuse their behavior by blaming their parents for the way they were brought up. Others blame their circumstances, saying, "If only we had more money' " or, "If only I weren't under so much pressure...."

**Nicky** I remember some years ago meeting a woman in hospital who was very ill with lung cancer. She asked me to pray with her and as part of my prayer I included an element of confession, asking God to forgive us for the wrong things we have done.

She immediately stopped praying, opened her eyes and said to me, "I can't say that I'm sorry for things I have done

> wrong. You see, I haven't done anything wrong. I try to be kind to everyone. I do occasionally have unkind thoughts about people but I put them out of my mind as quickly as possible. However, I wonder if you could pray for my husband because, you see, he has a terrible temper and treats me like his servant."
>
> I later talked to the nurses on the ward who told me that she was one of the most difficult patients that they had ever looked after.

It is never easy to listen to ways in which we have been responsible for hurting others. However, we need to try to see things from their point of view. When our husband or wife knows that we understand the extent to which they feel hurt, our apology will carry more weight. If they feel we do not understand how much hurt we have caused them, they will be afraid that we will easily do it again. Some incidents, as in Miles and Deborah's story, can appear trivial or even humorous to us, but we may discover that they have caused deep pain to our partner.

To be effective our apology must be unconditional. Rather than saying, "If you had been more reasonable, I would not have lost my temper," or, "If you hadn't made us late, I would not have forgotten to mail that letter," we need to swallow our pride and say simply, "I am sorry I lost my temper," or, "I am so sorry I forgot to mail the letter."

Equally we need to be sure that our tone of voice and body language do not contradict what we are saying. It is possible to say, "Sorry," in a way that means, "Sorry but..." or, "It was your fault really."

Genuine unconditional apologies are powerful in marriage because we no longer need to be on the defensive, determined to get our own back, volleying hurt back and forth in a tit-for-tat battle. We are suddenly on the same side again. This allows the anger to be dissipated and the hurt to be healed.

## Choosing to forgive each other

This is the third and for many the most challenging part of the process. Forgiveness is essential and has unparalleled power to bring healing to a marriage. The story that we told in chapter 3 of the reconciliation between James and Anna would not have been possible without forgiveness. We asked them to describe how it came about.

*James:* Anna left me early in January 1987. I remember clearly trying to tell my friends at work what had happened and—this part was considerably more difficult—why it had happened. The truth is that it had a lot to do with lack of communication, but even now some thirteen years later I still do not really know exactly why our marriage broke down. My friends were kind and sympathetic but the most hopeful thing they could say was, "Time will heal." But the days melted into months without any real sense of healing. In fact, the pain began to grow into an explosive cocktail of anger and regret and this brought with it still more pain.

I remember waking up in the morning and immediately feeling as if I was down an incredibly deep black hole. It was as if my mind was fractionally behind my heart and it would take a few moments before I recalled what had happened. I experienced similar feelings in the months following my father's death two years before.

One incident sticks in my mind. A couple of months after moving out, Anna wanted to come back to our house to pick up the remainder of her belongings. I remember changing the locks on the front door, not because I did not trust her, but purely because I wanted to hurt her. It was one of the most awful moments because I knew that my behavior was wrong but felt powerless to do anything to stop myself. Two days later I was flying over London on vacation to India and can recall crying uncontrollably as I saw London below and remembered what I had done.

It was this particular incident that came to mind when I found myself in Holy Trinity Brompton Church on the invitation of a work colleague in December 1987. I deeply regretted my behavior over the door lock and wanted to be free from the ever-lengthening shadow which had become my life. Again I wept, but these tears were different. Now I was asking, not for help to try to forgive Anna, but for forgiveness for myself. I was weeping for me, for my part in the breakdown, for my lack of sensitivity, for my single-minded pursuit of success at work no matter what the cost to our relationship. I left that service no happier—the circumstances had not changed: Anna was still living with someone else and still wanted a divorce. But I was feeling alive for the first time in nearly a year.

I cannot honestly tell you how the change occurred. I found myself able to forgive Anna and all the anger that had been like a poison in my body seemed to drain away. In that single moment God changed the direction of my life. And now when I look at Anna and our two beautiful girls, I thank Him.

*Anna:* James' forgiveness of me was so complete that in the early days I found it both liberating and perplexing. How could he really forgive every incident, every hurt, without ever once reminding me of something I had done or using it against me in some way? As I got to know Jesus and His forgiveness for myself, I began to understand that God had done an amazing work in James' heart and that however many times I said to him, "Are you sure you forgive me for that?" the answer was always, "Yes, don't think about it again."

*James:* I think people sometimes assume that this extraordinary turn of events was followed by a sort of heavenly romance in which there were no arguments, tensions, hurts, or misunderstandings. The act of forgiveness was done in a flash. But there were complex issues to sort out that had caused us to break up in the first place. Living out the forgiveness has been a process in which we have both wanted to participate.

For my part, I think of our new life together as an ongoing sequence of choices in which we live as openly as we can before God and before each other. When we trip up we are much quicker to run to each other, say we are sorry and forgive. This seems to be the point at which God can start to work and we know we need all the help he can give us.

---

*Forgiveness is not earned*

C.S. Lewis wrote, "Forgiveness goes beyond human fairness; it is pardoning those things that can't readily be pardoned at all."[2] This is why it is always costly to forgive; we have to sacrifice our pride, our self-pity, and our desire for justice. Our culture places tremendous stress on doing all we can to maintain our rights. When we forgive, we are laying down our right to justice and our desire for revenge.

We cannot demand that our partner earns our forgiveness nor can we be sure that they will not hurt us again in the same way. There are times when we suspect that they will do it again despite their best intentions. Jesus' instruction to forgive each other, if necessary, "seven times in one day" (Luke 17:4) is not just an exaggeration to make a point.

This does not mean that we are required to condone our partner's behavior where there is physical violence, verbal cruelty, sexual abuse, or unfaithfulness. Such violation of the marriage vows is a terrible betrayal of trust and must be confronted. Where such destructive behavior has become a pattern and there is a fear of provoking further abuse, the confrontation will best be done with a third party. For those in this situation we would recommend Gary Chapman's book *Hope for the Separated* and James Dobson's *Love Must Be Tough*.

*The flow of forgiveness*

The Christian message is that as we come to God, genuinely confessing our failures, He gives us forgiveness as a free gift. Jesus died in our place, taking the consequences for all we have ever done, said, or thought that is wrong. God freely forgives us, even when He knows we shall fail again. He is our model for forgiveness. The Apostle Paul writes, "Be kind and compassionate to one another, forgiving each other, just as in Christ God forgave you" (Ephesians 4:32).

As we begin to take in the incredible truth of God's ongoing forgiveness of our failings, He becomes not only the model but also the motivation for forgiving others. We feel inspired to echo His generosity in our relationships with others.

But even with a model, even with the inspiration, forgiveness can feel an impossible goal. Where are we to find the means to forgive? We can feel blocked. We find no forgiveness in our heart. We find only the desire for justice to be done. The Bible repeatedly encourages us to leave the consequences to God. "'It is mine to avenge; I will repay,' says the Lord" (Romans 12:19). We can leave the justice of our case to God. We are told: "Do not repay evil with evil or insult with insult, but with blessing, because to this you were called so that you may inherit a blessing" (1 Peter 3:9). As we give up our desire to repay, God promises to look after us and to pour His blessing into our lives.

A lake needs water flowing in and water flowing out to stop it becoming stagnant. We desperately need this dynamic flow of for-

giveness in all our relationships and especially in marriage. Forgiveness needs to flow into our lives from God. But it is no good if it is bottled up there. With God's help we must let it flow out into the lives of those around us and especially those closest to us.

*Forgiveness is a choice, not a feeling*

Forgiveness means choosing not to hold the past against each other. The question is not, "Do we feel like forgiving?" Often we do not feel like forgiving at all. Rather, the question is, "Will we forgive? Will we let go of the hurt?" Of course, there are some things that are much harder to forgive because the degree of hurt is much greater. Sometimes people say to us, "I can't forgive him/her." "I can't," is really another way of saying, "I won't," or, "I don't know how to." Very often people are waiting for the right feelings to come or for justice to be done before they forgive.

We do not want to underestimate how hard forgiveness is and, as James said earlier in the chapter, we shall often need to ask God to help us. But if we choose to forgive by an act of our will, the *feelings* of forgiveness will follow. For some this will happen quickly and for others by degrees over a longer period.

*Forgiveness sets us free*

When we forgive, that forgiveness may benefit our husband or wife, but ultimately we are the ones who benefit most by being free. According to the Christian writer, Philip Yancey:

> The word resentment expresses what happens if the cycle goes uninterrupted. It means, literally, "to feel again": resentment clings to the past, relives it over and over, picks each fresh scab so that the wound never heals.[3]

Corrie ten Boom was a Dutch prisoner-of-war in Ravensbrück concentration camp where she watched her sister Betsie die at the hands of the guards. In her book *He Sets the Captives Free* she recalls the moment after the war when she came face to face with one of their former guards, who had become a Christian and had come to ask for her forgiveness. Only through silently calling out for God's help could she fight every human instinct toward hatred and revenge, and do the impossible. She wrote later:

> At that moment, when I was able to forgive, my hatred disappeared. What a liberation! Forgiveness is the key which unlocks the door of resentment and the handcuffs of hatred. It is a power that breaks the chains of bitterness and the shackles of selfishness. What a liberation it is when you can forgive.[4]

Only through forgiveness can we be liberated from the pain of previous relationships. Irene was a young South African woman just out of university who enjoyed living and working in London. Soon she met Roger, an older man who swept her off her feet. He persuaded her to leave her job and move in with him; she became pregnant. They married and moved to a small village outside London. A few months later their son Timmy was born.

Isolated at home with a new baby, separated from family, friends, and job, Irene soon began to be plagued by horrible thoughts; she suspected her husband was having an affair. Roger explained his increasing absences and frequent need to use a pay phone as being linked with top-secret government work. It sounded far-fetched, but he was very convincing. Irene's worst fears were realized one evening when a middle-aged woman from the village turned up on her doorstep. She was holding a love letter which Roger had written to her sixteen-year-old daughter. He and the girl were lovers. The mother was particularly upset because she too was having an affair with Roger.

Soon it transpired that not only was her husband sleeping with both mother and daughter, but he also had a mistress in London. He later confessed to Irene that he had begun his first extramarital affair the day after their wedding. Roger was a sexual addict and a compulsive liar. Irene's world crashed down around her.

She and Roger had months of counseling. Gradually she put into practice principles from the Bible, learning to forgive and even to love him again, things she admits she never thought herself capable of. She felt they had been given a second chance to make things work. But a year later, Roger finally left Irene and Timmy and went to live with his secretary, who was pregnant with Roger's child. Abandoned and alone, Irene found anger and bitterness toward Roger rising constantly in her thoughts. On occasions she contemplated suicide.

Then one day while she was praying, she realized that her unforgiveness was like a parasite, feeding upon her and growing stronger as it was allowed to thrive. She determined by a decision of her will to forgive. Whenever she found herself replaying her mental video of the ways he had hurt and humiliated her, she would remind herself of all the things for which she had sought God's forgiveness. Then she would begin to pray for Roger and his new family. At first she did it through gritted teeth, but after a while she began to mean the prayers. Gradually the bitterness and unforgiveness faded. She began to feel a wonderful lightness and peace, and finally freedom—the freedom to start afresh.

Choosing to forgive enables us to move forward without being weighed down by the "chains of bitterness and handcuffs of hatred." At first, we may still feel acute pain, but forgiveness allows the recovery to start. It is like being stung by a bee. When the sting is taken out, the skin is not instantly restored, but it opens the way for healing to take place. When we forgive, we are still able to remember what happened to us, but as we keep forgiving the memories have less and less power over us.

Unforgiveness affects not only our relationship with the person or people who caused the hurt, but every relationship we have. A marriage can therefore be ruined if we hold on to anger against a third party. We have a Japanese friend who has done much to bring reconciliation between former prisoners-of-war and her own people. When husbands who suffered terribly during the war have been able to express forgiveness to those who ill-treated them, wives have often commented on the change in their marriage. Their husbands sleep well again and are less easily irritated by the small day-to-day issues.

Time on its own does not heal wounds. Only forgiveness can do that, but it involves a process. We often seem to forgive layer by layer, like the process of peeling an onion. We may find that we need to go on choosing to forgive for the same hurts on a daily basis in order to be set free. The less we forgive, the harder it is to do so. But if we forgive once, it becomes easier to do so the next time. And as we forgive, the emotional bruising gradually heals and our marriage moves on.

# Section 5 – The Power of Forgiveness

## Conclusion

If this process of resolving hurt and anger from the past is new to you, particularly if you have been married for some time, you will need to proceed sensitively and gradually. Ask God to guide you so that you go at His pace. We make ourselves very vulnerable when we identify how we have been hurt. We will need to be gentle with each other so that our husband or wife knows that we empathize with their feelings. Where trust has been broken, it will take time for this to be restored. Do not expect the one who has been hurt to be able to forget and recover immediately.

As part of his description of love, the Apostle Paul writes that love "keeps no record of wrongs" (1 Corinthians 13:5). Imagine for a moment that each day of your marriage is like the new page of a spiral notebook. Every day we do or say things, or fail to do or say things, that hurt our husband or wife, sometimes slightly and sometimes deeply.

On some days the list will be longer than on others, but every day there will be something on the page. If these things are not faced and forgiven, the page will be turned and the list left intact. We then start to build up a backlog of resentment and bitterness. Even if we cannot remember the details of each list, the record of the offenses remains and will in time become engraved on our relationship and quench our intimacy.

If we learn to forgive daily, it is like tearing off each page at the end of the day and throwing it away. We start each new day of our marriage with a clean sheet and no backlog. Neither of us will be on the attack or the defense. We shall then be acting in love, keeping no record of each other's wrongs.

## Fifth Golden Rule of Marriage

Practice forgiveness.

# Section 6 — Parents and In-laws

# 13

## How to Get Along with Parents and In-laws

*When I was a boy of fourteen, my father was so ignorant, I could hardly stand to have the old man around. But when I got to be twenty-one, I was astonished at how much the old man had learned in seven years.*

MARK TWAIN

*"Parents are strange," said Amy, "for their age."*

AMANDA VAIL[1]

We should not underestimate the profound impact of wider family relationships on marriage. Families are complex; some have caused untold heartache and pain that have rolled on down the years and even the generations; others have been a huge source of joy and happiness where the ripple effect on countless lives has brought much blessing and good. If our wider family relationships are to work for the benefit of each generation, we will first need to understand how our relationships with our parents should have developed as we grew up.

### THE PROGRESS FROM DEPENDENCE TO INDEPENDENCE

Our progress from complete dependence on our parents as children through to eventual independence is of vital importance for our marriage. We each move through different stages as we change from being a child to being a teenager, then an adult, and finally a married person. We have devised four diagrams which aim to illustrate appropriate parent-child relationships in these four phases. Of course no experience of family life will be quite as neat around the edges as these diagrams suggest. Some have been brought up by one parent. There are many very loving and highly effective single-parent families who create a healthy and happy home in which to grow up. There may have been divorce, death, remarriage, step-parents, and step-families. But the same general principles of moving through each stage apply to us all.

As a couple, look at these diagrams together, remembering that you were once the child in the equation. As we do this, we are seeking to understand more about our own and each other's upbringing, and whether our relationship with our parents changed as it should have done at each stage.

We need to talk openly about the strengths and weaknesses of our parents and their marriages. An adult relationship with them requires us to let go of the fantasies of childhood in which we idealized our parents, as well as the common disillusionment during our teenage years when they could do nothing right, and to see them as they really are. We hope that looking at the four different stages will help you to do this.

*Early years*

During the early years, our parents met our physical need for food, drink, sleep, cleanliness, warmth, and medication. They were also responsible for our emotional needs, as represented by the arrows on the diagram. These included affection, acceptance, security, encouragement, comfort, and so on. Our emotional needs were every bit as vital, even if not as immediately obvious, as our physical needs. The experience of parental love builds a child's self-confidence, an essential quality for making relationships later in life. Relationships always involve taking a risk and we all need self-confidence if we are to risk our love being rejected. Our experience of our parents' uncondi-

tional love enables us to takc this risk and to reach out in love to others.

The circle in the diagram represents the boundaries that our parents needed to set for our security. A young child's activities must be tightly controlled. Dangers must be avoided. Places which are unsafe to play in must be prohibited. As children we did not have the maturity to make sound judgements on such matters.

*Teenagers*

Do you remember yourself as a teenager? During these years, our parents needed to give us increasing independence, allowing us to make our own decisions in as many areas as possible. These may have included our choice of friends, the use of our spare time, our clothes, our hairstyles (if they dared), and how we decorated our rooms.

This gradual letting go is an essential part of the transition from total parental control to eventual independence. As young teenagers, however, we still needed boundaries around our activities. The change from a circle to an oval represents the increasing freedom within set limits. We were not mature enough to make all our own decisions and would usually have admitted, if pressed, that we appreciated the security that these boundaries brought. The ado-

lescent years involved much self-questioning as we established our own identity and we needed our parents' continued emotional support.

By now we might have started to recognize how we could be of help to our parents. This is represented by the faint dotted line.

*"Coming of age" / leaving home*

Between 18 and 21 years of age some of us were still living in our parental home. Nevertheless we were learning independence, making our own decisions over further education, choice of career, other relationships, use of money, and so forth.

Most of us at this stage continued to look to our parents for advice, financial support, and comfort (if things went wrong). But it

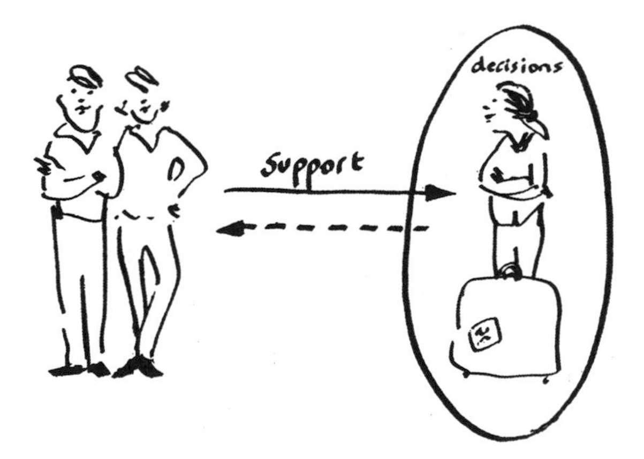

was now more of an adult relationship. Hopefully we were less self-focused and were accepting responsibilities toward our parents, such as making contact (if we lived away from home) and recognizing *their* need of appreciation, support, affection, or encouragement.

*Getting married*

Many situations look more complex than the one in the diagram below but, whatever our particular circumstances, the issue is the same. The circle around us as a married couple represents the need to establish our own home, make our own decisions, and meet each other's needs. Our first loyalty must now be to each other and we must leave behind any emotional dependence upon our parents.

This change of loyalty does not mean cutting ourselves off from

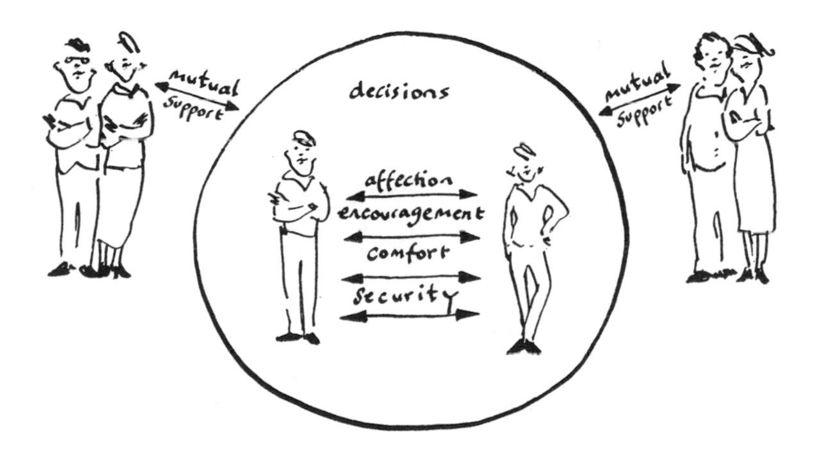


our families. When the relationship is on a proper footing, parents (and siblings) will be a huge support to a marriage. This has been our own experience and our parents have been a wonderful source of love, support, fun, and close friendship. We also greatly value the close and special relationship we have with our brothers and sisters and their families. Despite living hundreds of miles away these relationships play an important part in our own and our children's lives. They have had to be nurtured over the years, as it takes effort from both sides to stay in touch and spend time together.

Gatherings with our extended family around Christmas, New Year, and half-term holidays as well as special birthdays and anniversaries have all been valuable occasions for the different generations to meet. It is worth making the most of such opportunities because the demands and pressures of life can easily crowd out these unique relationships.

In the next chapter we will look at how to establish our independence as a couple. Here we consider how to develop a strong, mutually supportive and enjoyable relationship with our parents, parents-in-law, and extended family.

### BEING REASONABLE ABOUT WEDDING ARRANGEMENTS

The opportunity to start building for the future usually comes with the wedding arrangements. It is rare for any wedding to be organized without emotions running high. There are often strongly held views all around. Some parents have been anticipating and planning this day in their minds for many years.

Meanwhile the bride and groom hear friends say that this of all days is *their* day. In truth the day belongs predominantly to the couple, but it also involves the parents, partly because they may well be paying (and showing great generosity), and also because many of the guests will be older relations or long-standing family friends whose views matter to them.

It is natural that the parents should be involved in the plans and preparation. It is their final act of giving to their son or daughter before they get married and this helps them to let go. Organizing a wedding can mean hard work for many weeks and engaged couples are often shocked to discover how many decisions there are to make. Conflicting views, an emotional situation, and tiredness are a powerful cocktail for producing tension and arguments. Patient listening and compromise where possible are often required to maintain the peace.

## Showing our appreciation

All parents thrive on being shown appreciation by their children. The weeks before a wedding provide a good opportunity for this. Even if we have not come from a happy or harmonious home and have a difficult relationship with our parents, we can usually think of ways in which they have looked after us, perhaps as a young child or when we were unwell. Very few parents have made no sacrifices at all for their children. Some couples write a letter to their parents expressing their thanks. This can enormously increase the parents' joy and pride as they let go of their son or daughter as well as setting the right tone for their future relationship.

If we are already married, we can try to find opportunities to put our thanks in writing, perhaps in a birthday card or in a Mother's or Father's Day card. A friend of ours wrote a long letter to her father on his sixtieth birthday recounting her happy memories of his love and support during her upbringing. She has allowed us to reproduce a section of the letter here:

> I liked our journeys, especially when I was allowed one of those butterscotch sweets in a round tin. I also liked the way you put school dramas in perspective by sounding slightly amused or exasperated by some of the more teachery teachers. It gave me the sense that you were absolutely on my side and not theirs. I never doubted that you believed me far more than you would ever believe them. I now see that is unusual and wonderful.
>
> Same at parents' evenings when you would laugh at one of the teachers who terrified me. I would wait expectant in the hall. Always to be congratulated. But never overly. I always knew you counted me higher than any A grade. No pressure at all. Just plenty of space to make my own decisions.

Her father was unaware of what these things had meant to his daughter and her letter has helped to maintain the close and special relationship between them that has benefited not only her, but also her husband and children.

### Staying in touch

Once married it is important to work out together how to keep in touch with our parents. Regular conversations are of great value although the habit of talking to a parent on the telephone every morning or evening can lead to resentment in the other partner, particularly if such discussions are lengthy or take place when they have just got home in the evening. Make a conscious decision to keep the *best* time for talking for each other. For the sake of your parents, keep in touch. For the sake of your marriage, keep in control.

We must decide together how often to see our parents. If one of us tends to revert to being dependent or is unable to resist unhelpful pressure, it may be better to meet in our own home. If things are strained, shorter and more frequent visits may build the relationship more effectively. A congenial atmosphere can be maintained more easily for short periods; if we stay too long with nothing to do or to say, tension can build up.

One woman told us that she disliked her father-in-law and that spending time with him was very difficult. We cannot change such feelings overnight. But we can use the tools for building relationships described in the first five sections of this book, particularly considering which of the five expressions of love is most important to them. Then over time we will start to recognize more of their good qualities, and the relationship will improve as a result. This is a choice we must make for the sake of our husband or wife.

A friend discovered, by accident, the way to her father-in-law's heart and her relationship with him changed considerably:

> My father-in-law is someone who believes in concepts like duty and effort, particularly in family relationships. I always found this rather annoying, thinking that relationships should be easy, spontaneous and undemanding. Our relationship plodded on, not disastrous but mediocre. Then one birthday, I don't know quite why, I decided to try to make him a fruitcake. I think it came about as we had no clue what to buy him. He had said that he no longer wanted the gardening magazine subscription that had sustained us through the last three birthdays. I knew that he loved fruitcake. I also knew that I

had no clue how to make one. But it dawned on me that even if I bought the best fruitcake in the world, it would not convey the all-important concept of effort.

I struggled and eventually produced a very sad-looking cake. I put it in a tin and, apologizing, presented it to him on his birthday. He was totally thrilled: "It must have taken you so long, and you're so busy in your job?" My father-in-law finds it very curious that I, a woman, work in the (what he considers to be) male domain of the city. This was another problem between us: our views on women did not coincide. But this strange modern female had baked him a fruitcake—and she'd toiled and struggled just for him.

When we all tasted it, I forced him to confess that it was not the nicest fruitcake he'd ever tasted—and then there was laughter too! And from that day we have laughed, not only about the fruitcake, but about most things—including our differing views on women.

My father-in-law's love language, I realized when I was doing *The Marriage Course*, is deeds. If you do something especially for him, he feels loved. It didn't really matter whether the fruitcake tasted nice or not.

So I have learned the importance of love languages (and a sense of humor) not only in marriage but in this complex relationship with our in-laws.

We also need to decide to what extent we are going to be involved with our parents. Many parents are a huge support, particularly when a couple are under pressure with young children. But if we want them to paint the entire house, make all our curtains, or look after our children twice a week, we are inviting them to share deeply in our daily life. It would be extremely unloving and manipulative to show interest in them only when they were performing useful tasks. Having thought this through together, we may conclude that it is better to run our lives without their day-to-day involvement. We must maintain integrity with our parents and we must not exploit their love.

## TRYING TO RESOLVE CONFLICT

Even where there is a close relationship with parents and in-laws, there will always be some differences of opinion. Tense and difficult situations must be resolved with the same principles of talking, apologizing, and forgiving that we looked at in chapter 12.

We met one woman who had been married for seven years who felt continually undermined by her mother-in-law. They had little in common and conversation was difficult. Her husband meanwhile could do no wrong in his mother's eyes. The wife's feelings of hurt were compounded by frequent unfavorable comparisons with the other daughters-in-law. Certain remarks caused a strong emotional reaction within her, way out of proportion to the incident.

However, the relationship was maintained through the husband's understanding and encouragement and through the wife's determination with God's help to keep on forgiving and loving. As a result, things have gradually improved over the years and today, when they are together, the mother-in-law is less judgmental and the wife has more confidence.

It is important to clear up any unresolved conflict from the past, ideally before we get married. If we do not, anger, bitterness, resentment, or guilt will resurface later in some guise or other. Some people get married determined never to act like their parents. They may have had parents who frequently lost their tempers, who were uncaring and inconsiderate toward each other, who were emotionally distant or who had their favorites among their children. Yet after a few months of marriage they gradually start to behave in the same way. This is because they have not dealt with their own feelings of anger and resentment regarding their parents' behavior.

In the analysis of one marriage counselor, whatever we concentrate on in life, we tend to imitate. If we can forgive our parents and move on, our focus on their faults and weaknesses will cease and we will be free to shed any unconscious imitation of them.

If you, as the child, are even partially to blame for a breakdown in the relationship, you will need to apologize to your parents without blaming them or trying to rationalize your behavior. The effect can be far-reaching as Mary Pytches, an experienced counselor, illustrates:

> I remember being told the moving story of an elderly woman who was dying from cancer. Her son visited her in the hospital and then went back home to tell his wife that his mother was dying and that the doctors could do no more for her. On hearing this, the wife suggested that her husband had some unfinished business with his mother that needed sorting out before she died. She then reminded him of a time when he was much younger and he had walked out of his home and had lost touch with his mother for a whole year. "You need to put that right with her before she dies," said the wife. Her husband agreed and went back to the hospital and asked his mother to forgive him for his behavior all those years ago.
>
> She was very moved and willingly forgave him and asked him to forgive her for causing him to be so unhappy that he felt he needed to leave home. They were completely reconciled and the son went home. The following week his mother was discharged from hospital completely well. She enjoyed good health for many more years and eventually died of old age.[2]

## Considering their needs

While we were young, our parents (or another care-giver) took the initiative in looking after our needs; now we have the opportunity to reciprocate. Children move from a relationship of total dependence upon their parents to an adult relationship of mutual support until, for some, the role is completely reversed and the parent is totally dependent upon the child.

The actress, Sheila Hancock, writes affectionately of the care she received from her daughter, Melanie Thaw, whom she refers to by her nickname, Ellie Jane:

> Some years ago, I keeled over with cancer, and I let Ellie Jane look after me. I'm absolutely convinced I brought it on through obsessive stress. I used to rush around thinking I could save everybody, which was a way of avoiding looking at what I was doing in my own life. I went to the Bristol Clinic after I'd had the orthodox treatment, and Ellie Jane came too. She was so stable and supportive that our roles were reversed. She has a center core of strength, and I can't tell you how staggering all that was to me. If anyone had said that she would have been like this as a woman I would have laughed...I love her so much.[3]

While we cease to be responsible *to* our parents, we continue to have a responsibility *for* them. The fifth commandment, "Honor your father and your mother," does not cease to be relevant for us either when we come of age or when we marry. As parents grow older, their dependence will increase and we shall have the opportunity to return some of the love and sacrifices they showed toward us. This may include practical jobs around the home, help with finances, or planning for the future. Writer and broadcaster, Victoria Glendinning, describes how much care she receives from her adult son, Matthew, and how much he means to her:

> He always listens carefully, understands what I'm saying, makes measured and enlightening comments, gives himself entirely to the problem, and he doesn't try and hurry me on to something else.
>
> Once, recently, he had already got up to leave when I said

something about troubles. "Troubles? What troubles?" And he sat down again at the kitchen table as if he had all the time in the world.[4]

If a parent lives alone, his or her greatest need is likely to be for conversation and company. Some friends of ours with teenage children have the only surviving grandparent living in part of their house. Not only has this arrangement allowed both the couple and the grandmother sufficient independence, but it has also led to very special friendships across three generations.

## VALUING THE EXTENDED FAMILY

Sometimes new couples blindly, unkindly, but rather bravely, discard the tribes they came from. Sometimes they have to, because on religious, racial or class grounds, the tribe is being so foully bigoted about the marriage. More often, I suspect, they do it out of sheer thoughtlessness: moving away, striking out into the wider world together, starting anew.

But with the birth of children comes a time when it is healthy, even pleasant, to let the tribe creep forward again and surround the new family with its old echoes. In other words, however decrepit your family tree looks to you, don't be too cavalier about chopping off the branch you sit on. When you start to be a family, the one which is there already turns out to have all sorts of unsuspected advantages. As well as only-too-well-suspected problems.[5]

Of course, no extended family is perfect. Far from it, yet in the diversity of age, personality, and viewpoint, there is the chance for plenty of color. We live in an age of neat nuclear families, who often close the front door on others of the same surname and lineage. But we easily become one-dimensional, and even claustrophobic, as we do so. Why not get together on special occasions? Libby Purves recommends that:

> The family year needs milestones, something on the calendar to look forward to. You can justify them by saying they represent cultural heritage, or religious faith, or you can just take them as a bit of fun, especially at the duller times of year. We have celebrated, in our time, not only all four birthdays and Christmas but New Year, Epiphany, Pancake Day, Easter, Harvest Supper...Guy Fawkes, May Day, St. Nicolas's Day, and Pudding Thursday (a bit obscure that, but all you do is eat Yorkshire pudding). Give me time and I shall devise ways of marking Shakespeare's birthday, Michaelmas, Midsummer's Eve, St. Andrew's Day, St. Patrick's Day (for the Scottish and Irish connection), and if any Americans should drop in, I will include Thanksgiving and Groundhog Day with pleasure. Celebrating does not have to be expensive: a paper flag or two to paint, a meal around the table, a game if you can.[6]

The gathering of the clans has its plus points: we adults get a chance to be mothered and fathered by the older and wiser, and we get some living examples of what our children are about to turn into. Children enjoy cousins, especially badly behaved ones, and we all love a doting granny or an eccentric uncle. This is part of the hurly burly of real life, and it shapes us. If we do not have an extended family, there are other ways of creating the same atmosphere. A friend of ours (a single mother) held a Pancake Party on Shrove Tuesday this year to which she invited twenty colorful representatives of all the generations.

Just as large family events have their place, so too does the nurturing of special relationships across the generations. It is not only we who will benefit from a close relationship with our parents; a grandparent can play a very special role in a child's life.

**Nicky** When I was a young child I would often go with my mother to visit my grandmother at her home on a Saturday morning. These times have become a special part of my childhood memories. It must also have met the needs of my grandmother, though I did not think of that at the time.

Through maintaining contact with our parents, we enable our children to get to know their grandparents and we ourselves may come to see our own parents in a new light.

**Nicky** I came to appreciate more fully the wonderful qualities of gentleness and humor in my own father through seeing him play with our children. I suppose that I had forgotten these gifts in my own childhood or had taken them for granted. In retirement he had more time to spare, and his grandchildren were the main beneficiaries.

Some grandparents can take on a very special role in their grandchildren's lives. And a new baby in the family can mend or cement wider family relationships. Justine, daughter of the founder of *The Body Shop*, Anita Roddick, writes:

> Mum really surprised me because she adored my baby from the moment Maiya was born, and I saw her re-emerge in a whole new maternal way. I had the worst post-natal depression, and I came to Mum: she stayed up all night looking after the baby....Now that Sammy [Justine's sister] and I have obviously moved away from

> home, I think Maiya has cemented the family; she's given my mum and dad another bond, so she helps their relationship.[7]

Many grandparents comment on the joy of having children around them for whom they are not ultimately responsible and whom they can hand back at the end of the day. But grandparents vary. Some would happily give up anything to spend time with their grandchildren. If this is so, grandparents may be involved in frequent childcare and will inevitably have more influence on our children's upbringing. Others are less enthusiastic about prolonged childcare, or perhaps come into their own when the children are older. We must not expect too much of our parents. After all, they did not choose to have their grandchildren and are not responsible in the way that parents are.

If our parents have died, or live far away, it is worth trying to help our children make friends with others of an older generation. It is wonderful where we have seen this happening within our church, leading to great enjoyment for both age groups.

## UNDERSTANDING EACH OTHER

Even when relationships between ourselves and our parents and parents-in-law are healthy and enjoyable, there is potential for conflict. We are a generation apart, and the gap of two generations between grandparents and grandchildren is yet more gaping. Just as our lives are entering their most intense phase, our parents' lives will tend to be slowing down. We may well need to work hard to understand each other. We may have to face not only the pain of ill health, but the complicated logistics involved in prioritizing our responsibilities to our children and to our parents.

If at times we cannot understand the attitudes and opinions of parents and parents-in-law, perhaps we should stop trying. Instead, we could relax a little and appreciate them for who they are, rather than judge them for who they aren't. They will not be around forever.

Sheila Hancock's thoughts on getting to know her mother reflect the kaleidoscope of emotions many experience:

> After my father's death, I brought my mother up to London and she lived in a little flat near me. I had Ellie Jane by then, so there were resentments about her interference between us. There she was in this little place all on her own when she wasn't with me, and I didn't want her with me all the time because I was getting on with my own life. She must have been so unhappy, and I would have been so much nicer to her but she didn't show me she was in pain.
>
> Now I understand what it's like when your children grow up and you feel outside their world. I'm really sorry I didn't put my hand out to her more. I bitterly regret that I didn't know my mother better as a woman. Right at the end of her life, when I was nursing her, I remember washing her, and I said, "You've got a beautiful nose." She said, "I've gone through my life hating my nose. I thought it was so ugly." I was stunned that my mother had any anxiety about the way she looked. I said, "I can't believe that. It is a wonderful nose. Mine's a funny nose. And you're so beautiful." She had no idea that she was beautiful. But I probably never told her that. All I said was "You're not going to wear that at speech day."
>
> I think underneath all that coping was quite an insecure woman, particularly when her uppity girl went to grammar school, and became educated beyond her. She was both hugely proud of me, and frightened for me. I think I was extremely unkind sometimes, and I showed off my new knowledge in a way which was not exactly humiliating but extremely upsetting. Intellectually, I began to outstrip my parents, and I didn't, at the time, value the kind of wisdom they had. I certainly do now.
>
> The RADA archive has a letter to the principal from my

> father saying, "Are you sure our daughter has talent?" My parents were very frightened and hugely ambitious for me. I was very pleased that they saw me beginning to be successful, but they were very overwhelmed by that world—as was I. When I was in rep, my mother wrote to me saying, "Look after your husband," and things that you wouldn't say to girls nowadays. My girls are ashamed and embarrassed by me in a different way. I'm a bit flamboyant, and I state my views very firmly; I shout when I'm driving, and my language is appalling. When they were at school, I would turn up, dressed wrongly—just like my mother! Now I wish I had valued more how extraordinary my parents were. Similarly, I look back now with such admiration at where my parents came from, and their achievements. [8]

Whether we have happy or sad memories of childhood, whether relationships between ourselves and our parents are peaceful or tense, we share each other's past; we feature on the same family tree; we emanate from the same blood; we share each other's memories. It is natural to want to be part of each other's present: to care about each other's lives; to share each other's failures and successes; to support each other's weaknesses, and value each other's strengths.

# 14

## How to Leave Behind Parental Control

*We have to leave our parents in the sense that we don't hang about waiting for them to give us something more.*
ROBIN SKINNER AND JOHN CLEESE[1]

Laughter, tears, lumps in the throat, anticipation, nervousness, and excitement are all part of a wedding day. This is true for the bride and groom and it will normally be true for their parents also. In the Book of Genesis, the significance of the wedding day is put very simply: "For this reason a man will leave his father and mother" (Genesis 2:24).

We spoke recently to a father on the day after his son's wedding. We knew that they were a close family and that he was fond of his new daughter-in-law, and we asked if he had enjoyed the wedding day. He hesitated before answering, "It is hard to put into words what I felt—it was more complicated than I had anticipated."

Despite the fact that his son had lived away from home for a number of years, this father had understood that a vital part of the marriage was the *leaving* of father and mother. As a result, the day produced for him a mixture of joy and of loss, of looking forward with pride and back with nostalgia.

**Nicky** When I am taking a marriage service, there is one particularly poignant moment: when the father of the bride gives me his daughter's hand for me to pass to the groom. This action symbolizes the fact that both sets of parents are letting go of their son or daughter, passing them from the parental hands into each other's care. It is the culmination of years of responsibility from their child's conception to their marriage, when a new family unit is formed. The parents of the bride and groom, once the most important people in their child's life, must now for the sake of the marriage take a step back to love and encourage in a new way.

Some parents find letting go of their child the most difficult part of parenting, as Victoria Glendinning recalls:

> I found this process so painful that when Simon, the youngest, left home, and for the first time there was no "child" in the house, I had to write myself a stern memo—I was on a train, I remember, and wrote it with tears trickling down my face—to the effect that I had no rights in them, they were only lent to me, and that if I expected them all to ring me up virtually on a daily basis I was a monster and a fool… Some want more contact than others. Some are more naturally communicative. This has absolutely no bearing on who loves whom most.[2]

The need to leave our parents, an essential aspect of marriage, is easily missed today because, in the West at least, most people who are getting married moved out of their parental home some years earlier. Yet the significance of leaving is not so much the *physical* move as the *psychological* and *spiritual* one. For many years the home we were born into was the center of gravity from which we moved out in ever-widening circles of exploration and independence.

But the center remained, the home to which we initially had to return and to which later we would choose to return when comfort was sought, advice was needed, money was short, or the laundry had piled up. The family home was the place of authority, provision, and security. After marriage, there is a new center, a new decision-making structure, a new home. Our highest commitment and loyalty must now be to each other; the apron strings must be cut.

Even if we have been married for many years, we need to ask ourselves if we have fully left our parents. Consider together the following questions. Is one of our parents more important to us than our partner? Are we still emotionally dependent on our parents? Are they trying to control our lives? Do we expect our marriage to be like their marriage? In this chapter we will look at strategies which will help us to leave behind unhelpful parental control in order to protect and nurture our own marriage.

## Recognizing our first loyalty

One woman who was about to get married described her mother to us as "my best friend." She was rightly grateful for a wonderful upbringing but it was an important development for her to see her husband as her best friend, in whom she could confide and from whom she would receive emotional support.

The new center of gravity must now be our new home and our relationship with each other. Even if our parents are going through difficulties themselves, our loyalties must change. Author and journalist, Julie Myerson, writes about her own experience:

> My mother had been left by the man she loved, and I'd met the love of my life. Has Jonathan replaced my mother as the most important person? Probably. Jonathan pointed out how I hadn't separated emotionally from her. I had been a fourteen-year-old girl who told my mother everything, and I became a twenty-one-year-old who told her everything. But you have not to do that after a while.[3]

In many marriages this need to change loyalties is never addressed. In some cases an unhealthy and unhelpful influence continues to exist from parent to child, causing resentment from their partner and placing strain on the marriage. In other families it is because the parents have failed to recognize their child's need to make their own decisions. Insecurity and fear on the parents' part may have led to excessive control. Other parents have sought to hold on to their children in order to meet their own need for affection and support.

It is not common for parents to try to break up their child's marriage. If they interfere inappropriately with unsolicited advice or criticism, it is most often because they think that they are helping. Our joint responsibility is to resist such interference kindly but firmly

This will be difficult if we have been compliant all our life or if a

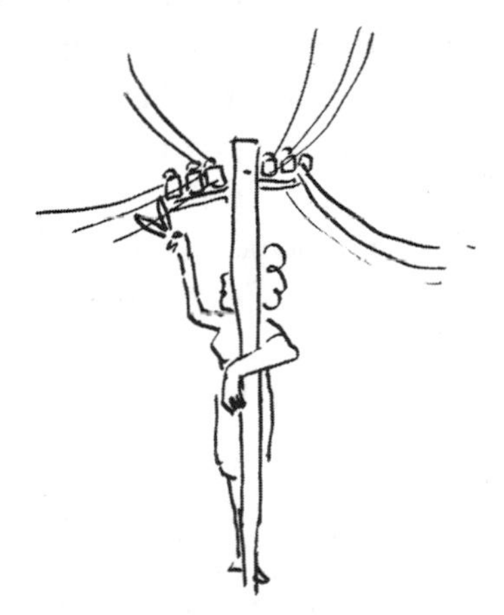

parent is controlling and manipulative. Emotional pressure may be brought to bear with the suggestion that we are being uncaring or ungrateful. It may feel like disloyalty not to go along with what our parents want. We have to remind ourselves where our first loyalty now lies.

## Making our own decisions

It is crucial to a marriage that issues are discussed and decided upon as a couple. We must make our own decisions regarding vacations, the use of our money, the decoration and furnishing of our home, our choice of employment, the raising of children, the frequency of visits and so on.

When Tom and Christine got married a year ago, they moved into her home. Owing to a debilitating illness, Tom is only able to work for four days a week and it happens that his parents live close by. We asked Christine how she was finding married life, and she told us of a particular incident that had caused friction between them. She returned home on one of the days that her husband was not working to discover that he and his mother had rearranged some of the furniture in their house. It could easily be put back and in that sense was not of major significance. But she felt very upset about it, way out of proportion to what had happened, and it took Tom some time to understand why she minded so much.

We asked her if her reaction was stronger because it had been her house prior to their marriage. She recognized that this had something to do with it. The real issue, however, was that the decision about the furniture had been made, not by Tom and herself, but by Tom and his mother. This was a small incident and yet the feelings it caused were very strong indeed. If allowed to continue, this kind of situation can cause serious division between a couple.

Parents will often have valuable advice to offer because of their own experience, and it makes good sense for a couple to listen to it. But it is most important that they are free to take or leave the advice given. We must never make an important decision with one of our parents without discussing it with each other first. Nor must we give our husband or wife the impression of valuing a parent's opinion above theirs. This will undermine our partner's confidence and lead to tension and conflict.

Even when a couple is being supported financially by parents, they must be free to decide how they use that help. We know of one situation where the husband is American and the wife English. They now live in America in a house built for them by his parents, who live nearby. The wife particularly has felt constrained in her ideas for the decoration of their home, knowing that her parents-in-law have not always approved of her taste. As a result the couple have found it hard to make their home feel truly theirs as there has always been a sense of control from outside.

This interference in decision-making can often be exacerbated when children are born. Most couples have little or no experience of caring for children before they have their own. Advice from parents can easily be taken as criticism and interference, particularly if the couple is feeling insecure in the new role. There may in addition be some areas where we will decide to bring up our children differently to the way that we ourselves were brought up.

**Nicky** Our own parents gave us all the encouragement and freedom we needed to develop our family life in our own way. Yet we have encountered differences of opinion that could have caused difficulties. A relatively trivial example makes the point.

When I was growing up, my hair was firmly brushed from left to right with a straight part at one side (although over the last twenty years my part has widened so much that it is now hard to see which side it is). By contrast, Sila and I have taken a more liberal attitude toward our children's

> choice of hairstyle. They have brushed it forward. They have brushed it backward. They have brushed it upward. They have had center parts. They have bleached it. At times they have had it cut to within millimeters of the scalp.
>
> For us this is a way of allowing our children to make their own individual choices and to express their own personality. Our parents, from a more traditional approach, have not always liked these hairstyles and have usually said as much. Depending on whose parent makes the comment, one of us will be tempted to agree, as loyalty to our parents is deeply ingrained in us. At such times we have had to make a conscious decision to stand together on what we have agreed for our own family life.

We heard recently of a marriage that had broken up after thirty years. The reason given was that the wife had never broken free from her very dominant mother. Even after this length of time, parental interference can still be an issue. It cannot be ignored in the hope that it will resolve itself.

## Supporting each other

Some friends of ours, soon after having their first child, had a difference of opinion with his parents that precipitated heated emotions. The couple had decided to use a pacifier for their baby to suck on as a way of stopping his crying. The wife knew that her mother-in-law would strongly disapprove and became increasingly anxious about it, particularly as she was about to stay with her parents-in-law while her husband was away on business. She knew she could not hide it for a whole week. In her own words, "I was terrified of facing her."

When she told her husband of her feelings, he said, "No problem—I'll give her a call and sort it out." His mother exploded down the telephone, "No child of mine ever had a pacifier and no grandchild of mine will ever be seen with one.'" After a very heated exchange, the husband finished the conversation by saying to his mother, "That's it. I've said my piece and I don't want to talk about it again."

Even before going to stay with her parents-in-law, the husband's intervention had a powerful effect upon his wife. She said, "I felt we had made this decision together and he stood up for me—that was all I needed. I didn't care what my mother-in-law said about it after that." In fact the mother-in-law never said a word about the pacifier all week and it has never been mentioned again.

David Mace, formerly director of the American Association of Marriage and Family Counselors, gives this advice:

> When a husband and wife have an agreed policy and stand firmly together putting it into effect, attempts at exploitation and manipulation invariably fail. But any weakness, any crack in the unity of husband and wife enables the in-laws to drive a wedge between them.[4]

We must present a united front. This will mean refusing to take sides with our parents and standing up for our husband or wife against criticism if necessary. Supporting one another consistently over time has a powerful effect, not only uniting us as a couple, but also sending a clear but kind message to parents.

### SETTING BOUNDARIES, IF NECESSARY

One couple on *The Marriage Course* told us that the husband's father had been on his own for many years. The father would telephone his son once or twice each day, often just as they were about to sit down for a meal in the evening or were about to go to bed. The husband's mother had died when he was fifteen and, as the eldest son, he had formed a very special and close relationship with his father. This caused no problems before he got married.

Once married, however, it was a big issue for his wife, and she became increasingly upset. As her father-in-law was on his own and the relationship with his son was so important to him, she felt guilty about saying anything to her husband.

Eventually she knew she must tackle the situation and said, "I am finding your telephone conversations with your father more and more difficult. The timing of them is bad for us, and it makes me feel left out when your dad gets to hear your news first. Then by the time you talk to me, you can't face going through it all again." They discussed the situation and came up with a solution: that the husband would talk to his father once a day at the office.

At first, it did not work as the father would still call every evening. So the husband said to his father, "When you get up in the morning, give me a call at the office, and I'd love to talk to you then; otherwise this isn't going to work."

The father tested it several times over the next few days. Each time he called in the evening, the husband would say, "Sorry, Dad, I can't talk to you now. Would you mind calling me in the morning and we can have a really good talk?" But after two weeks, in the husband's words, "He got the hang of it." The wife said that as a result a lot changed in their marriage, "My husband was putting more emphasis on our marriage, making it the priority, and that made me feel really great." She also commented that both her own and her husband's relationship with his father became closer than before.

In such situations, the first step must be to discuss the quandary together and to try to understand each other's feelings. This will not be easy. We instinctively want to excuse our parents or accommodate their wishes, particularly if we have idealized them or if they are ill or on their own. This in turn can cause us to become defensive or dismissive of the other's perspective. We may not even recognize the problem. We need to listen carefully to our husband or wife (as described in chapter 4) and to acknowledge that there is an issue for them. Sympathetic listening will usually go at least halfway to resolving the situation. We also need to recognize that our partner is not attacking our parents or family but being rightly protective of the marriage relationship. We are then in a good position to work out together what action to take, obtaining outside advice and help if necessary.

A newly married husband and wife spent an hour describing to us the difficulties they were facing with her parents. The parents clearly wanted to continue to control their daughter's life, and they had made no effort to build a relationship with their son-in-law. Having listened to and understood each other's feelings, they decided that the best way forward would be to arrange a meeting with her parents. We do not know exactly what they planned to say but we recommended that they included the following:

- their appreciation for the ways that her parents had sought to help and support them.
- their desire for a close ongoing relationship with her parents.
- an explanation (with some real examples) of why the husband was feeling excluded and why this was putting a strain on their marriage.
- a few practical suggestions as to how they could work together to improve the situation.

They went to see her parents one Saturday and bravely raised the awkward subject about an hour before they had to leave. The atmosphere was tense. The parents were reluctant to listen to what they had to say. However, over the following weeks the couple went out of their way to maintain communication, and the situation steadily improved. The confrontation was painful, but very worthwhile in the long run.

### PUTTING EACH OTHER FIRST

Eric, who is now divorced, admits that when his young wife was grappling with a four-year-old, a baby, a part-time job, and a big and chilly house in a strange neighborhood, he regularly used to stop off at his parents' cottage, near his work, for a drink and a talk on the way home.

There, with a deep-pile carpet beneath him and a bowlful of homemade cheese straws at his elbow, he would relate the triumphs and trials of his day to his Mum. She was an interested, intelligent, stimulating listener. As we all will be one day, when we can get some sleep and not be responsible for anyone's socks but our own. When he went home to a wife physically exhausted by the babies' bathtime and still staring hopelessly at the contents of the fridge, he could not help comparing the two homes and the two women. Aloud. It was his father who eventually blew the whistle on him by coming in on one of his evening sessions with Mother and remarking (with great vision for his generation) that perhaps his own wife might like some help with getting the babies to bed. But it was too late by then. Eileen and the children went home to her own mother[5]

But it does not have to be like that if we get our priorities right. Melanie Thaw explains how her relationship with her mother, Sheila Hancock, is now stronger, though different:

Motherhood has definitely brought us closer together, but it also changes the relationship because you have a shift in responsibilities. My responsibility now has to be my partner and my child. I don't want it to seem as if I'm pushing Mum away, but maybe that's how it feels. She's not the only important person in my life any more. Her role has changed....And Mum is a brilliant granny...[6]

# 15

## How to Address the Effects of Childhood Pain

*Love...has the power to remake situations.*
ALAN STORKEY[1]

Our past affects the present, which in turn affects the future. Nowhere is this more true than in family relationships—for good and bad. This chapter is written for those whose childhood and upbringing are casting a shadow over their own marriages. They may be struggling to come to terms with a traumatic past or may be unaware of the connection between their experiences then and their behavior now.

Ted's mother was a dynamic and forceful woman. She had boundless energy, which was channeled into pushing her three children to achieve success in everything. She was driven by obsessive ambition, which she had not fulfilled in her own life. Ted's older brother excelled at sports and his sister played two musical instruments to a high standard.

Ted was always expected to follow in their footsteps. "You'll get into the first team, Ted—just like Robert," said his mother. "I've organized two weeks of coaching for you in the holidays." "No, you can't go and stay with Phil because I've booked you in for a week's dinghy sailing so you can race next summer with Jane." Ted's life had been organized and planned for him since

> the moment he was born. He was never allowed to disagree nor permitted to express his feelings.
>
> When Julia, his wife, suggested that they might go for a biking weekend in the Lake District, his cutting and hurtful reply, "Why are you always trying to control my life?" sparked a heated argument. Accusations flew back and forth, the issue of the biking weekend forgotten in the exchange of fire. Ted had by now perfected the art of finishing the exchange with a sarcastic comment that usually left Julia in tears.

Ted's resentment of his mother's attempts to control his life and his pent-up anger had remained over the years. It poured out, however, not against his mother, but against his wife, Julia. Their confusion about the source of so much conflict in their marriage eventually caused them to seek help.

No parents are perfect and none of us had a perfect upbringing. Sometimes it was not the fault of our parents, and sometimes it was. Unresolved pain or anger could have resulted from death or from long absence abroad. Or it may have stemmed from our parents' divorce, from abuse (either physical or emotional), from excessive control, or the suppression of emotion.

Some have grown up in a home where the love they received was conditional upon their intelligence, their looks, their abilities, how well they did at school, or how well they behaved at home. The failure of parents to show unconditional love is likely to leave deep wounds. The key is whether our memories of our childhood are happy or painful. For some these memories are so painful that amnesia has set in, and they cannot easily recall anything of what they felt during their upbringing.

As a result of experiences from childhood, we may find that at times we react irrationally toward our partner or another third party. These reactions can be very disturbing for our husband or wife.

Soon after Miranda got married, she began to experience great difficulty in her relationship with her father-in-law. Having had only sons, he was not used to relating to women of his children's generation. The more vulnerable she felt, the more dogmatic he became. On several occasions when they visited Patrick's parents, Miranda ended up in tears, much to Patrick's bemusement. It became so bad that she felt physically sick and full of dread in weeks before their visit at Christmas. Patrick realized that there was a problem, and together they sought help.

It transpired that Miranda's childhood had been traumatic. Her sister had always been treated as the favorite. At the age of eighteen Miranda had been beaten by her father and told to leave her home and family and not to come back. Her parents had subsequently divorced. As Patrick and Miranda talked it through, she realized that her difficulties in relating to her father-in-law were an overreaction as a result of her own deep pain from the past.

In a loving marriage and with God's help, hurt such as this can be healed. Looking for a quick cure is unhelpful, but, over time, feelings can be changed and our ability to relate intimately can be restored.

We should be aware of two dangers with regard to childhood pain. One is a sense of hopelessness in the person who has been hurt. They might say, "I cannot help behaving and reacting the way I do. I'm a victim. It is just the way I am, and it is my parents' fault." We must not abdicate responsibility like this. At any moment, even while carrying hurt from the past, we can choose to look outward to the needs of others, including those of our husband or wife.

The second danger is a lack of understanding by their partner, who may blame them rather than seek to help. Their partner needs to understand that, while healing is possible, it often takes time. Those who have been deeply hurt may need the help of an experienced counselor. During the process of healing, they will benefit greatly from the love, encouragement, and prayers of their partner.

If you have particularly painful memories of childhood that may be affecting your marriage, we would encourage you to talk about the following points together. If you get stuck at any stage or encounter feelings that seem uncontrollable and dangerously strong, it is wise to seek the help of a Christian pastor or a counselor.

### RECOGNIZE THE SOURCE OF THE PAIN

At the start of the last chapter, we looked at the role of parents in providing for the physical and emotional needs of their children. Refer back to the two diagrams for the "early years" and "teenagers" and ask yourself if your parents, or any others who took care of you, met these needs in your childhood.

It can be hard to face the situation honestly. For most people there is a sense of deep loyalty to their parents, and they do not want to appear ungrateful to them. Those with unmet childhood needs easily think it was their own fault that they were not shown love. They assume that they could not have been lovable or worth bothering with, and that is why their parents did not affirm them. It is important to take an honest look at what was lacking and the consequences this is having on our relationships now.

We should not be surprised if, as we do so, we encounter a strong sense of anger, or other emotions such as sadness, rejection, fear, and shame. These emotions will have been suppressed over a long period. A young woman who came on *The Marriage Course*, who has had a difficult relationship with her mother, described how she spent an evening throwing shoes around her bedroom. She had not previously recognized the buried anger.

If we experience such emotions, we can always tell God what we feel and look for His comfort. The more honest we are in prayer the better. The Bible uses imagery that portrays God as father *and* mother, full of compassion toward us and encouraging us to bring every need to Him. The psalmists were able to express to God the whole range of human emotions—anger, frustration, pain, regret as well as gratitude, and joy—and so can we. In the words of the Apostle Peter, "Cast all your anxiety on Him because He cares for you" (1 Peter 5:7).

### Grieve with each other

Unmet childhood needs constitute a type of bereavement. If a husband or wife can talk about what was lacking in the past, their partner can seek to provide emotional support through their willingness to listen, without trying to explain away the feelings or minimalize the effect. The Bible tells us to "mourn with those who mourn" (Romans 12:15). This very process of speaking openly of the sense of loss to someone who cares brings healing and assists the grieving process.

If your spouse recalls a lack of affection, affirmation, or support in his or her childhood, you must be particularly careful not to compound the pain by ignoring these ongoing emotional needs within your marriage. Those who lay bare their childhood pain need to receive comfort, without demanding it, from their partner.

### Forgive those who have caused the hurt

In chapter 12, we wrote about the process of forgiving. Here are the main points again. First, to forgive is an act of the will. We must forgive those who have hurt us even when we do not feel like doing so. For some, childhood experiences will have become a "no-go area." We received a letter recently from a woman named Jennifer who had come on *The Marriage Course* and had realized that she needed to forgive her step-father. She wrote:

> I had a step-father named John. My mother married him when I was seven and divorced him when I was fifteen. The application for divorce was made on the grounds of "mental cruelty." My childhood was a nightmare. My biggest wish was to grow up as quickly

as possible to get away from the situation.

I am now thirty-three. I have carried the burden of these memories and the hate around for eighteen years, despite becoming a committed Christian two years ago. It was the one part of my life that was simply a no-go area. I was desolate. How could I possibly "forgive" John for what he had done? Where would be the justice in that? I was a child. I was the victim. I haven't seen him since I was fifteen—he wasn't even asking (I would have preferred begging) for forgiveness.

The combination of *The Marriage Course*, Philip Yancey's book *What's So Amazing About Grace?* and God's work in my life enabled me to see clearly that I needed to deal with this once and for all—unless I wanted eighteen years to turn to twenty-eight, thirty-eight, forty-eight... with no end.

I prayed, lay awake for several nights, cried, and prayed some more. Then I wrote John a letter, forgiving him for the hurt and anguish I had experienced as a child in his care. As I wrote, I had no idea if he was even aware of the impact that that part of his life had had on mine; I decided to leave that part up to God. But I knew as I mailed the letter that I had been set free.

We subsequently heard that Jennifer's step-father made contact with her. He was unable to see the damage that he had caused or why he needed her forgiveness. Despite his response, Jennifer still experienced complete freedom from the pain that he had caused her.

Forgiveness is first an act of the will. Second, it is an ongoing decision. Where we have been deeply hurt, we will need to keep on deciding to forgive, even on a daily basis, for the same offense. When we forgive as a conscious act, like Jennifer, the feelings will follow.

Third, as we saw in Jennifer's story, our forgiveness is not to be conditional either upon our parents' (or step-parents') understanding of where they have failed us or upon a change of attitude in them. Forgiveness means giving up both the desire to repay and the expectation that our parents will now meet our needs. This is part of letting go of our dependence upon them.

It will not always be advisable or indeed possible to express our forgiveness directly to those who have hurt us. If both parents are dead or all contact with them has been lost, we still need to let go of any anger toward them, and we suggest below the outline of a prayer that could help you release those feelings to God.

### Seek God's love

We can ask God to heal our sense of loss, inviting Him as the perfect parent to give us the security that we did not receive from our parents. His promise to us is this: "I have loved you with an everlasting love and am constant in My affection for you" (Jeremiah 31:3). His love, therefore, is able to meet our deepest needs for acceptance, security, attention, encouragement, and so on. Parental love even at its best could only ever be a pale reflection of the strong, steady, and unconditional love that God has for us.

God invites us to become part of His family and to experience Him as Father: "Yet to all who received him [Jesus], to those who believed in His name, He gave the right to become children of God" (John 1:12). When we put our lives into God's hands, He gives us His Spirit, who fills us with the assurance of His love: "God has poured out His love into our hearts by the Holy Spirit, whom He has given us" (Romans 5:5).

Below is a suggested prayer that you might like to use if you are carrying hurt from your upbringing:

> Lord, thank You for your unconditional love for me and Your willingness to forgive me freely. Thank You for the good things my parents gave me. [Here put good memories into words.] I now bring before You the ways they failed me and ask You to help me to forgive them.

> [Then say:] My father/mother (or whatever term you normally use), caused me to feel like this through failing to ...[name the unmet childhood needs]... but I choose to forgive them.
>
> Lord, thank You that You are a perfect Father. Please fill me now with Your Holy Spirit that I may know Your love in my own experience. Thank You for Your promise to give Your Spirit of love to all those who ask You. Amen.

We have listed at the end of the chapter some of God's promises. Dwell on these words. Dare to believe God's unconditional love for you. As you do so, God will gradually replace the pain of unmet childhood needs with a sense of security and comfort.

## MOVE ON

As we forgive our parents, we may become aware that, because of the unseen motive to satisfy childhood needs, we have acted irrationally and upset others, especially those we love most. There may have been angry explosions at our husband or wife for no obvious reason, or denial, self-hatred, and the pushing away of those who try to love us and get close to us. We may have visited and telephoned our parents too often, telling them of our achievements and longing to hear the "Well done" that was absent in childhood. Though at times it may feel impossibly difficult, with God's help and the encouragement of our husband or wife, and others if necessary, we can leave this behavior behind.

Change, however, makes us feel insecure. Victor Frankel describes the liberation of surviving Jews from the concentration camp, Dachau, at the end of the war. The prisoners walked out into the sunlight but were so dazzled by it that they went back into their cells.[2] Sometimes we would rather return to the familiarity and safety of our obviously imperfect relationships and old patterns of behavior.

As we move on, we may well feel exposed and need reassurance. We should not be surprised or put off by this.

If one partner has had to bear the brunt of some irrational behavior, they should not expect changes to be instantaneous. It takes time for old ways of responding to be replaced with new ones. Be gentle, patient, and encouraging.

## TAKE HOPE

We have written this chapter not for everyone, but for those whose unresolved pain and anger from their childhoods have put great strain on their relationships. If this chapter has relevance in your life, we would encourage you, for the sake of your marriage and despite the emotional energy required, to work through these painful issues together and with someone else if necessary. Attempts to restore relationships with the wider family may or may not be reciprocated. It is still worth it for the sake of your own marriage.

We have in God a perfect Father, "... slow to anger and abounding in love" (Jonah 4:2), always ready to listen, to comfort, and to help. If our own parents failed to love us, we may at first find this hard to accept. The well-known words from 1 Corinthians 13, "Love always protects, always trusts, always hopes, always perseveres," are an inspiration and encouragement to see the process through.

We have written here a selection of God's promises of love which many have found reassuring.

> In a desert land He found him, in a barren and howling waste. He shielded him and cared for him; He guarded him as the apple of His eye, like an eagle that stirs up its nest and hovers over its young, that spreads its wings to catch them and carries them on its pinions (Deuteronomy 32:10–11).

But while he was still a long way off, his father saw him and was filled with compassion for him; he ran to his son, threw his arms around him and kissed him (Luke 15:20).

As a father has compassion on his children, so the Lord has compassion on those who fear Him (Psalm 103:13).

So do not fear, for I am with you; do not be dismayed, for I am your God. I will strengthen you and help you; I will uphold you with My righteous right hand (Isaiah 41:10).

Because you are His children, He sent the Spirit of His Son into our hearts, the Spirit who calls out, "Abba, Father" (Galatians 4:6).

And so we know and rely on the love God has for us (1 John 4:16).

# Section 6 – Parents and In-laws

## CONCLUSION

This is the experience of one married woman's relationships with her wider family:

> As I listen to friends struggling with manipulative mothers and cold distant fathers, interfering grannies and obsessive grandpas, I find myself wondering if my upbringing was boringly simple. But I now see that it must, at times, have been mind-stretchingly complex.
>
> Mum and Dad provided my brother and myself with a very real, normal family life. We all argued from time to time of course, my brother and I hourly between learning to walk and learning to drive (according to my mother).
>
> But through the highs and lows of family life (and despite all of our imperfections) we always communicated—and we still do. We sat down virtually every evening to supper and we discussed our respective days, asking everyone's advice and caring about everyone's struggles.
>
> My first boyfriend arrived one evening on his motorbike dressed in full leathers. He was instantly invited to join us for supper with absolutely no fuss, whispering or raised eyebrows. It all carried on exactly as normal, apart from my father saying, "Why don't you take your jacket off, old boy? The tassels are dragging through the creamed leeks."
>
> And so it went on.
>
> And then I got married, and the relationship grew between Tim, my husband, my brother and, of course, my parents. My own relationship with them expanded to include Tim and it must have changed too—but I've no idea how.

> I guess that without really thinking about it, we allowed ourselves to regroup and to rearrange ourselves into our new roles. Then we had children and we probably rearranged again.
>
> We talk on the phone; we call to find out how many times you can reheat mince; we ask Dad how to build shelves and hope he might offer. We meet for lunch and supper. They sometimes have the children and we escape. They are incredibly busy. So are we. We had to live with them for a while between houses with an eighteen-month-old son with a tendency to empty cupboards and wake at dawn. But that's another story. Yes, the whole thing is spectacularly underwhelming. And I love the lot of them—absolutely.

While the members of that family were far from perfect—indeed they would stress their many imperfections—they experienced firm foundations in childhood upon which to build their own marriages.

For many people, this is not the case. We have seen examples of difficult and sometimes extremely painful family situations in these chapters.

Where our past has been painful, our marriage need not be jeopardized. Indeed marriage itself can be a healing relationship. A friend of ours told us the other day how painful she had found it as a child to discover that she was adopted. She could not accept that she had no known blood relation. When she became pregnant and started her own family, she found her pain was healed. The healing came through her marriage and her experience of family life.

Another man, who had a difficult relationship with his own father, spoke of the thrill of forming a healthy and loving relationship with his father-in-law. It convinced him finally that there was nothing wrong with him. He was an acceptable man.

Those who had neglectful or cruel parents sometimes worry about their own ability to be a good parent. But as they discover the joy of having and loving their own children, again the past can be healed. Victoria Glendinning writes:

> I had a difficult childhood myself. I rewrote it, in happiness, through my children's childhood.[3]

For all of us, marriage can be a healing relationship. It is the place where the insecurities and self-doubt which we carry with us from the past can be revealed and reversed. Through God's love, and the love of our husband or wife, the gaps can be filled, the hurtful words repealed, and our confidence in who we are rebuilt.

## Sixth Golden Rule of Marriage

Honor your parents but do not be controlled by them.

# Section 7 — Good Sex

# 16

## Sex – What Is It All About?

*Sex has a purpose...to abolish isolation. Some people choose isolation. They do so not because at heart they prefer isolation but because they fear rejection and estrangement. Yet, if I do not expose myself, how will I ever discover the wonders of being enfolded by and lost in another?*

JOHN WHITE[1]

Sex is the greatest natural intimacy builder. We have left the subject until now, not because it is an unimportant part of marriage, but because every other part of our marriage affects our lovemaking and our lovemaking affects every other part of our marriage. When our sexual relationship is a vital expression of our love for each other, we experience a togetherness which permeates every level of our being.

God loves sex. He invented it. We are designed to revel in the attraction we feel toward our husband or wife. The ability to express love through the joining of our bodies is a gift from the one who is pure love. He intends us to enjoy it to the full within the loving commitment of marriage where there is nothing to hide or hold back from each other. Mike Mason describes this act of "total nakedness":

> To be naked with another person is a sort of picture or symbolic demonstration of perfect honesty, perfect trust, perfect giving, and commitment, and if the heart is not naked along with the body, then the whole action becomes a lie and a mockery. It becomes an

> involvement in an absurd and tragic contradiction: the giving of the body but the withholding of the self. Exposure of the body in a personal encounter is like the telling of one's deepest secret: afterwards there is no going back, no pretending that the secret is still one's own or that the other does not know. It is, in effect, the very last step in human relations, and therefore never one to be taken lightly. It is not a step that establishes deep intimacy, but one which presupposes it.[2]

Our own perception and experience of sex may well be very different. In the second half of the twentieth-century sex has been overdone, overportrayed, and overemphasized. We have seen it everywhere, at times cheapened, at times sentimentalized, at times idolized, but nearly always out of the context of marriage. Some have become addicted to it. Others have gotten fed up with it, such that a broadsheet headline recently declared: "Why sex isn't sexy any more."

Many people (us included) learned about sex from their peer group who seemed at an incredibly young age to be a great authority on the subject. Later it emerged that they were equally ignorant or misinformed.

Our education will have played a part in how we view sex. Libby Purves wrote of the attitudes she encountered at school: "There were one or two excessively modest [teachers], like the Mistress of Discipline who banned radios from the bathrooms in the morning because it was not decent for deep, male voices to be heard in a room where a young girl was unclothed."[3] What a contrast to the attitude of many schools today where no particular boundaries are taught, except that, if possible, sex should be safe.

Historically the church must bear some of the blame for a false understanding. The Bible is clear that sex within marriage is good, but the church has not always reflected this teaching accurately. In the fourth century, Augustine spoke of "the shame that attends all sexual intercourse." Other theologians went further. Some warned married couples that the Holy Spirit left the bedroom when they engaged in sexual intercourse. Therefore the less sex, the better.

But perhaps the greatest influence on the shaping of our attitudes is our parents' view of sex. In some homes the subject is never discussed openly, or it is talked about inappropriately—in cheap jokes or bad language. For others their parents' fear and overprotectiveness have caused false guilt and left them feeling all sex is dirty. Tragically some people struggle with a distorted view of sex having suffered the horrors of sexual abuse, while others bring into their marriage the painful consequences of past sexual relationships.

There is supposedly great openness about sex and sexuality today, yet many people are still embarrassed to talk honestly with each other about sex in their marriage. This is a strange paradox: sex is bandied about in society, but privately we don't mention it, especially if we have problems.

Before we discuss sex at a practical level, we will outline four biblical principles that provide the setting for a fulfilling sexual relationship within a loving and lifelong marriage.

## SEX—A POWERFUL FORCE

> The man said, "This is now bone of my bones and flesh of my flesh; she shall be called 'woman,' for she was taken out of man." For this reason a man will leave his father and mother and be united to his wife, and they will become one flesh (Genesis 2:23–4).

The modern equivalent of Adam's words when he first set eyes on Eve might start with a long drawn-out "Wow!" God's great plan for marriage is that the longing that a husband and a wife have to be together culminates in the sexual union. When practiced lovingly, it both expresses and creates oneness.

This is why sex outside marriage is damaging. The joining of a man and a woman sexually will always be more than a temporary physical bond. Whether we intend it or not, it affects us at a deep emotional, psychological, and spiritual level. The two sheets of paper that we spoke of in chapter 1, glued together to become one sheet, cannot be torn apart without damage to both.

Sex is designed by God to be an expression of the exclusive and committed relationship between a man and a woman. Each time we express our love for each other through this physical joining of our bodies, the bond between us is made deeper and stronger.

### SEX—A LIFETIME OF DISCOVERY

The second reference comes from the Song of Songs. In the middle of the Bible there is a beautiful erotic love poem describing the passionate relationship between a lover and his new bride. The writer unashamedly celebrates the mysterious power of God's gift of sexual love. The poetic imagery, although obscure at first reading, leaves us in no doubt that God intends us to enjoy exploring each other's bodies and delighting in our mutual attraction, arousal, and climax. There is no hint of shame, guilt, or embarrassment.

> Eat, O friends, and drink;
> drink your fill, O lovers (Song of Songs 5:1).

The lovemaking in the Song of Songs gradually matures over the course of the poem as the couple's relationship develops. Perhaps this gives a further glimpse as to why God's purpose is for sex to be kept within marriage.

By contrast, the impression given by countless films today is that sex is most exciting when a relationship is new or adulterous. This myth causes many to assume that, as a husband and wife grow familiar with each other, the excitement will inevitably wane. Only the adventure and secrecy of an affair can provide the sexual high again.

But this is not the way that God designed our bodies. It is rather that, as we grow in understanding how to arouse and bring pleasure to each other, our sexual relationship develops and the enjoyment increases with the years, nourishing the entire marriage as we express and receive love. This conviction led the writer of Proverbs to state with such feeling "... may you rejoice in the wife of your youth... may her breasts satisfy you always, may you ever be captivated by her love" (Proverbs 5:18-19).

A couple in their late sixties write about their own experience after thirty-six years of marriage:

> Sexual intercourse is first of all for deepening a couple's relationship of love. If this were not so, God would not have allowed this part of our being to go on with vigor and ardor well beyond the years of child-bearing into our fifties, sixties, and seventies (we are so glad that this is so!).[4]

When a husband and a wife take a long view, they will be amply rewarded. The Christian author and psychiatrist, John White, comments:

> Sex was intended to end aloneness...the communion (the close-

> ness, the intimacy, the knowing-and-being-known, the loving-and-being-loved) is a complex living structure that takes years to grow. It begins as a delicate and beautiful plant, vibrant with life. It grows into a sturdy tree with deep roots to sustain it through drought and storm.[5]

Because of the power of sex to create pleasure and intimacy, the passionate sexual imagery of the Song of Songs is also used as a metaphor for the close personal relationship God desires to have with us.

### SEX —AN ESSENTIAL INGREDIENT

The third reference comes in Paul's first letter to the church in Corinth, a city noted for its sexual license and red-light district.

> The husband should fulfill his marital duty to his wife, and likewise the wife to her husband. The wife's body does not belong to her alone but also to her husband. In the same way, the husband's body does not belong to him alone but also to his wife. Do not deprive each other except by mutual consent and for a time, so that you may devote yourselves to prayer. Then come together again so that Satan will not tempt you because of your lack of self-control (1 Corinthians 7:3-5).

These verses have at times been misused, particularly by husbands making demands on their wife to satisfy their every sexual whim and wish. This contradicts the main point of this passage which is to remind husbands and wives of their *duties* toward each other rather than of their rights. Neither a husband nor a wife is to withhold physical lovemaking except by mutual agreement for a limited period. Both need to recognize that their sexual relationship is not the icing on the cake of their marriage but an essential ingredient of the cake itself.

As we saw earlier, Roman law gave a husband absolute rights over his wife. Paul's teaching about this mutual giving of a husband's and a wife's body to each other was therefore revolutionary in the first century. Today it is just as relevant.

An article in *The Sunday Times* reporting on the British National Survey of Sexual Attitudes and Lifestyles showed that, while outside marriage sex is widely regarded as a normal part of relationships, within marriage thousands of couples "have spurned sex in favour of chastity...Research reveals that up to one in thirty of all couples are opting for celibacy in their relationships because they have neither the time nor inclination for sex."[6]

It is widely assumed that sexual relationships have a natural life span. Liz Hodgkinson, author of *Sex is Not Compulsory*, writes, "For some that may be a week, for others it could be twenty years. But if you try to extend your sexual relationship beyond its natural life, then you are asking for trouble because then it no longer becomes spontaneous or enjoyable."[7]

This is a sad misunderstanding about the way that sex works. God designed sex for a lifelong marriage relationship and intended it to be fulfilling (although changing) throughout our lives. As we get to know each other more deeply over the years, the potential for intimacy and joy through the sexual bond increases—not decreases. Far from giving up when sexual desire diminishes for a while, a couple needs to discover new ways of arousing and satisfying each other.

If we neglect the biblical command and withhold ourselves from regular times of making love (except for reasons such as ill health or recovering from childbirth), we become separate at every level. Lack of lovemaking in a marriage must be taken seriously. It can lead to feelings of isolation and aloneness. And when we feel lonely we are vulnerable to temptations from elsewhere.

## SEX—AN ACT OF GIVING

The fourth reference comes from the fullest teaching about marriage in the New Testament. It is not exclusively about the sexual relationship but certainly includes it.

> Submit to one another out of reverence for Christ. Wives, submit to your husbands as to the Lord. Husbands, love your wives, just as Christ loved the church and gave Himself up for her...In this same way, husbands ought to love their wives as their own bodies. He who loves his wife loves himself. After all, people have never hated their own bodies, but feed and care for them, just as Christ does the church—for we are members of His body. "For this reason a man will leave his father and mother and be united to his wife, and the two will become one flesh." This is a profound mystery—but I am talking about Christ and the church. However, each one of you also must love his wife as he loves himself, and the wife must respect her husband (Ephesians 5:21-22, 25, 28-33).

Good sex requires both husband and wife to think how best to give each other pleasure through their lovemaking. Much of the stimulating and satisfying of sexual desire today has become self-oriented.

The emphasis is upon *my* right to satisfy *my* desire in the ways that *I* choose. Sex, however, is not a gift for self-gratification. It is a way of giving ourselves to one another, submitting to each other's needs and desires.

Sexual intercourse is the most intimate way of showing love to your husband or wife and it involves making sacrifices for each other. A couple needs to learn how to give to each other. At various times and for various reasons we will each have a different level of sexual desire, especially during periods of stress or with the arrival of a child. For one, sacrificial love might mean showing restraint. For the other, it might mean making love despite tiredness.

The concept of giving through sex can be difficult to grasp. We are so easily preoccupied with getting rather than giving. Many people grow up thinking that sex is something to take, to earn, or to manipulate. The art of giving oneself to another person can therefore feel foreign at first; but this art must be cultivated in every area of marriage, particularly in the area of sex.

> We do not marry to copulate...We marry to make an alliance of mutual help and service, and as an expression of love. [Sexual] intimacy in such a context is the seal of commitment. It is also a delicate communication of love and trust by which a man and woman know each other ever more deeply.[8]

# 17

## Six Qualities for Great Lovers

*[Sex] celebrates what is happening in the rest of the couple's life.*
ALAN STORKEY[1]

The most basic yet most important fact to grasp about our sexuality is that men and women are made differently. Someone described the differences like this:

> Men can't get enough sex; women can't get enough romance. Men are thinking about the destination; women are thinking about the road. Men are like gas cookers: they heat up instantly and cool down rapidly. Women are like electric cookers: they take time to heat up but stay hot for much longer.

God designed men and women to be aroused in different ways and it is the combination that can produce a long and fulfilling sexual relationship. If women were made like men, it would all be over in thirty seconds and sex would not be the great intimacy builder God intended it to be.

Both husbands and wives have to understand and enjoy these differences; otherwise they can seem like insurmountable problems. A husband has to learn to be gentle and patient and give time for his wife to be aroused. Meanwhile, a wife needs to understand her own as well as her husband's sexuality. For her the process of arousal is generally more complex than for her husband, and sex may not be so easily divorced from the rest of life. These differences in our sexual responses often lead to misunderstanding and conflict, which will affect the whole marriage for the worse. What follows is the first of six important qualities that will enable lovemaking to develop.

### Communication

The whole subject of sexual intimacy is for many people deeply private. However, if we can be open and honest with each other, it will greatly strengthen our mutual trust and our closeness.

A couple who attended *The Marriage Course* described the effect of talking more openly:

*Carol:* Before we did *The Marriage Course*, for me our sex life was fine. I thought my husband had all the problems and I didn't have any. I was quite happy with the way things were.

*Richard:* If you had asked, "Do you have any problems with your sex life?" I would probably have said, "No." But there was an issue for me. I always seemed to be having to ask, "Do you feel like it?" I felt helpless. There seemed no way in which I could influence Carol's response.

*Carol:* During the course we had to write down a score to assess the friendship, spiritual intimacy, and physical intimacy in our marriage.

It came as quite a shock to me when my husband showed me what he'd put: out of 20, our friendship was 18; our spiritual relationship was 19 and our physical relationship was 2! Really it was like that! Then when we talked together, for the first time I actually listened to Richard and tried hard to understand what a problem it was for him. I took it seriously. Until then I thought that he was always demanding and that he didn't understand me; but now I began to realize how important this part of our marriage was to him.

Before *The Marriage Course* I had never really held a Christian view of sex. I had not seen how crucial it is. I thought we were great friends, that we were spiritually aligned and that if our sex was not very good, it didn't really matter. During the course I realzsed that I was suffering from certain hang-ups, and these were preventing us being free with each other sexually.

When I was twelve years old, I walked into my parents' bedroom while they were making love. Nobody, including my parents, had ever talked to me about sex. I had no understanding of what they were doing, but it didn't *sound* as if it had anything to do with love. I was so embarrassed by the incident that I went to school the next day before my parents were up. That evening they sat me down and, looking extremely awkward, they tried to explain. From that day, sex became a highly embarrassing subject for me. A few years later I discovered that my father had been unfaithful to my mother, and deep down I started to believe that it was impossible to trust men sexually.

I had not told Richard about any of this before *The Marriage Course* but he was living in the shadow of its effect upon me. When I told him one night, in the dark, feeling a mixture of shame and embarrassment, he was so kind and gentle. I then spent some time talking and praying about this with one of the leaders of the course and, with Richard's love and support, it was resolved.

*Richard:* It was so good for me to be able to be honest and give us a 2. The best part was to be listened to and taken seriously, rather than feeling like a whingeing sort of animal, which is how I felt treated before. The second thing was that I decided to cool down a bit and we started experimenting with making agreements. We agreed to make love once a week. Meanwhile I would try to be more romantic.

Holding a Christian perspective is really great because it means that sex is more than an instinctive physical process. It has become something that is part of our intimate relationship. Also I realized I had been behaving like a victim and not being straight over my requests.

*Carol:* Since we completed *The Marriage Course* I have discovered how wonderful sex can be. Now that our physical relationship is no longer something separate, our growing together has suddenly become a reality. I used to think that if we talked about everything, our marriage would be fine. Now I see that our sexual relationship is a way of communicating in marriage that is as important as the words we say.

Many husbands have a stronger sex drive than their wives which, without good communication, leaves many women feeling sexually inadequate or intimidated. We need to learn to be open with each other, expressing our desire to make love, telling our partner what we enjoy or do not enjoy. Assumptions about one another or generalizations about gender are unhelpful. Some wives have a stronger sex drive than their husbands, and some husbands feel inadequate because they don't live up to the expectations our culture puts upon them. No couple is a stereotype. We all differ in the peaks and troughs of our sexual desire. Listening to each other and expressing our feelings about sex is as important as any other area of communication in our marriage.

During lovemaking, wives need to tell their husbands what arouses them and when they are ready for intercourse, while husbands need to tell their wives what *not* to do if they are struggling to delay orgasm. The more we discover about one another, the more we shall enjoy making love. Any embarrassment quickly disappears once this kind of communication has begun.

Past sexual experiences can affect us deeply: there may be a reluctance to give ourselves for fear of being hurt again, or bad memories may inhibit our freedom. It is important to expose our deepest fears to each other in this complex area of our personality. For it is as we communicate verbally (often with painful feelings of vulnerability) that our husband or wife is able to comfort and encourage us, and our feelings of rejection and estrangement will be replaced by warmth and welcome. And this acceptance can then be expressed through a loving sexual relationship. The issue thus becomes a virtuous circle: as we make love, we heal the bad memories, which in turn leads to less fear and more desire.

## Tenderness

Sexual intimacy arises out of tenderness; they are two sides of the same coin. Tenderness is a vital aspect of our relationship, and love-making will feel empty and one-dimensional without it. Tenderness involves taking time over making love. Time to unwind from the pressures of the day. Time to build romance and desire. Time to enjoy being physically close. Time to love each other with our words: kind, tender, affirming words. It does not matter if the same words are used again and again if we really mean them.

Just as an orchestra starts with the oboe and then the other instruments in the orchestra tune to it, so tenderness means tuning in to each other's emotional needs. If we do not take time and are looking only to achieve orgasm, sex will be mechanical.

Some husbands only touch their wives when they want sex. This sends terrible signals to her. Indeed it can lead to a marriage with no physical contact at all as the wife backs off, resenting her husband's attitude and intentions. If she feels in any sense *used*, her body will shut down. For a woman to give herself to her husband, she must feel safe. She needs to feel loved. She must feel special. We are not suggesting that tenderness and passion are mutually exclusive but, for a woman particularly, the emotional fulfillment can be as satisfying as reaching orgasm.

The BBC "six O'Clock News" recently reported that at some stage in their lives one in three wives in the U.K. experience domestic violence. That is a terrible reversal of those words in Ephesians that we referred to in the last chapter: "Husbands, love your wives, as Christ loved the church" (Ephesians 5:25). In a traditional Jewish wedding, instead of putting a ring on his wife's finger, the man takes off his coat and puts it around her as a symbol of his promise to protect her.

A number of women were asked what makes a man a good lover.

Their replies revealed that it is neither athletic prowess nor the size of a man's muscles nor the size of anything else, but rather *tenderness*. This was put far higher than physical technique. Sexual love cannot work against a background of selfishness, exploitation, criticism, or harshness.

When a woman feels safe, special, and beautiful, her mind and body will respond sexually toward her husband, and this will enhance their mutual fulfilment. The bedroom should be the place where the wife knows, "I am cared for, loved, and cherished. In a world that may undervalue, scorn, or ridicule me, there is a man who knows me like no other and is tender toward me."

## RESPONSIVENESS

Many husbands like Richard, if asked about their sex lives, will reply that their wives are not very responsive. The Bible speaks of a woman as a secret garden, "… a garden locked up… a spring enclosed, a sealed fountain" (Song of Songs 4:12).

**Sila** There is an old and beautiful English garden that I know and love. In front of the house are herbaceous borders. As you turn the corner, stretching away beside a long lawn is a yew hedge, broken by an arch. Through the arch you walk down some steps into a hidden sunken garden. On the far side is an opening in an old wall which leads through to a small and intimate rose garden with a circular pond in the middle. Beyond this, past climbing wisteria, roses, and clematis, you come upon a large walled vegetable garden. In summer there are beds of pink, orange, and red poppies, mixed together. The garden leads on into an orchard full of apple, plum, and damson trees with a gate at the far end out into the fields.

Whatever the weather, whatever the season, this garden excites curiosity and invites exploration, always offering some new discovery in a hitherto unseen corner. It is in this sense that the Song of Songs uses a garden as a picture of a wife's sexuality; there is enough to discover and delight in over a lifetime.

The imagery in the Song of Songs resonates with pleasure and delight for both lovers. This woman is aware of her own sexuality and is wonderfully untainted by self-consciousness or restraint. She takes the initiative in welcoming her husband into the garden, "Awake, north wind, and come, south wind! Blow on my garden, that its fragrance may spread abroad. Let my lover come into his garden and taste its choice fruits" (Song of Songs 4:16).

A wife's responsiveness is the secret to her husband's pleasure. A husband needs to know that his wife finds him attractive. He needs to know how much his wife desires his love. He needs to hear his wife say how special (in physical as well as other ways) he is to her. A husband needs to sense the excitement and anticipation of his wife's desire and all the delights that she wants to share with him.

Knowingly or unknowingly, the wife holds the key to unlock the garden. She must choose to explore it together with her husband. Some women, however, do not know that the key, or indeed the garden, exist; others fear what lies beyond the gate; for others their past experience of the garden has been negative and traumatic.

Within the safety and commitment of marriage these issues can be dealt with. A wife needs to believe in the possibility of pleasure and fulfillment through the act of lovemaking. In some cases great courage is required. She will need help and support from a patient, caring, and sensitive husband in order to give herself freely to him. The ideal is that the husband and wife enter the garden, hand in hand, and start to explore and enjoy it together.

Later in the poem the bride says, "Let us go early to the vineyards...there I will give you my love... at our door is every delicacy, both new and old, that I have stored up for you, my lover" (Song of Songs 7:12-13). Most husbands would look forward to coming home if they heard propositions like that from their wife.

## Romance

Romance has the potential to draw us into a world that belongs only to the two of us: a world in which our imagination is awakened and our senses stimulated. It stops sex becoming mechanical and routine. Romance creates the setting for lovemaking that involves every part of our being and draws us together, and typically plays a bigger part in sexual arousal for women than for men.

**Nicky** One *Mother's Day* I decided to make a special supper for Sila. I then asked her what she would like to do for the rest of the evening. She had earlier watched the first half of *Jane Eyre* on television with our children and had videotaped the rest. She suggested that we watch it together. Not an inch of bare flesh below the neck was revealed throughout the film, yet I could not believe how arousing this romantic love story was for Sila!

If romance is neglected and our marriage revolves around doing the chores and paying the bills, we can end up as teammates rather than as lovers. There may even be an awkwardness between us regarding sex, inconceivable as that would have seemed at the start.

Husbands and wives can create romance for one another. This need not involve great expense. We just need to do something different from the normal routine: a walk along the river, a picnic in the park, or a trip to the movies. If you can get away together for a weekend, a change of environment often creates feelings of romance.

**Nicky** I have made various attempts at romance over the years, not all of them successful. One particularly uncomfortable memory is a visit to the theatre to see the musical *Les Miserables* on our tenth wedding anniversary. I had hoped somewhat naively to combine it with a picnic in a park halfway through. Not only was there no park in sight and an impossibly short interval but, owing to the exaggerated size of my romantic picnic, I had to spend the entire evening with a very large basket digging into my knee.

**Sila** Nicky was determined to see his plan through and not to let the romantic picnic supper go to waste. We ended up spreading out our rug on the stairs between the upper circle and the grand circle. I sat down on one side of the narrow

Edwardian stairway while Nicky sat on the other, passing me a red rose to accompany a glass of champagne and a plate of delicious cold food, while people cast us curious glances as they went up or down the stairs.

It was a memorable evening (in fact I shall never forget it!) although I was very glad not to have recognised anyone in the audience or more particularly on the stairs. And Nicky's intentions meant a lot to me even if the evening didn't quite work out as he had planned.

### Anticipation

One of the secrets to good sex is realizing that our mind is our most important sexual resource. In a healthy relationship, anticipation builds desire that leads to the most satisfying lovemaking. As one husband put it, "The best sex starts at breakfast."

Some couples develop a secret code to create anticipation. One wife told us of an evening that she and her husband had set aside to spend together. They were about to go upstairs to bed when a friend called to say she was bringing around some food for a party the following day. Thinking quickly, the wife asked her to leave the pasta on the doorstep. Since that evening, the words "pasta on the doorstep" have gained a whole new meaning for them.

**Nicky** Because of the importance of the mind for our lovemaking, a husband must keep his sexual thoughts for his wife, and

> vice versa. Many men at some point in their lives, often during their school days, have been exposed to pornography. Today, with pornography on the *Internet*, the temptation is worse than ever. The danger of pornographic material is that it arouses our sexual desires in a way that leads to lust rather than to a loving relationship. It can easily become an addiction.
>
> Pornography dehumanizes us and can rob us of true sexual fulfillment. Women become objects to arouse and then satisfy men's sexual desires. In today's culture, it is difficult for a man to avoid some degree of arousal through what he sees in advertisements, magazine covers, or films. For the sake of his marriage, it is vital that any erotic thoughts are directed toward his wife.
>
> We may in addition need to find ways of protecting ourselves. For those who are required to travel and stay in hotels alone, the television can be a great snare, especially where pornography channels are available. This will be a particular temptation to a man who is tired and missing the close companionship of his wife. A friend of ours asks the hotel to remove the television from his room or, when it is fixed to the wall, gives the TV remote control to the hotel reception.
>
> I have another friend who has a program on his computer to block pornography from his web browser. Self-imposed boundaries like this are not a sign of weakness but rather of wisdom, and the marriage relationship will be the stronger for it.

If a husband (or wife) has a problem with pornography, we strongly suggest finding another person of the same sex with whom to talk this through, and then to ask for God's forgiveness and help in breaking free from the addiction. It will be important to remain accountable to that person in the future, allowing him or her to ask at regular intervals how it is going.

**Sila** While for many men false pleasure comes through pornography, for many women there is the danger of fantasizing. One famous actress being interviewed for a Sunday paper spoke candidly about her sexual relationships and told the journalist that she would regularly think of other men when making love to her husband. This may have increased her sexual desires but it would not have helped her marriage.

A woman can become addicted to fantasy through what she reads or sees, making real life seem by comparison dull, routine, and empty of the love and intimacy she craves. Many popular novels encourage such fantasizing. But seeking to escape from reality on a regular basis through what is often regarded as harmless entertainment can be dangerous for a marriage.

The New Testament emphasizes the need to discipline our minds: "Finally, brothers and sisters, whatever is true, whatever is noble, whatever is right, whatever is pure, whatever is lovely, whatever is admirable—if anything is excellent or praiseworthy—think about such things" (Philippians 4:8).

## VARIETY

The sixth and final quality essential for good lovemaking is creating variety. All of us tend to take extra care of new things. About eight years ago we bought a brand new car, and we treated it with kid gloves. In the early days the children were not allowed to eat anything in the back; but nowadays, we think nothing of consuming a three course Macdonald's meal complete with ketchup, drinks, and melting ice cream. Our attitude has totally changed. We take less care of something when it is no longer new. Familiarity produces complacency.

It is at the point of familiarity in our sexual relationship that the thought of an affair can seem appealing. A good sex life needs cre-

ativity, thought, and variety. Some of the following suggestions may seem impractical, but it is amazing how much effort people put into conducting an affair. We need to use a similar amount of imagination, and more, in our marriage.

- *Vary the place we make love.* It doesn't always have to be in the bedroom. What about on the sofa, in the shower, or in front of an open fire? If there are other adults living in our house it is worth making one night a week our own particular evening in! We can be clear about the time we need alone.

  When children are around the options are more limited. Having a discreet but efficient lock on the bedroom door when children are old enough to wander in is important both for the children's sake and to make it possible for us to be totally relaxed. Relaxation is essential for good sex.

  Planning a night or two away in a different setting can be a great antidote to boredom and over-familiarity. This does not need to be expensive. Once or twice a year you could ask friends to look after your children, or even swap houses, as we suggested in chapter 1.

- *Vary the times we make love*, not always last thing at night when we are feeling exhausted. Again, this is obviously more difficult with children. Making love as soon as we are sure they are asleep is one possibility, or, if they are older, ask them if they would like to spend a night with a friend every so often.

  Try making love before eating. Neither men nor women are at their best sexually after a huge meal, especially if it is eaten late. Alcohol can also have a detrimental effect. Two or three glasses of wine can impair a woman's ability to have an orgasm and a man's to maintain an erection. Some changes in our eating and drinking habits may regenerate the quality of our sex life. Setting aside time to make love is as important as making time to go out together.

- *Vary the atmosphere*. For example, put on some music or try different lighting. Making love under a 100-watt bulb does not create the most romantic atmosphere. Experiment with candlelight, darkness, moonlight, or firelight.

  In the Song of Songs, the lovemaking involves each of

the five senses being evoked and enjoyed. As one woman put it, "Lovemaking is at least 75 percent sensuality and at most 25 percent sexuality."[2] Sensuousness stimulates the imagination and enhances the enjoyment.

- *Vary the routine.* We can so easily fall into a pattern of always making love the same way because it works. We get comfortable with what we know and are used to. While being sensitive to each other's enjoyment, be creative. Vary which of you initiates things. Variety and romance help us to put proper erotic thoughts and desires into each other's minds and increases our passion for each other.

  There will be times, however, when too much experimentation is inappropriate, particularly if a woman is getting over childbirth and feeling a bit uncomfortable about sex.

People sometimes ask us what the Bible *allows* in terms of sexual practice in marriage. It is not specific about details but there are certain principles which act as safe boundaries, the most important of which is that whatever we do must be mutually agreeable and show respect for one another's dignity. Does this practice bring enjoyment and satisfaction to both of us? Or does it make our partner feel uncomfortable, embarrassed, or used? Could it lead to mutual orgasm? Does it cause us to focus our thoughts exclusively on our husband or wife?

God intended us to love one another through sexual intercourse within marriage; He is not surprised or shocked by our enjoyment of it. It was His idea. He made us spiritual, emotional, and sexual beings. He intended that our bodies should be desirable and pleasurable to each other and deliberately created in the sexual union a lifetime of exploration and possibilities.

# 18

## Protecting Our Marriage

*Foolishly I once tried to classify people who had extramarital affairs such as ornithologists classify birds. But I gave up the attempt. Adulterers cannot be classified. They may be old, young; cultured, crude; lusty, refined; selfish, generous; kindly, cruel, and even, if we use the term with the slightest degree of flexibility, spiritual or carnal...Any married person can commit adultery. A Jew, a Catholic, a Quaker and a Pentecostal can all be committers of adultery; a business convention and a religious revival can both be occasions for it while cars, doctors' offices, homes and church offices are all possible places for the practice of it.*

JOHN WHITE[1]

Not one of us is exempt from the danger of an affair. We are all capable of being attracted to another person, sometimes when we least expect it. King David, the most famous Old Testament king, succumbed one evening as he walked on his palace roof: "From the roof he saw a woman bathing. The woman was very beautiful and David sent someone to find out about her" (2 Samuel 11:2-3). The woman, named Bathsheba, was the wife of a loyal soldier in David's army. Already it was too late. Even before he summoned her to his bed, David had gone too far. By the time he had allowed himself to entertain thoughts of adultery, he had set the direction for his actions, which were to have dreadful consequences for his family for many years to come.

The prevalence of affairs and their wide acceptability today does not lessen the pain that they cause for each individual involved. This story about a teenager named Judy appeared in a national newspaper:

> Judy thought her parents' twenty-three-year marriage was unshakeable, but on a dull afternoon eighteen months ago, her father told her that he had been having an affair for two years with a family friend. She described her feelings of betrayal, hurt, and anger at her father's infidelity, "I don't know if I can forgive him...Friends say to me, 'He is your Dad. Look at all the things he did for you," and I think, 'Well, sure, he read me bed-time stories, but it does not excuse what he has done.'" It is one of the most selfish things you could ever do. We were the typical happy family, three kids, two cats, and a dog. I feel sorrow, real sorrow, that my Dad did this and thought that it would all work out. My only contact with him now is the money he pays into my account every month.[2]

Affairs are easily entered into but the ensuing hurt and damage are not so easily repaired. A marriage is built on trust and, once abused, the reestablishment of trust is a slow and painful process. An affair appears alluring in the short term, promising emotional closeness, intimate conversations, and exciting sex. But in the long term it leads to many regrets when a marriage is broken and family life is destroyed.

In the Christian wedding vows, we echo Scripture as, in the presence of our family and friends and in the sight of God, we vow to "be faithful…forsaking all others." When a husband or a wife breaks that vow, the spouse (and their children, if they have any) faces a terrible sense of betrayal.

> For the betrayal of an oath is the betrayal of a person. It is not copulation that is the "wicked" thing in betrayal. Copulation is good (just as apples are good). It is stealing and cheating that make adultery bad, not copulation. A stolen apple can be sweet and eating it

> a profoundly healthful experience. Never in my life have I tasted anything so good as trout we caught by poaching on the Isle of Skye once. We cooked them on the shore on a fire of driftwood as the sun went down and the blue-green waves pounded the rocky beach. My heart was light and full of joy. I did not really feel bad about the poaching. But our enjoyment of the poached trout did not make poaching right.[3]

Nowadays people prefer to run their lives on feelings rather than on rules, but our feelings are changeable and notoriously deceptive. God gives us a law prohibiting adultery, not to spoil our fun, but to protect family life and to keep us from hurting each other, and ourselves. In the New Testament we are told, "Marriage should be honored by all, and the marriage bed kept pure," (Hebrews 13:4).

There will be some readers, however, who are already conducting a relationship which is secret from their husband or wife, others who know that their partner is having an affair, and still others who feel themselves being drawn toward one and who are torn between the desire to remain faithful and the power of the attraction.

## Be wise

An affair is not usually premeditated. Catherine, a married woman, who felt herself being drawn toward a relationship with another man, spoke to us of her experiences. She was taken by surprise by the suddenness and strength of her emotions. Because the attraction was not sexual it felt "pure and good" to her, at least initially. She had been married for seven years and found herself strongly attracted to Rob, a colleague at work. She struggled privately with her feelings for six weeks.

Then one evening she went out with a group from work, including Rob. After a few drinks she found herself telling him of her feelings. He wanted to pursue the relationship. For Catherine the draw was the sense of closeness to a man who listened to her and seemed to understand her. His desire was for a sexual relationship with a woman he found attractive.

Catherine told us that two realizations saved her from starting an affair. The first came through a Christian book on marriage which enabled her to distinguish between the initial attraction, for which she was not responsible, and the choice to pursue those thoughts, for which she was.

The second realization was that she was not strong enough to deal with the temptation on her own. She cried out to God, asking for His forgiveness and help. As a result she confided in an older woman whom she could trust, seeking her support and advice. Having poured out her inner turmoil, she felt no longer alone in the struggle and could see the issues much more clearly. Catherine then determined to put boundaries in place to avoid being unfaithful. As her work forced her together with Rob, she was prepared to change jobs if necessary, although as it happened he was transferred to another office.

Meanwhile, as she had kept these thoughts secret from her husband, Simon, a distance had grown between them. He had felt her shutting down deep communication without knowing why. Having started to take action to prevent an affair, Catherine felt able to tell him the reason for the change in her. She then asked for his forgiveness.

Since bringing it out into the open, Catherine has determined to focus her thoughts on her husband and on all that is good about their marriage. Simon has taken more care to listen to her and to encourage and affirm her. Not only has their marriage been saved but they have grown closer as a result of this near-crisis. Indeed, friends who knew nothing of these events have commented spontaneously that they look like a couple who have just fallen in love.

## INVEST TIME AND ENERGY INTO THE MARRIAGE RELATIONSHIP

Almost always the root cause of an affair is a lack of intimacy in the marriage. For a while at least, the affair meets a dissatisfied husband's or wife's longing for attention, respect, affection, or excitement. The best protection against unfaithfulness is therefore to take care of our marriage, so that the relationship grows in strength, closeness, and depth. Charlotte, mother of two and a banker in the City of London, describes what can happen:

> Although I didn't realize it at the time, when I married John, my attitude toward him changed and I began to take him for granted. He'd been looking forward to the togetherness of marriage, but I still wanted to be a girl about town—so I'd go out playing all the time, safe in the knowledge that I had my husband's support at home. We carried on leading separate but perfectly happy lives until we had our first child. I adored being a mother but I still tried to go out as much as I could. That's when things went badly wrong between John and me, because we just didn't have time for each other any more. I never stopped loving John, but I became more and more irritable and bad-tempered with him. I had no idea he was becoming less and less enamoured with me, but the resentment was building up and by the time our second child was born he was having an affair.[4]

By failing to work at their relationship, Charlotte and John grew apart. They had failed to grow roots which intertwined.

If we do not spend time together, do not communicate deeply, do not make love, do not resolve our hurts, our relationship will have weak foundations. And if our love is only surface-deep, we will be more prone to temptation, more critical, less understanding, less forgiving. We may struggle to accept the changes brought about by age or the arrival of children. We may idealize other people's relationships and fantasize about other men or women. Like a rootless tree, we will not withstand the storms.

And we also miss our opportunity. Joy is not found in a new and shallow relationship, not in hotel rooms with false names, nor on guilty holidays. Real joy is found in "the beauty of those hands, recognizing the sound of the footsteps on the pathway or looking at the face which you can read down to the last millimeter of muscle movement."[5]

### SET BOUNDARIES

Infidelity starts or stops in the mind. This was true for King David. It was true for Catherine. It has been true for everyone down the ages irrespective of age, culture, or gender. We cannot always prevent ourselves being attracted to someone, but we can decide whether or not to control such thoughts. For the sake of our marriage these thoughts must be put out of our minds before they are allowed to become habitual. Jesus' teaching sets in place boundaries that protect our hearts and our minds:

> You have heard that it was said, "Do not commit adultery." But I tell you that anyone who looks at a woman lustfully has already committed adultery with her in his heart (Matthew 5:27–28).

Jesus' point applies equally to a woman thinking lustfully about a man. When we are aware of a growing attraction, we have to determine not to spend time alone with the person concerned or sometimes not to see them at all. An invitation to have lunch alone together has to be refused. Saying no early on can avoid many problems later.

Many affairs begin not with immediate sexual attraction but through intimate conversation. When a person of the opposite sex allows us into the private world of their thoughts and emotions, a dangerous (and alluring) closeness is created. As we are drawn further in, we may start to feel better understood or more needed by them than by our husband or wife. If we ever sense that we may have (even slightly) overstepped this boundary, the best course of action is to tell our husband or wife as soon as possible about the contents of the conversation.

### Talk to someone about the feelings

Where strong feelings have been allowed to develop or have taken us by surprise, talking to someone else will often rob them of their power over us. One couple told us that in their first year of marriage they both found themselves at different times strongly attracted to other people. The longer they kept their thoughts a secret, the stronger they became. Only when they confessed their feelings to each other did the bubble burst and the infatuation quickly die down. If talking to our husband or wife seems impossible, we need to find someone we trust and confide in them.

The longer unfaithfulness continues, the harder it becomes to turn back. People who have set off down the road of infidelity often speak of the power of what they feel. They say that they have never before experienced such intense emotions for another person, and that these emotions seem authentic and good. They sometimes maintain that they feel alive for the first time and that this may be the only opportunity they have in their lifetime to experience such "love." They feel that they are being swept helplessly away to a future of freedom and happiness.

Such feelings are highly unreliable. A long-term perspective is needed: in due course this infatuation (like any other) will wear off, at which point their marriage partner will not seem so inadequate, and they will frequently look back with deep regret on the marriage and family life they have destroyed. Though the ending of an affair may be the hardest decision they ever make, in years to come they will look back and see it as the best.

### Take a firm stand

What should we do if we discover that our partner is having an affair? Are we required to forgive and to continue loving in the hope of winning him or her back? Certainly both forgiveness and love are essential. But that does not mean condoning a partner's behavior when it is destructive to the marriage. There are times when to act most lovingly requires us to be tough and to take a firm stand. Gary Chapman gives the following advice:

> Some things are not permissible in a marriage. When physical abuse, sexual unfaithfulness, sexual abuse of children, alcoholism, or drug addiction persist in a marriage, it is time to take loving action.[6]

Such attitudes and actions, if left unchecked, will destroy both ourselves and the marriage. Love requires us to forgive, but also at times to confront.

Lisa had never stood up to her husband Martin's bullying tactics. He always got his own way and she lost all confidence in herself. After eight years of marriage, she discovered that he was having an affair with a neighbor. He promised that he would break off the relationship for the sake of their marriage and three children. But on three further occasions she discovered that the affair was continuing. Each time he assured her that it would end. Finally, on the advice of a friend, she took action.

She told him that he had undermined the trust in their relationship and that he must move out. If he persisted in being unfaithful, the marriage would be over. If, however, he proved with his actions as well as his words that he wanted to come back, there was a chance that their marriage could be saved. For the first time in their marriage, Lisa stood up for what she knew to be right.

We met them when they had been separated for several months, by which time Martin was wanting to return home. His respect for Lisa had grown since she had drawn a line over his behavior. He realized that he could not have it all his own way. He had to make a choice between the affair and his family. Lisa's firm stance was more loving than her previous acquiescence, because it gave the most hope for them to get back together and for their marriage to be restored.

## DO NOT GIVE UP TOO QUICKLY

Charlotte, the city banker, did not give up hope of her husband, John, returning to her. Eventually he told her that the affair was finished and he agreed to come home. Charlotte explains:

> He made the commitment to stay, but it took another year for him to be happy at home, and during that time he wouldn't touch me in bed, barely talked to me, seemed furious to be back, and kept telling me he was still in love with this other woman.
>
> The summer after he came back I went on vacation with one son, leaving our other son with John. It was a wonderful vacation and I didn't ring John once. On the fifth day he rang me, though, saying how much he was missing us. That was the turning point. Two years exactly from the time he'd moved out, he came back to me.
>
> Slowly we began to rebuild our marriage.[7]

If either you or your partner are or have been engaged in an affair and are struggling to rebuild your marriage, we would recommend reading one of the books listed in the recommended reading at the back under "Rebuilding a Marriage." We know couples, some of them quoted in this book, who are back together again after an adulterous relationship, determined to nurture and protect their marriage. But it is important to recognize that it takes time for trust to be rebuilt. An unfaithful husband or wife cannot expect their partner to act as though nothing has happened. They will need to be sensitive and patient, understanding the range of emotions from anger to fear that their partner will probably go through.

For some, forgiveness will need to be a daily decision. One man, whose wife recently had an affair, told us that each time they have an argument, he thinks, "What right does she have to disagree after what she's done?" But he knows that forgiveness means not holding the past against her. He must allow her and their marriage a new start. Meanwhile his wife has had to learn how to be free from constant guilt through believing that both God and her husband have forgiven her past behavior.

# 19

## Keeping Sex Alive

*Sexual union says truthfully, "I love you," and the message bears much repetition.*
ALAN STORKEY[1]

A failure to address any one of the areas raised in this book can open a marriage to the risk of an affair, but a failure to develop our sexual relationship makes us especially vulnerable. Our sexual desires and responses are complex. Even the strongest marriages have their seasons when desire wanes and difficulties arise. These must be addressed and worked through without delay. If sexual intimacy is allowed to exit quietly from our marriage, our relationship will lose its special quality.

There are some couples who find sexual intercourse difficult because of a debilitating illness. But the sexual dimension of their relationship is still vital, and there are means other than full sexual intercourse by which we can meet our partner's need to be loved and cherished in a sexually fulfilling way.

This section is not a comprehensive guide to every sexual difficulty. We shall not be dealing with the painful area of sexual abuse, violence, or the discovery that a husband or wife has homosexual tendencies. Nor shall we be looking at the consequences of infertility, miscarriage, or abortion. These may leave emotional scars, suppressed grief, nagging guilt, and feelings of fear or despair surrounding sex.

We would recommend talking in confidence to a person (or a couple) well-qualified to offer advice on these painful issues. A doctor or church leader may be able to refer you to a specialist counselor. We have included at the back a list of recommended books with a Christian viewpoint on these subjects as well as a directory of organizations for special help. If you identify with one of the issues above, do not give up. We know many who, through a new discovery of the love and power of God, have found healing for their past and hope for the future.

Most marriages will be susceptible to difficulties at some time or another. Some couples remain stuck in a passionless rut, either because they do not know how to resolve the difficulty or because they have let it go on so long that they are no longer close enough to face it together. We have seen couples get out of the deepest ruts simply by facing their situation, talking together, and being willing to change.

What follows are five common reasons why the sexual relationship in a marriage can run into difficulties, fizzle out, or never get going. Any one of them can be addressed and rectified.

### Low self-esteem

Our self-esteem and our attitude to our body have a profound effect upon our sexual desires. The Song of Songs speaks explicitly about the physical attributes of the man and the woman which attracted and captivated them (see Songs of Songs 1:15-16; 4:1-7). The biblical perspective is an open acceptance of our own body and of our partner's body. God did not create us all with bodies like supermodels or athletes. He made each one of us unique and there is infinite variety. He made us tall or short, big or small, black, brown or white, and many shapes and shades in between.

Today, the media dictate to us what it means to be beautiful. Specific details change as models come and go, but the message remains clear: you need to be a very thin woman or a muscular man with "six-pack-abs." The pressure to conform to a particular shape may be felt particularly by women. According to some surveys, over 80 percent of women in the U.K. are dissatisfied with their bodies and 30 percent have disordered eating. An increasing number of women do not know their natural and most healthy body weight and live on a semi-starvation diet. Deviation from this diet then results in weight gain which can lead to feelings of guilt and disgust. It is important to seek help if you think you may have anorexic or bulimic tendencies or are slavishly overexercising to maintain body weight (see some suggested books at the back).

But we can choose to help ourselves and each other. We must not compare our partner's body or our own to the current fashion. For a woman especially, sexual enjoyment is profoundly affected by how she feels about herself. Poor body image and feeling self-conscious will short-circuit her ability to be aroused and to reach orgasm.

Each one of us can build up our husband's or wife's self-esteem through telling them on a regular basis how attractive and beautiful they are. (If we don't, they are likely to listen to someone else who will, and we open our marriage to the danger of an affair.) There needs to be an unspoken rule between us never to criticize or to have unreasonable expectations of each other's body.

At the same time it is important to recognize that we need to continue *within marriage* to make an effort with our appearance for one another, as we did when we first went out together. Otherwise we can easily find ourselves in a vicious circle. We think, "My partner is not interested in how I look anymore," or, 'He never says how attractive he finds me," or, "These days she never tells me that I turn her on." And then we lose the confidence and the motivation to try to be attractive for each other any more: it is too awkward and it seems unnecessary. But our partner was almost certainly physically attracted to us when we got married, and there is much we can do to make that continue.

As we make love verbally and physically, tenderly and passionately, we shall bring out the beauty inherent in each other. We have often noticed that when someone *knows* they are loved they increase in beauty. There is an inner beauty which shines out of them and can lead in subtle ways to a change in their physical appearance. Beauty grows in a culture of love.

### Unresolved emotions

Sex should never be used as an alternative to resolving problems or conflicts. Unexpressed feelings such as anxiety, mistrust, or resentment all affect our sexual intimacy. Typically a man may use sex as a temporary escape from pain or anger, whereas negative emotions will often cause a woman to withdraw and shut down.

Lack of desire for sex or the inability to give ourselves 100 percent can be the result of unresolved hurt within the marriage or from previous sexual relationships or even from our upbringing. If necessary, refer to chapter 12 again for the process of talking through ways you have hurt each other and to chapter 15 for ways of addressing pain from childhood. Many couples have spoken to us of the benefit to their lovemaking when they have faced these issues together. New energy is released and a new level of intimacy is experienced.

### Physical problems

There are three physical problems which affect many couples. First the failure of a wife to reach orgasm. Second, an inability by the husband to control ejaculation for the length of time needed for his wife to be aroused to orgasm. Third, a husband's difficulty in maintaining an erection (that is, impotence). These problems are possible to overcome with help and information from a doctor, a specialist counselor or even a good book. Only rarely are any of them caused by a physical defect. Almost all women are physically able to achieve orgasm and most men can learn how to control ejaculation. Impotence is not a hopeless condition and a great deal of cases can be cured, either with medication or good advice.

A helpful book for overcoming such physical problems, written from a medical and a Christian perspective, is *Intended for Pleasure* by Ed and Gaye Wheat. As well as general advice on how to develop the sexual relationship, the book contains detailed descriptions of ways to help each other in these three areas.

## TIREDNESS

Tiredness is probably the most common factor that disrupts a couple's sex life. This can happen at any stage of a marriage, whether in the early months, a few years on when children arrive, or as a career becomes increasingly demanding. Whatever the pressure, physical and mental exhaustion usually result in our sex lives being the first casualty. The neglect can be imperceptible at first, but if allowed to become a pattern, sex can all too easily become nonexistent. Bill

Hybels writes:

> God asks us to be sexual beings in an imperfect world. As the initial hormones and romance fade from our marriages, day-to-day reality steps in, demanding our time, energy, and commitment. No longer is it just "me and you" but "me and you plus the babies, the job, the dog, the church, the bills, and the broken washing machine."[2]

Tiredness often means that the easiest thing to do in the evenings is to flop down in front of the television and cease to communicate either verbally or physically.

There is no easy remedy. Being aware of the danger to our sexual relationship is half the battle. Some changes in our lifestyle can also help. Strangely enough, more exercise can make us less tired. Many of us do little or none. We sit in the car or at a desk or at home all day. Exercise is beneficial to our health in every way (unless it becomes obsessive) and especially to our enjoyment of sex. We feel more energized. It is worth finding a form of exercise that works well for you, perhaps fifteen minutes of fast walking a day or cycling to work.

For others clearer boundaries have to be made concerning work and home time. Creating times of relaxation and romance together, and planning a weekly marriage time, will help to prevent exhaustion.

In the long term, despite feeling tired, less sleep than we might like or think we need is worth the sacrifice if it means that this essential dimension of our marriage remains alive and active.

## ADJUSTMENT AND CHANGE AFTER CHILDBIRTH

During pregnancy and around childbirth a woman is at her most vulnerable. Inevitably there is a dramatic change in a couple's lovemaking. A husband needs to be at his most sensitive, caring, and protective. There *is* life after birth (sexually) but unselfish love and understanding are required from both husband and wife.

A husband must appreciate fully the physical changes that occur for his wife before, during, and after giving birth. He can then show the necessary tenderness and be guided by her as to when they can resume lovemaking. The change in shape of the vagina, the tendency for it to be less well lubricated, and the possible scarring caused by tearing all need to be taken into account.

A husband has a delicate road to walk between the two extremes of being overly anxious about touching his wife for fear of hurting her, and being overly enthusiastic to resume their sexual relationship before she has healed physically.

Each couple must work out what is right for them. This requires openness and honesty, particularly by the wife as she explains how she is feeling physically and emotionally. Breastfeeding and the accompanying tiredness affect a woman's libido. Don't despair! Time brings healing, as do pelvic floor exercises. These are designed not only to regain a pre-birth figure but also to ensure that a woman continues to enjoy fulfilling orgasm (see *Intended for Pleasure* for more details about the pubococcygeus or P.C. muscles).

In the short term a mother will often avoid sex as she bonds with and nurtures her new baby. This is natural. What is unnatural is when this is used as an excuse for continuing to avoid sex for many months or even a year. A wife has to understand the difficulty her husband experiences as he sees her role change from being wife and lover to wife and mother. Her breasts, which have been a source of pleasure only for him, are now apparently monopolized by someone else. A wife needs to help her husband to adjust to the new situation and to recapture his image of her as a sexual being.

The more involved a husband and wife are together with the baby they have created, taking joint responsibility, and both learning as they go along, the closer and more attracted they will feel to each other. If the husband acts as though nothing has changed, isolation and separation can easily set in. For a wife, the most desirable husband is one who is with her in the whole experience. She sees him in a new light and that creates intimacy and sexual attraction. More than at any other time, couples must realize what it means to give themselves to each other in caring, cherishing ways. It is not unusual for a woman to take a year before she feels normal about sex again.

Finally, we need to be careful about taking a baby into our bed. Obviously when they are tiny this is a natural thing to do for the nighttime feeding, though even then many mothers prefer to get up and sit in a chair. However, after the newborn stage has passed, having a baby in one's bed quickly becomes unhelpful. Patterns are hard to change in young children and trying to do so with a child of eighteen months can be traumatic for everybody. A child in your bed (or in your bedroom) will seriously damage your sex life! Our suggestion is not to let a habit develop in the first place.

The birth of a child should not lead to a decline in sexual enjoyment—indeed, quite the reverse—as a couple take in the miracle of creating a new life through their lovemaking.

> Even if you are doing [everything you can] to stop another miracle happening just yet, that feeling remains: the miracle of Life trying to happen. And the extraordinary fact is that sex is actually better—if different—on the far side of childbirth. Men and women who understand this stay together. The ones who don't—the women who cool off entirely, or grant themselves grudgingly as a favor, the men who see no difference and grumble at the roundedness and tiredness of the maternal woman—are most likely to fall into the

miserable chaos of affairs and estrangements. Take your pick. Be prepared to accept change, as spring turns to summer and later to autumn. As in so many areas of family life, you can't have everything, but you can, with patience and humor, get a great deal of it.[3]

# Section 7 – Good Sex

## Conclusion

Our culture bombards us with much misinformation about sex. "Do it with lots of different partners; you will become a more mature person and a better lover." "Sex is just one way of enjoying yourself. If it feels good, do it!" "If you love each other, have sex. There's no need to wait until you're married."

And then there are the lies about sex within marriage. "Marry someone you're physically attracted to and sex will be instantaneously wonderful" "Don't expect to be sexually fulfilled with one man or woman your whole life. Experiment! Fantasize! Flirt with others! Be realistic. Sex always peters out."

It is easy to be deceived and confused. The truth is that God gives us sex as a gift of love. Countless thousands of couples have discovered that the best sex is experienced within a loving marriage. Such sex goes way beyond physical gratification. It creates a deep emotional, psychological, and even spiritual bond which has the power to communicate love in a way that transcends words. Our sexual relationship can express our love for each other tenderly, regularly, and passionately over years of married life.

When wrongly used, sex has the power to plunge us into the depths of pain and isolation; but, when rightly used, to lift us up to the heights of togetherness and ecstatic joy.

## Seventh Golden Rule of Marriage

Do not neglect sexual intimacy.

# Epilogue

# 20

## The Opportunity of a Lifetime

*A cord of three strands is not quickly broken.*
ECCLESIASTES 4:12

An elderly couple were celebrating their platinum wedding anniversary. A radio reporter was sent to cover the story and did his best to make the old man (who was very deaf) understand his questions. "Seventy years is a long time," he shouted in the old man's ear. "Have you ever contemplated divorce?" The old man toyed with the question. Then he replied, "Divorce? No, I can't say I have. Mind you, I've considered murder, several times!"[1]

The secret of a long and happy marriage is found, in the words of the psalmist, where "Love and faithfulness meet together" (Psalm 85:10). You will, we hope, know couples who have been married for twenty-five years or more, whose lives have been woven together into an intricate interdependence.

They have developed over the years a deep understanding of each other's needs and desires; their love has matured and grown steady with the passage of time; they have together weathered the storms of life's disappointments and tragedies; they appreciate each other's strengths and accept each other's weaknesses; they have learned to apologize for their own acts of selfishness and to forgive each other's; they have supported one another through the physical strain of parenting young children and the emotional exhaustion of guiding teenagers; they now relish the new opportunities of togetherness presented by the "empty nest."

In such a marriage, love and faithfulness have met together, and it was for this that God gave marriage to be a great blessing to humankind. Indeed, this is the potential for your marriage and ours. For we have been created for love by the God who is love. We are capable of friendship, companionship, romantic love, and sexual love. We were created to feel loved and to give love. Besides which, we have been created for faithfulness by the God who keeps His promises. We are capable of commitment and are able to choose honesty and loyalty.

Love with faithfulness is the most powerful force for good in the world, and God planned it to be at the heart of the marriage relationship. In the words of Martin Luther King, Jr., this kind of love "is the most durable force in the world. It is the key that unlocks the door to ultimate reality."

Many people are asking why marriage is in such trouble today. The overwhelming reason is that love and faithfulness have been torn apart. Commitment has gone out of fashion. Love *without* faithfulness is fickle, damaging, and painful—it is at best no more than a physical infatuation that departs as randomly as it arrived, evaporating like the dew.

Behind all the humor (and despite the various weddings) the climax of the film *Four Weddings and a Funeral* is an accurate reflection of our Western society's fear of commitment. Early on in the film, the main character, Charles, began his speech at his best friend's wedding, "I am of course in bewildered awe of anyone who can make a commitment like this." The film concludes with him making a somewhat lame non-proposal to the heroine Carrie. The final pictures create the impression that they then lived happily ever after.

The problem is that in real life close relationships are built on commitment. Tom Marshall, in his book *Right Relationships*, says, "...because intimacy produces vulnerability it requires commitment for its security. ...The tragedy today is that people are so hungry for intimacy yet so afraid of commitment that they seek intimacy in uncommitted relationships and time and again reap devastating hurt."[2]

Marriage, in biblical terms, is a covenant in which a man and a woman make binding promises to each other. Some couples who cohabit assert, perhaps correctly, that they are more committed to each other than some married couples they know. Certainly being committed 80 percent is better than being committed 60 percent. But that is not the point. Marriage is about 100 percent commitment to each other, knowing that our husband or wife is not going to walk out if the disagreement is too serious or the lovemaking not good enough. That is the only way for real trust to be built.

Within such a covenant there is safe ground on which to build a strong and intimate marriage. Without such commitment each partner inevitably holds back for fear of disappointment. Commitment provides security and trust: there is no issue that will not be faced and worked through.

Faithful love requires us to go against the contemporary culture. The long-term building of relationships carries a higher cost than the short-term fulfillment of our desires. For some couples, the first year, even the honeymoon, is agony. Each day the painful adjustments tempt them to look back over their shoulder questioning their decision. Mike Mason paints a realistic picture of what is involved:

> A marriage ... may be compared to a great tree growing right up through the center of one's living room. It is something that is just there, and it is huge, and everything has to be built around it, and wherever one happens to be going—to the fridge, to bed, to the bathroom, or out of the front door—the tree has to be taken into account. It cannot be gone through; it must respectfully be gone around. It is somehow bigger and stronger than oneself. True, it could be chopped down, but not without tearing the house apart.

> And certainly it is beautiful, unique, exotic: but also, let's face it, it is at times an enormous inconvenience.[3]

Faithful love means that we must be prepared to change and adapt ourselves to each other. A father whose daughter played the violin spotted an expensive instrument in a junk shop at a very cheap price. He was delighted—until he discovered that the tuning knobs were immovable. Someone had glued them in place. But of course the violin had not stayed in tune. Tuning up is an essential routine for every musician. So it is in marriage. There need to be frequent adjustments.

For many people, the most significant achievement of their lives will be the building of a loving marriage. Their children will benefit from the security of a loving and stable home. Their friends will enjoy the overflow and warmth of their love. Their society will be the stronger and healthier for their contribution. Barbara Bush, former First Lady of the United States, said in her address to students graduating from Wellesley College:

> As important as your obligations as a doctor, lawyer, or business leader will be, you are a human being first, and those human connections—with a husband or wife, with children, with friends—are the most important investments you will ever make. At the end of your life, you will never regret not having passed one more exam, not winning one more verdict, or not closing one more deal. But you will regret time not spent with a husband or wife, a child, a friend, or a parent ...Our success as a society depends not on what happens in the White House, but on what happens inside your house.[4]

Building a strong marriage not only yields the highest rewards but also fulfills a noble and holy place in the purposes of God. Dietrich Bonhoeffer, the German pastor executed during the Second

World War for his opposition to the Third Reich, wrote a letter from prison to his niece on the eve of her wedding:

> Marriage is more than your love for each other. It has a higher dignity and power for it is God's holy ordinance through which he wills to perpetuate the human race until the end of time. In your love you see only your two selves in the world, but in your marriage you are a link in the chain of the generations, which God causes to come and to pass away to his glory, and calls into his kingdom. In your love you see only the heaven of your happiness, but in marriage you are placed at a post of responsibility towards the world and mankind. Your love is your own private possession, but marriage is more than something personal—it is a status, an office.[5]

The Bible sees marriage as a commitment to give our lives away out of love for another person. "Christ loved the church and gave Himself up for her" (Ephesians 5:25). His example of loving us is our model for loving our husband or wife.

> When we get married we are giving ourselves away lock, stock, and barrel to each other. Making love, which is the central act of marriage, is simply another form of giving ourselves away. The total abandonment of it all is the nearest thing this side of heaven to the spiritual ecstasy and intimacy we will one day have with God. That is how Christ loved us. He lavished himself upon us and gave himself completely. There was no holding back.[6]

On our wedding day, the two strands of our separate lives are knotted together, and during our marriage those strands wrap themselves around each other, twisting together into oneness. But how can they be held together in harmony without unraveling, fraying, or even breaking? What are we to do in the harsh reality of day-to-day life when love seems to run out or dry up? What if we can't find the resources or the will to go on loving our husband or wife? Are there any answers?

We believe that the only certain answer lies outside ourselves: "A cord of three strands is not quickly broke" says the writer of Ecclesiastes in the Old Testament (Ecclesiastes 4:12). There is a third strand, a third person in the relationship. This is Jesus Christ, who nourishes the marriage from its core, so that we need not lean on human willpower alone. He is the invisible strand who turns the twofold twist of human relationship into the strong threefold cord, woven together by the hands of God.

O Lord, make me an instrument of Thy peace;
Where there is hatred, let me sow love;
Where there is injury, pardon;
Where there is discord, union;
Where there is doubt, faith;
Where there is despair, hope;
Where there is darkness, light;
Where there is sadness, joy.
Grant that we may not seek so much to be consoled
as to console;
To be understood, as to understand;
To be loved, as to love.
For it is in giving that we receive,
It is in pardoning that we are pardoned;
And it is in dying that we are born to eternal life.

*The Prayer of St. Francis of Assisi*
*(1182–1226)*

# Appendix A

## Ready for Marriage?

How do we know that we are right for each other? Am I making a dreadful mistake? What happens if we are not compatible? If I have doubts, am I wrong to marry him or her? When we are contemplating marriage, these may well be some of the questions that we are asking ourselves. Such questions must be faced honestly.

In this appendix we list *seven tests of love* which are designed to reveal whether we have the foundations upon which to build a strong marriage.[1] These tests will show not only if we are right for each other but also if we are ready for marriage. Marriage must be based on more than infatuation. Feelings of "in loveness" will not sustain a marriage for a lifetime. Infatuation wears off, but these following seven aspects of love can grow stronger over the years.

### Test 1: Do I want to share the rest of my life with this person?

Marriage is about two individual people, who have been leading individual lives, coming together and sharing everything. Does the thought of doing so fill me with excitement or uncertainty?

Marriage does not allow us to remain as two independent people living in the same house, using the same bed, and spending a lot more time together. Marriage means being ready to share our whole lives with another person.

Am I ready to share my time? I have been used to organizing my own agenda in my own way. Now we will need to work out *our* agenda together. Marriage does not mean spending every minute together, but it does mean always taking each other into account when we make our plans.

Am I ready to share my money? Could I honestly say, "Whatever is mine will become ours"? In marriage there is nothing that remains mine alone for we promise that "all my worldly goods with you I share." Every possession I have, large or small, valuable or sentimental, is to be shared with another person. Am I ready for that?

### Test 2: Does our love give me energy and strength or does it drain me?

If the relationship is healthy, we shall feel more alive when we are together and more motivated to live to our full potential. The other person's love should set us free to be the person we were created to be. Marriage (contrary to many people's perceptions) can be liberating. The experience of a strong marriage is of living a life that is renewed by another's love.

Our closest friends or family are often the people who recognize most accurately the effect of the relationship on us. If we bring out the best in one another, other people want to be around us. Does being together make each of us more rather than less of a person?

This second test reveals whether our love motivates and inspires us. For some couples the sheer effort involved in keeping the relationship going drains them and causes them to feel trapped. That is not a healthy basis for marriage.

### Test 3: Do I respect this person?

There will be different aspects that attracted us to each other. Respect, however, goes deeper than mere attraction.

Do I respect this person's character? We discover someone's character by seeing the way they relate to others: how they treat older people, younger people, their family, their peers, those from a different background, culture, or race. Do they show kindness, compassion, courage, perseverance, patience, consistency, and any other qualities we value highly?

Do I respect their judgment? What about the decisions they make, big or little, about career, money, or family? Are we compatible in our core beliefs and values? It would be unwise to marry someone with strongly opposing views on those things we hold most dear. For example, do we agree on matters of faith, ethical issues, education, children? To find out that our partner does not want children can be a very painful discovery with implications for the rest of our lives.

If you are a Christian, the Bible's injunction not to "be yoked with an unbeliever" (2 Corinthians 6:14) is important advice for those considering marriage. Does this person want to follow and serve God wholeheartedly in every aspect of their lives? Does he or she look to God as the One who has a plan and purpose for their life (and therefore for your life together)?

Can I say to myself, "I would be proud to be attached to this person"? A telling question to ask is, "Would I like this person to be the mother or father of my child?"

### TEST 4: DO I ACCEPT THIS PERSON AS THEY ARE?

None of us is perfect. We all have our weaknesses and our bad habits. We need to be sure that we could live together and love each other even if none of these things were to change. We must not get married on the installment plan, hoping to change this or that about our partner once married. We will usually be disappointed.

### TEST 5: ARE WE ABLE TO ADMIT OUR MISTAKES, APOLOGIZE, AND FORGIVE ONE ANOTHER?

Conflicting ideas and negative feelings are an inevitable part of any close relationship. John Gray in *Men Are from Mars, Women Are from Venus* says, "Some people fight all the time, and gradually their love dies. Others suppress their honest feelings in order to avoid conflict and argument. As a result of suppressing their true feelings they lose touch with their loving feelings as well. One couple is having a war, the other is having a cold war."[2]

Neither of these approaches works. When we hurt one another, we need to be able to bring it out into the open, let go of our pride, apologize, and forgive. This requires good communication. Have we as a couple settled disagreements between us in a constructive way? The point of this test is not the existence or absence of conflict but our ability to resolve it.

### TEST 6: DO WE HAVE INTERESTS IN COMMON AS A FOUNDATION FOR FRIENDSHIP?

Friendship is built between people who do things together. "Shared time, shared activities, shared interests and shared experiences lead to shared feelings and shared confidences."[3] Have we found interests that we both enjoy? Do we derive pleasure from doing things together? It will be important to continue with these and other joint activities within marriage to keep our friendship growing.

### TEST 7: HAVE WE WEATHERED ALL THE SEASONS AND A VARIETY OF SITUATIONS TOGETHER?

Have we seen each other through a summer and a winter—in shorts as well as in an overcoat? Or have we only seen each other with washed hair and ready to go out? Do we know the whole person? Have we known each other not only when things are going well but also when times are difficult? How do we each respond under stress or in a crisis?

Some people rush into marriage because they have been hurt by a previous relationship or a tragedy in their lives. Getting married as an escape from pain is an insecure foundation for any relationship. Only sufficient time together will reveal the real person. As someone has said, "Love is what you've been through with somebody."

---

We have happily married friends who could have answered yes to all seven tests but on their wedding day were still wrestling with hesitation and doubts. It takes courage to tie the knot and to say words that will affect the rest of our lives.

We know others who have been brave enough to break off an engagement within a few weeks or even days of their wedding. Some have subsequently gotten married to someone else; others have remained single. They have not regretted their decisions. Better by far to be single and independent, using our freedom to serve God and to reach our full potential in Him, developing many friendships along the way, than to suffer the consequences of an ill-chosen husband or wife.

# Appendix B

## Engagement, Sex, and the Honeymoon

### Engagement

Engagement is a time of preparation, not just for the wedding, but for marriage. It is a time to develop our friendship, to understand more about one another, and above all, to discover the expectations that each of us brings to married life. We hope that discussing the contents of this book will help. Some tension and misunderstandings are common and the wedding plans often act as the catalyst. Learning to resolve disagreements is a valuable part of the preparation.

### Sexual boundaries during engagement

Engagement can also be a time of learning to control our physical desires. God's plan is that the moment of giving ourselves to each other sexually follows the commitment we have made in our wedding vows. Mike Mason writes of the act of intercourse:

> As a gesture symbolic of perfect trust and surrender, it requires a setting or structure of perfect surrender in which to take place. It requires the security of the most perfect of reassurances and commitments into which two people can enter, which is no other than the loving contract of marriage.[1]

Some maintain that we must discover if we are sexually compatible before marriage. But living together on a trial basis is not a fair test.

In July 1998, *The Family and Child Protection Group* appointed by the Lords and Commons sent a report to the Home Secretary entitled "Family Matters." The group found that "cohabitation does not build a secure relationship in the experience of the vast majority of cohabitees...." The rate of divorce among those who cohabited before marriage is almost double that for those who did not cohabit.

The reason for this is that a sexual relationship makes us vulnerable. Such vulnerability requires trust, and this trust can only exist within the framework of the marriage vows. Within a relationship of total commitment we are truly free to give ourselves unreservedly to each other. It is not sexual experience, physical endowments, or the right chemistry that matter; rather it is committed, self-sacrificing love that produces the best sex.

The refrain in the Song of Songs, repeated three times, recognizes this need to keep physical desire in check until the right moment arrives to give ourselves to each other: "Daughters of Jerusalem, I charge you... Do not arouse or awaken love until it so desires" (Song of Songs 2:7; 3:5; 8:4). Because of the power of sexual desire, we have a responsibility to each other not to "arouse" or "awaken" each other beyond the limits of our self-control. We discovered a lot about the value of sexual boundaries in the four years that we were together before getting married.

**Nicky** After we had known each other for sixteen months we were deeply in love, deeply committed to each other, and it seemed natural to start sleeping together.

**Sila** I was eighteen, I was independent, and I loved Nicky as much as I could imagine ever loving anybody. In retrospect I recognize that our relationship took on an intensity of mood when we started sleeping together and, even though buried at quite a depth, a sense of guilt. I knew my parents' views on sex outside marriage but had always dismissed them as traditionalist Christian principles that had no relevance for me.

My love for Nicky was different. I was deeply committed to the relationship; I was not jumping in and out of bed with different men, and it seemed the most natural way to express my overwhelming love for him. I convinced myself that this reasoning would do because I wanted it to.

Initially in early 1974 when Nicky and I started discussing Christianity, I had no real understanding of the implications for our relationship.

**Nicky** Gradually as I started to consider and explore the Christian faith, my conscience told me that if I were to commit my life to Jesus Christ it would mean not sleeping together again before marriage. That produced a fear that we might then start to drift apart. As a result I kept my thoughts on this subject from Sila for as long as I could.

At the point where I knew I had to make a decision one way or the other, I remember writing down a sort of prayer: "God, I think You are there. I think I believe that Jesus Christ is the Son of God and that He rose from the dead, and therefore I need to make a commitment to You. But I don't have the strength to do so unless You convince Sila as well."

**Sila** When I heard David MacInnes talk about Jesus Christ, he spoke as if he knew Him personally—like I knew Nicky. This was a revelation to me. Gradually I began to see that if I embraced the Christian faith, this would change areas of my life, including our sexual relationship. It was not that anybody had told us. It was a gradual realization that culminated in a clear conviction of the best way for us both. The evening we committed our lives to going God's way we knew that we had to wait until marriage before we made love to each other again.

**Nicky** We discovered over the following weeks that the close intimacy of sleeping in the same bed without making love was too difficult for us, so I slept on the floor. Some months later we realized we would find it easier not even to sleep in the same room. We had come to see that this degree of intimacy is best kept for marriage.

The change was a process for us and we were grateful for the way in which God took us gently from one stage to the next. Far from pushing us apart, He brought a new freedom to our relationship, a closeness that we had not known before, and a greater trust of each other.

In the two-and-a-half years between the time we stopped sleeping together and getting married we learned a lot. The physical side of our relationship wasn't always easy, but we grew to understand why God created sex for a lifelong, committed marriage relationship. We learned the difference between lust and finding ways of showing our love through care and appropriate physical affection.

Now we can see that this was an important lesson to learn, because even within marriage we have the capacity to hurt one another through our sexual relationship. It is possible to seek only to gratify our own desires rather than to love and to give ourselves to each other.

We also learned the need to help each other. It is easy to play a game which involves one of us arousing the other in order to get them to do something to us that arouses us that then causes us to do something to them... and so on. And if we go further than we had intended, "It is not *my* fault because *you* led me on!" We came to recognize that we both needed to take responsibility to help each other.

We have put below some practical tips that we and other couples who have sought to keep sex for marriage have found helpful:

- Recognize what each of you finds particularly arousing, whether through sight, words, or touch. In general, men are quickly excited through sight, while women are stimulated through emotional intimacy. (These differences are also important to recognize *within* marriage when we deliberately seek to arouse each other.)
- Try not to put yourselves in situations where you could go to bed together with no fear of being disturbed or discovered. For example, to stay the night alone in a house or to go on vacation alone will for many couples produce more temptation than they are able to resist. Go with other friends. Chaperones may sound old-fashioned but they are particularly effective!

- We would strongly suggest not sleeping in the same bed, even if you have decided not to make love. That level of intimacy naturally leads to intercourse. Couples who have put themselves in situations which require enormous self-restraint find that this can easily lead to feelings of guilt about sex *within* marriage. One couple who regularly slept in the same bed worked so hard to restrain themselves before marriage that once married they had great difficulty letting go.

- In terms of how far to go physically before marriage, each couple will need to work out their own boundaries. Our own limits included aiming not to lie down together and avoiding being naked or partially naked together. Such disclosure should rightly be kept for the marriage night.

Practicing such restraint is hard, but we will retain the wonderful anticipation of giving ourselves to each other at the most perfect moment. A friend of ours wrote:

> Before I became a Christian, I had been to a lot of weddings. Like Charles in *Four Weddings and a Funeral,* I found that hardly a Saturday passed without one. They were generally heartwarming affairs full of beautiful dresses, kind words, and good wine. However, I shall never forget the first wedding I went to where I knew for certain that the wedding day marked the beginning of the couple's sexual relationship. There was something different in the air: a perceptible lightness, a feeling of awe, a sense of fragility, preciousness, and purity. The look in their eyes as they made their vows is a look I shall describe to my children.

## Our past sexual history

God's intention for us is that both husband and wife are virgins when they marry. We have already spoken of the reasons for celibacy. But if because of past sexual experiences, there is pain, guilt, jealousy, or unforgiveness, these emotions need to be addressed before going into marriage.

A previous sexual relationship, whether secret or not, can tarnish our marriage. Far from providing helpful experience, it can give rise to mistrust, jealousy, and destructive memories. The Christian answer is to bring our sexual past to God and to ask for His forgiveness and cleansing for the mistakes we have made.

We would suggest revealing past sexual relationships to our fiancé(e) and asking for his or her forgiveness. We do not need to go into details as these will be hurtful and may cause further harm. God can then bring healing and the freedom and joy of a new start.

We may be afraid of hurting our fiancé(e) but secrets are dangerous in marriage. When secrets, suddenly come to light later in the relationship, much more hurt and damage can be caused. If you are worried about how to tell each other, a good church leader or counselor would be able to help. Courage may well be required but such confessions will ensure that your future together is firmly based on a foundation of trust, openness, and forgiveness.

It would be wise to ask advice before talking about areas such as abortion, addiction, pornography, prostitution, cross dressing, or homosexual experience. Find someone who understands such issues. This could start a process for dealing with the past that may take months or even years, in which case each other's support will be essential.

Some couples feel guilty about having gone further in their physical relationship with each other than they intended before marriage. Their sexual desires have got out of control and one of them has led the other on to arousal against their true wishes. These regrets can be brought to God and to one another for forgiveness and restoration. As we come openly and honestly to God, His promise to us is that, "If anyone is in Christ, there is a new creation: the old has gone the new has come!" (2 Corinthians 5:17) Wonderfully, we can then enter marriage knowing a freedom from our past.

## THE HONEYMOON

*Be prepared*

We suggest that a month or so before your wedding both of you read a good book on sex from a Christian perspective (see the recommended reading at the back) so as to be well-informed. Once married, try going through such a book together. This will make it easier to start discussing your sex life openly (with each other!). It will also stand you in good stead should you encounter problems later on. Every lifelong relationship will have some periods when things don't go so well. Many men will experience a degree of impotence at some stage, most often through stress, and many women have a lower sexual desire when children arrive.

If there are any anxieties or unanswered questions a doctor should be able to help. Or talk to a married friend you know and trust.

*Be realistic*

Recognize your need to recover from the heavy demands of your wedding day. Try to organize a honeymoon that will be the most relaxing you could imagine. It is probably not the moment to go overland to Antarctica, up the Amazon in a canoe, or to climb the Himalayas. The purpose of a honeymoon is to spend time relaxing, adjusting to, and enjoying each other. Too much hard traveling or sightseeing defeats the purpose. This is not the moment to plan your vacation of a lifetime. Save that for a year or so into marriage; it will probably be a lot more fun then.

*Don't expect too much too soon*

The honeymoon is only the beginning of a lifelong discovery. Take a long view. With regard to sex, don't expect all your Christmases to come at once. This is a time for gentleness, tenderness, and patience.

Keeping a sense of humor will help you to stay relaxed. Don't panic if things don't work out as they do in the films—instant, spontaneous, multi-orgasmic sex. It may well take some time for you to experience mutual or simultaneous orgasm.

Don't be afraid to talk about what gives pleasure and what doesn't, both during and after times of making love. This will deepen your understanding of how to arouse each other. At first this may seem awkward and unnatural but communication is essential if our physical relationship is to develop. Any embarrassment will soon disappear.

*Talk about your expectations*

It is easy to have unrealistic and uncommunicated expectations of each other. You should not feel under pressure to make love the second you cross the threshold of the bedroom. But feel free to. Make sure that you have discussed this moment so that you do not start your marriage with uncertainty and misunderstanding. Suddenly to have crossed the boundary from not okay to okay may seem strange and you may react differently.

One husband told us that his wife of nine hours was so exhausted by the wedding that she fell asleep as soon as she got into bed, while he was still in the bathroom. He stayed awake all night deeply disappointed and thinking he had made a terrible mistake getting married at all. Things improved considerably when they talked about their different expectations the next day and they went on to have a wonderful honeymoon.

*Maintain a sense of humor*

Honeymoons can be unpredictable. One couple told us that they got so badly sunburned on the first day of theirs that they could not touch each other all week. Thankfully they saw the funny side of it. Another newlywed husband described how things did not go to plan on the first night:

> When we finally got to the hotel it was eleven o'clock at night. It looked smaller than it had appeared in the brochure and I felt my heart sink. Just about the only contribution I'd made to the wedding arrangements was to choose the hotel. The day had gone well and my wife was looking radiant. I so wanted the evening to be memorable. We found our room and it was lovely, and Jane smiled when she saw the chilled bottle of wine and roses on the bed. I began to relax; everything was going to be great.
>
> And it could have been. But to my horror I noticed that there wasn't a double bed but two singles. I quickly found the manager. "This is our honeymoon, and this is meant to be your honeymoon suite," I said.
>
> The manager was very apologetic but explained that due to an oversight another couple were in the honeymoon room and were well settled.
>
> "But there are single beds in here," I pleaded. At that point I should have argued and demanded my rights. But when the man-

ager suggested a solution I went along with it as he said it had worked before.

"I'll send you up some rope," he said, "and you can tie the beds together."

"Send it up fast!" I exclaimed.

And so on the night I'd waited twenty-eight years for, the night I'd long dreamed of, I was giving it my best effort when the beds parted. Jane and I both crashed to the floor. I looked up at the ceiling and wanted to die, but just then Jane leaned over and whispered into my ear, "Darling ... I think I felt the earth move."[2]

# Appendix C

## Working Out a Budget

According to a survey by the Marriage Guidance Service, *Relate*, most arguments about money come down to spending priorities. If money causes problems in your marriage, it will be beneficial to make an agreed plan of how, as a couple or family, you are going to use it. A budget is of course no magic formula but the very process of working it out together has a number of benefits. The first is that our true financial position becomes clear to both of us. Second, we have to discuss how we are going to spend our money. Third, when we have allocated an amount for each area of our expenditure, we are both free to choose what we buy within a set limit.

Like any other area of conflict, money can either be an issue that comes between us and affects our whole relationship or a problem that we work at together, drawing us closer to each other in the process.

Working out a budget can remove the fear of feeling out of control, the guilt attached to reckless spending, and the conflict arising from mutual blame where there is a shortfall. We know of marriages that have been transformed from acrimony to harmony through discussion and decisions about finances.

If money is a source of tension we recommend the following three steps. (They sound very obvious and straightforward but it is amazing how few of us ever sit down and work these things out together.)

## Discover your true financial position

*Work out how much you own or owe*

Find a time when you are not tired or distracted and are unlikely to be disturbed. Then collect bank statements, unpaid bills, savings accounts, credit card statements, and so on. Being honest with each other if we have overspent and are in debt can be hard but it will be well worth it. Anxiety about money can easily become a dark secret. When fears are out in the open they lose much of their power over us.

Be gentle with each other—none of us gets it entirely right. If we find we are in debt, part of our discussion will need to be about how we can get out of it. Do not be afraid or embarrassed about seeking help from people with experience. The sooner the problem is faced, the more easily it can be solved.

*Calculate your income*

In order to plan our spending we need to know how much money is coming in and where it is going out. The simpler part is working out our joint income. We need to write down all sources and amounts of income after deduction of income tax and Social Security. This can then be worked out as an average amount for each month. Enter these figures onto a "Monthly Budget Planner" such as the one at the end of this appendix.

*Work out what you spend*

Many couples find themselves stretched financially but are not aware of where their money goes. As a result they can blame the wrong items for pushing them into debt. In order to form an accurate picture of our expenditure, it may be necessary to write down over the course of a month or two everything we spend our money on. This information, together with our bank statements and any credit card statements, should enable us to work out our expenditure for an average month. (With expenses that are not incurred monthly, such as car expenses, household insurance or vacations, work out an annual figure and divide by twelve.)

Record this information in your budget planner, creating as many other categories as necessary. Start with those areas of expenditure that are fixed such as a mortgage or rent, gas and electricity, insurance, and travel costs. Then put down those areas where there is room for more flexibility, such as food and housekeeping, clothes, presents, hospitality, and sports.

Next, we need to subtract what we spend from what we earn. (If the result does not tally with our bank records, either the bank has made a mistake or we have left something out!) We may find of course that we are left with a minus figure. We are spending more than our income and we need to take urgent action.

### Discuss the future

The second step is to plan the use of our money, allocating specific amounts to different areas. The aim is to set a budget that is within our income and that reflects our agreed priorities, putting aside enough for the unexpected.

Sacrifices may have to be made by both husband and wife but most couples find it easier to discuss the future than to explain the past. If you cannot agree, break off discussions to allow both of you time to consider (and pray about) the other's point of view. Find another opportunity to talk again when you are at your most reasonable.

The great advantage of reaching agreement is that we can then spend money up to the agreed limit without feeling guilty or having to hide it from each other.

### Decide how to keep control

*Appoint a financial director*

Setting a budget is one thing; sticking to it is quite another. It is helpful to decide which of us is best equipped to keep track of the finances, to pay the bills, and to initiate a regular review.

*Watch the credit card*

For many people the greatest difficulty in keeping their spending under control is the credit card. There are two dangers. One is that we do not feel as if we are spending real money. The other is that there is no automatic means of keeping track of how much we have left in our budget. Some couples have therefore cut up their cards and reverted to cash. Though less convenient, it has enabled them to control what they spend and has prevented a great deal of conflict in their marriage.

*Ten suggestions for guilt-free spending.*

Here is one easy system. It took us about ten years to work this out.

1. Take a sheet of paper. Keep a record of the total amount of money you have allocated for essentials (food, drug store, etc.) this month.
2. Every time you spend money on essentials, make a note of it, deducting it from your total. Both of you have to confess.
3. If you take money out of an ATM, you will probably spend it on essentials. Deduct that also. It is easy to forget ATM withdrawals, especially if you want to.
4. At the end of one week, see how you are doing. Are you going to have to cut back next week or can you relax a bit? Be honest with yourself. Put the steak back if necessary.
5. Start a new page at the beginning of each week with your new total. Keep deducting anything you spend on essentials.
6. In the last week of the month it is not uncommon either to lie, give up, or eat a lot of baked beans. They are very good for you apparently.
7. Other expenses such as new clothes and going out can be categorized (sadly) as nonessentials.
8. Note: We don't have to buy nonessentials. We will live (albeit painfully) without the take-out Chinese food or the football game or the new boots. At times we will need to say

no, preferably to ourselves, rather than to each other.

9. Keep the same system for "nonessentials" as for "essentials." The desire to lie, forget, or omit may become more pressing.
10. When the cash is available, shopping, candlelit dinners, a weekend at a health farm, or an away game can all be enjoyed to the full.

We have to admit that the system is only as good as its operators. There have been some periods in our marriage when money has been tight and we have had to administer it rigorously. At other times there has been more, and we have been more lax in keeping a record of what we spend. Sooner or later, however, we have had to review our finances and revert to our system to get us back on track.

Occasionally when a couple cannot make ends meet the problem is that they do not have enough income to support themselves. Most often the problem lies with their expenditures. Rob Parsons writes about his own upbringing:

> My father was a postman and my mother a cleaner. We lived in a rented house, and life was simple to say the least. Nonessentials like heating in the bedrooms, fitted carpets, and toilet paper (don't ask!) belonged to another world. I didn't eat in a restaurant until I was sixteen. But I had everything I needed in that home, including wise advice from a father who would take me aside regularly and recite to me the words of Mr Micawber from Dickens' David Copperfield: "Annual income: twenty shillings; expenditure: nineteen shillings and sixpence—result: happiness. Annual income: twenty shillings; expenditure: twenty shillings and sixpence—result: misery." A belief in that principle meant that my father was never in debt. You may think that he paid an unacceptable price for that. He never had a vacation away from his own home, or had his own bank account, and he never did get to taste pasta—but I have never known a man so content.[1]

## Monthly Budget Planner

| | | Actual | Budget |
|---|---|---|---|
| **Average Monthly income after taxes (work out annual figure)** | | | |
| Joint salaries | | | $_________ |
| Other sources of income | | | $_________ |
| Total (1) | $_________ ÷ 12 = | | $_________ |
| **Fixed regular expenses (work out annual figure)** | | Actual | Budget |
| Rent/mortgage | | $_________ | $_________ |
| Property tax | | $_________ | $_________ |
| Utilities (gas, electricity, water) | | $_________ | $_________ |
| Health insurance | | $_________ | $_________ |
| Loan repayment | | $_________ | $_________ |
| Transportation | | $_________ | $_________ |
| Auto insurance | | $_________ | $_________ |
| Charitable giving | | $_________ | $_________ |
| Other | | $_________ | $_________ |
| Total (2) | $_________ ÷ 12 = | $_________ (monthly) | $_________ (monthly) |
| **Flexible "essential" expenses (estimate annual figure)** | | | |
| Household (food, pharmacy, etc.) | | $_________ | $_________ |
| Clothes/shoes | | $_________ | $_________ |
| Car repairs, gasoline | | $_________ | $_________ |
| Telephone | | $_________ | $_________ |
| Other | | $_________ | $_________ |
| Total (3) | $_________ ÷ 12 = | $_________ (monthly) | $_________ (monthly) |
| **Flexible "nonessential" expenses (estimate annual figure)** | | | |
| Entertainment/hospitality | | $_________ | $_________ |
| Gifts | | $_________ | $_________ |
| Sports/leisure | | $_________ | $_________ |
| Vacations | | $_________ | $_________ |
| Cable TV, subscriptions | | $_________ | $_________ |
| Other | | $_________ | $_________ |
| Total (4) | $_________ ÷ 12 = | $_________ (monthly) | $_________ (monthly) |
| **Monthly sum for savings/emergencies** | | | |
| Total (5) | | $_________ | $_________ |
| **Add together total monthly expenses** (2, 3, 4, 5) | | $_________ | $_________ |
| **Compare to total monthly income** (1) | | $_________ | $_________ |

# Appendix D

## Praying Together

For some who are reading this book, the thought of praying is a most bizarre and alien concept. Some think that prayer is a sign of weakness or shows intellectual immaturity. They have been taught that growing up is all about learning to cope on our own. As a result, people dare not admit to themselves, let alone to their partner, that they are struggling in any area of their lives.

Others find the idea of praying aloud highly embarrassing. A woman on *The Marriage Course* told us that she would rather run down the road naked than pray with her husband. It might well make us feel exposed and vulnerable since prayer is a highly personal and even intimate activity, but it does not need to be quite as difficult as that.

Praying together means that we are drawing upon a source of wisdom, love, and power outside ourselves. It engenders a sense of hope rather than despair. This is what some couples we know have said about the effect of joint prayer on their own marriage:

- "Prayer mainly takes the worry out of our lives. Give it to God, and we both relax a bit."
- "We try and pray briefly before we go to sleep at night. It's like a glue for us."
- "We try to pray on Sunday evening. It means we worry much less as the things we would otherwise have been anxious about have been put into God's 'in-tray.'"

- "Life seems a lot more bumpy when we don't pray together, because as we come before God it brings a unity to us."

## How to get started

For ourselves, praying together has played an important part in our marriage, particularly once we had overcome some initial unrealistic expectations. These were matched only by the expectations we had regarding our capacity for eating.

**Nicky** When we first got married, Sila would regularly cook a gourmet dinner, with enough food to feed at least six people. Several evenings a week she would do a new recipe until, after three months of bloated stomachs and an exhausted wife, she could keep it up no longer, and we switched overnight to a diet of toast and cheese or Chinese take-out.

Our praying together started much the same way. There always seemed so much to pray about and, if we managed to pray at the end of the day, it seemed to go on far longer than we could handle. It was usually late and we were often too tired. After a while neither of us would suggest praying as we could not face the prospect of another long session.

Then somebody recommended we tried praying together for five to ten minutes at the beginning of the day and that made all the difference for us. We timed it so that we would only have ten minutes before one of us had to leave for work. This removed any danger of it going on for too long.

For the last twenty-four years, our aim has been to start the day by praying together for a short time, and we have adjusted the timing according to the ages of our children and the schedule and demands of our jobs. We do not by any means manage it every day but having that as our goal helps us to achieve it more often than not, and the benefits make us want to do it again.

## How to pray with and for each other

Praying together on a regular basis need not be strange. We need to start by praying as we can, not as we can't. For some that might mean using a book with written prayers that they pray aloud. For others reading a few verses from the Bible and praying silently for each other might be the place to begin. The books *30 Days*[1] or *Daily Light*[2] with some verses from the Bible for each day of the year, has proved helpful for many.

Others will be familiar and comfortable with saying their own prayers out loud. Our advice would be to start where you feel comfortable and to aim for simplicity and honesty.

A few months ago we met a couple who were about to celebrate their fortieth wedding anniversary. We asked them what they had found most important in building such a strong marriage. They said a number of kind things about each other and described how they had grown together.

But it was what they said next that was most revealing. They both agreed that the thing that had made the most difference to the strength and harmony of their marriage was praying together every morning.

Thinking that they had done this every day for the last forty years, we asked them when they had begun. They replied, "About eighteen months ago." And they added that, if someone had suggested even a few years previously that this would become important to them, they would have thought it very strange.

It is never too late to start. Equally it is never too soon. Below we have set out some suggestions that have helped us enormously in making joint prayer achievable.

*Start with thankfulness to God*

Thankfulness reorients our thinking. If we feel under pressure or overwhelmed, choosing to be thankful can dramatically change our perspective. The Apostle Paul wrote several of his letters under the strain of imprisonment, yet they overflow with thankfulness and gratitude to God. "Be joyful always; pray continually; give thanks in all circumstances, for this is God's will for you in Christ Jesus" (1 Thessalonians 5:16-18). This attitude goes against the current trend of dissatisfaction and striving for more and bigger and better. Thankfulness to God, including being thankful for each other, will change our perspective.

*Pray for each other*

The main aim of this time is to discover each other's needs or anxieties about the day ahead and to bring them before God. Sometimes it will be about one of our children; sometimes it will be because we are short of money; at other times it is because we feel inadequate in the face of the day's challenges. If one of us is struggling to relate to a particular person, we have asked the other to pray that God would change our heart and fill us with His love for them.

Our pride and stubbornness can easily get in the way of our coming to God and asking for His help. But God wants us to pray about everything, especially those things for which we have no human answer.

*Don't worry about needing the same prayer daily*

Jesus tells us, "Ask and it will be given to you; seek and you will find; knock and the door will be opened to you"(Luke 11:9). The tense in the original text means we are to go on asking, seeking, knocking, and not to give up after one attempt.

**Sila** When our children were small, I found myself asking Nicky to pray the same thing for me day after day. I endlessly needed more patience and more physical energy and Nicky's prayers made an amazing difference in my relationship with our children. The fact that we need to keep on asking for the same thing does not mean that God is not answering our prayers—rather it is a recognition of our dependence upon Him.

*Ensure that prayers are vertical, not horizontal and manipulative*

Praying is not a way to get at each other. I (Sila) should not pray, "Please, Lord, help Nicky to stop working so hard and spend more time with the children," unless of course he has asked me to pray specifically for that. Nor should we use prayer as an opportunity to communicate things to our husband or wife when they are less likely to interrupt.

*Don't give up*

This will be particularly relevant for those who have young children. This stage of parenting can seem to go on forever, and we remember thinking that we were never going to manage to pray together again for even five minutes. We seemed to spend a lot of physical and emotional energy taking a child back to their bedroom with a toy or a tape and saying, "We are praying. It is not time to get up yet." Then we would rush back to our room to get in another minute's prayer before the door would open and we would repeat the whole procedure.

Was it worthwhile? Looking back, even when we only managed one prayer for each other two or three times a week those few minutes definitely helped us, as well as allowing our children to see the importance we attached to it. Children do grow up and praying together becomes easier again.

*Look to the promises of God*

Becoming familiar with many of the promises of God in the Bible is a great resource for us. We grow in wisdom through reading the Bible individually and together. As we learn to apply its advice to our everyday life, it shapes and changes our attitudes and behavior.

Just as there is power in prayer, there is power in reading the Bible together. We have often found that the few verses we have read from a psalm or the Gospels before we start praying seem to apply to us very personally for that particular day.

## Conclusion

Many people think that God is out to trap them or to accuse them or to restrict their lives. Nothing could be farther from the character of God revealed to us in Jesus Christ. God longs to give to us, to help us, to set us free from the past, and to enable us to look outward to others in love. He does not force Himself upon us but waits for us to respond to His overtures of love.

The biblical instruction, "Submit to one another out of reverence for Christ," is set in the context of seeking *God's* will for our lives: "...find out what pleases the Lord," and, "...do not be foolish, but understand what the Lord's will is" (Ephesians 5:21, 10, 17). When both husband and wife determine to seek God's will for the major decisions in their lives, they will discover a freedom from worry that will profoundly affect their marriage.

The Apostle Paul wrote, out of his own experience, "Do not be anxious about anything, but in everything, by prayer and petition, with thanksgiving, present your requests to God. And the peace of God, which transcends all understanding, will guard your hearts and your minds in Christ Jesus" (Philippians 4:6-7).

Praying could be the most important thing we do together.

# Notes

### Introduction

1. For an answer to the question, "Why did Jesus die?" we recommend reading *Questions of Life* by Nicky Gumbel (Kingsway, 1993), particularly chapter 3.
2. From the Anglican Marriage Service, *The Alternative Service Book*, 1980.

### Chapter 1 – Taking a Long View

1. Mike Mason, *The Mystery of Marriage* (Triangle, 1997), p. 160.
2. John Bayley, *Iris, A Memoir of Iris Murdoch* (Duckworth, 1998), p. 57.
3. Extract from Sonnet No. 116 from Stanley Wells (Ed.) *Shakespeare's Sonnets and a Lover's Complaint* (Oxford University Press, 1987), p. 130.
4. Frank Muir, *A Kentish Lad* (Corgi, 1997), pp. 404-405.
5. *The Guardian*, 24 October 1998, p. 3.
6. Quoted on audio tape by Sam Thompson "Communion in Marriage" Part 2, tape 2 Anaheim: VMI 1984.
7. Quoted in Selwyn Hughes, *Marriage as God Intended* (Kingsway Publications, 1983), p. 13.
8. *The Daily Mail Weekend*, 9 January 1999 [Interview with Lynda Lee-Potter].
9. *The Times*, 15 February 2000 [Interview with Celia Brayfield].

**Chapter 2 – Planning to Succeed**

1. Virgil: 29BC *Georgics* Book III.
2. John Fitzgerald Kennedy, *The Observer,* 10 December 1961.
3. Rob Parsons, *Loving against the Odds* (Hodder & Stoughton, 1994), p. 39.
4. Raymond Snoddy & Carol Midgley, *The Times*, 22 April 1998, p. 5.
5. Ibid.
6. *Vanity Fair,* October 1999, p. 135.
7. *The Daily Mail,* 20 April 1998.
8. Gary Chapman, *The Five Love Languages* (Northfield Publishing, 1995), pp. 29, 36.
9. Alan Storkey, *Marriage and its Modern Crisis* (Hodder & Stoughton, 1996), p. 25.
10. Dr. Henry Cloud and Dr. John Townsend, *Boundaries* (Zondervan Publishing House, 1992), p. 160.
11. Rob Parsons, *Loving Against the Odds* (Hodder & Stoughton, 1994), p. 39.

**Chapter 3 – How to Talk More Effectively**

1. Libby Purves, *Nature's Masterpiece*, *A Family Survival Book* (Hodder & Stoughton, 2000), p. 221–2.
2. *Speaking for Themselves,* The personal letters of Winston and Clementine Churchhill, Edited by Mary Soames (Black Swan, 1999).
3. *The Mail on Sunday.*
4. Cherry Norton, *The Independent on Sunday*, 3 October 1999, pp. 6–7.
5. Libby Purves, *Nature's Masterpiece*, *A Family Survival Book* (Hodder & Stoughton, 2000), p. 221.
6. Sonia Leach, *Good Housekeeping,* August 1994—"Do Men Understand Intimacy?"
7. *The Message*, a translation of the Bible in contemporary idiom by Eugene H. Peterson (Navpress, 1993).
8. Frank Muir, *A Kentish Lad* (Corgi, 1997), pp. 404–405.

**Chapter 4 – How to Listen More Effectively**

1. Mary Catterwood, 1847–1901, U.S. writer, *Mackinac and Late Stories* (Marianson).
2. Gerard Hughes.
3. These five categories of poor listeners have been developed by the Acorn Christian Healing Trust.
4. Gary Chapman, *The Five Love Languages* (Northfield Publishing, 1995), pp. 61–63.
5. Stephen Covey, *The Seven Habits of Highly Effective People* (Simon & Schuster), p. 239.
6. Bilquis Sheikh, *I Dared to Call Him Father* (Kingsway Publications, 1978), pp. 40–41.
7. Stephen R. Covey, *The Seven Habits of Highly Effective People* (Simon & Schuster, 1999), p. 237.
8. Dale Carnegie, *How to Win Friends and Influence People* (Simon & Schuster, 1964).
9. Diane Vaughan, *Uncoupling: Turning Points in Intimate Relationships* (Oxford University Press, 1984).

**Chapter 5 – The Five Expressions of Love**

1. Louis de Bernière, *Captain Correlli's Mandolin* (Vintage, 1994), p. 281.
2. Gary Chapman, *The Five Love Languages* (Northfield Publishing, 1995).
3. Richard Bausch, *The Eyes of Love* (Macmillan, 1995), pp. 258–9, 261–262, 264.

**Chapter 6 – Words and Actions**

1. Ella Wheeler Wilcox, "An Unfaithful Wife to Her Husband," in Charles Mylander, *Running the Red Lights* (Ventura, Calif.: Regal Books, 1986), pp. 30–32.
2. Louis de Bernière, *Captain Correlli's Mandolin* (Vintage, 1994), pp. 43–44.

**Chapter 7 - Time, Presents, and Touch**

1. Jean Anouilh (1910–1987) from *Adele* (1949).
2. Alan Storkey, *The Meanings of Love* (IVP, 1994), p. 117.
3. Gary Chapman, *The Five Love Languages* (Northfield Publishing, 1995), p. 107.

**Chapter 8 –Appreciating Our Differences**

1. Frank Muir: A *Kentish Lad*, (Corgi Books, 1997).
2. Richard Hooker (1554–1660), English theologian.
3. Paul Tournier, *Marriage Difficulties* (SCM Press, 1971), p. 26.
4. Susan Quillam and Relate, *Stop Arguing Start Talking* by Relate (Vermilion, 1998).
5. Bill and Lynne Hybels, *Love that Lasts* (Marshall Pickering, 1995), p. 12-14.
6. *Ibid.*, pp. 15–16.
7. Judith S. Wallerstein and Sandra Blakeslee, *The Good Marriage* (Houghton Mifflin Company, 1995).
8. *Ibid.*
9. Richard Selzer, *Mortal Lessons: Notes in the Art of Surgery.*
10. *Red* magazine, March 2000.

**Chapter 9 – Focusing on the Issue**

1. Quoted in Philip Yancey, *What's So Amazing About Grace?* (Zondervan Publishing House, 1997), pp. 97–98.
2. Philip Delves Broughton, *The Times*, 12 February 1998, p. 9.
3. *Marriage in Mind* (The Church Pastoral Aid Society, 1993), p. 34.
4. Libby Purves, *Nature's Masterpiece, A Family Survival Book* (Hodder & Stoughton, 2000), p. 227.
5. Colossians 4:6; Philippians 4:5 from *The Message*, a translation of the New Testament in contemporary idiom by Eugene H. Peterson (Navpress, 1993).
6. Rob Parsons, *Loving Against the Odds* (Hodder & Stoughton, 1994), pp. 65–66.

**Chapter 10 – Centering Our Lives**

1. Gabriel García Márquez, *Love in the Time of Cholera* (Penguin Books, 1989), p. 209.
2. *Children's Letters to God*, compiled by Stuart Hemple and Eric Marshall (Collins, 1966).
3. The Alpha course offers the opportunity to hear and discuss the relevance and truth of the Christian message. It is currently being run in over seven thousand churches in the U.K. and in many other churches worldwide. We know personally many couples whose marriages have been transformed as a result of doing this course.
4. For those who would like to know more about prayer, a good basic introduction may be found in chapter 6 of *Questions of Life* by Nicky Gumbel (Cook Communications, 1999).

**Chapter 11 – How Can Intimacy Be Lost?**

1. John Taylor, *Falling* (Victor Gollancz, 1999), pp. 3–4.
2. For this section, we are particularly grateful to David and Teresa Ferguson for the inspiration and insights gained through their book, *Intimate Encounters* (Nelson, 1997) and family life courses.
3. C. S. Lewis, *The Four Loves* (Fount, Harper Collins Religious, 1998), p. 116.
4. Valerie Windsor, "Telling Stories," *Fresh Talent* (W. H. Smith), pp. 39–40.

**Chapter 12 – How Can Intimacy Be Restored?**

1. Martin Luther King Jr., cited in Philip Yancey, *What's So Amazing About Grace?* (Zondervan Publishing House, 1997).
2. *Readings for Meditation and Reflection*, ed. by Walter Hooper (New York: Harper Collins, 1996), p. 63.
3. Philip Yancey, *What's so Amazing About Grace?* (Zondervan Publishing House, 1997), p. 97.
4. Corrie ten Boom, *He Sets the Captive Free* (Kingsway Publications, 1977), p. 38.

**Chapter 13 – How to Get Along with Parents and In-laws**

1. Amanda Vail, *Love Me Little*.
2. Mary Pytches, *Yesterday's Child* (Hodder & Stoughton, 1990), pp. 147–48.
3. Ann McFerran, *Motherland—Interviews with Mothers and Daughters* (Virago Press, 1998), p. 22.
4. Victoria Glendinning, *Sons and Mothers* (Virago Press, 1997), p. 248.
5. Libby Purves, *Nature's Masterpiece* (Hodder & Stoughton, 2000), p. 260
6. *Ibid*. pp. 337–38.
7. Ann McFerran, *Motherland – Interviews with Mothers and Daughters* (Virago Press, 1998), pp. 119–20.
8. *Ibid*., pp. 15–17.

**Chapter 14 – How to Leave Behind Parental Control**

1. Robin Skinner and John Cleese, *Families and How to Survive Them* (Mandarin, 1990), p. 298.
2. Victoria Glendinning, *Sons and Mothers* (Virago Press, 1997), p. 256.
3. Ann McFerran, *Motherland—Interviews with Mothers and Daughters* (Virago Press, 1998), p. 168
4. Dr. David Mace, *Getting Ready for Marriage*.
5. Libby Purves, *Nature's Masterpiece* (Hodder and Stoughton, 2000), p. 262.
6. Ann McFerran, *Motherland—Interviews with Mothers and Daughters* (Virago Press, 1998), pp. 28–29.

**Chapter 15 – How to Address the Effects of Childhood Pain**

1. Alan Storkey, *The Meanings of Love* (IVP, 1994).
2. Victor Frankel, *Man's Search for Meaning* (Hodder and Stoughton, 1992).
3. Victoria Glendinning, *Sons and Mothers* (Virago Press, 1997), p. 255.

**Chapter 16 – Sex—What Is It All About?**

1. John White, *Eros Defiled* (IVP, 1997), p. 20.
2. Mike Mason, *The Mystery of Marriage* (Triangle, 1997), p. 100.
3. Libby Purves, *Holy Smoke* (Hodder and Stoughton, 1998), p. 85.
4. Michael and Myrtle Baughen, *Your Marriage* (Hodder and Stoughton, 1994), p. 62.
5. John White, *Eros Defiled* (IVP, 1977), p. 86.
6. *The Sunday Times*, 2 November 1997, News, p. 14.
7. *The Guardian*, 17 October 1998, p. 3.
8. John White, *Eros Defiled* (IVP, 1977), p. 15.

**Chapter 17 – Six Important Qualities for Great Lovers**

1. Alan Storkey, *The Meanings of Love* (IVP, 1994), p. 98.
2. Michael Castleman, *Sexual Solutions* (Simon & Schuster, 1983), p. 162.

**Chapter 18 – Protecting Our Marriage**

1. John White, *Eros Defiled* (IVP, 1977), pp. 75–76.
2. Kathryn Knight, *The Times*, 17 March 1996.
3. John White, *Eros Defiled* (IVP, 1977), p. 81.
4. *Good Housekeeping*, March 2000, p. 64.
5. Alan Storkey, *The Meanings of Love* (IVP, 1994), p. 83.
6. Gary Chapman, *Hope for the Separated* (Moody Press, 1982), p. 78.
7. *Good Housekeeping*, March 2000, p. 64.

**Chapter 19 – Keeping Sex Alive**

1. Alan Storkey, *The Meanings of Love* (IVP, 1994), p. 164
2. Bill Hybels, *Tender Love* (Moody Press, 1993,), p. 106.
3. Libby Purves, *Nature's Masterpiece* (Hodder and Stoughton, 2000), p. 225.

**Chapter 20 – The Opportunity of a Lifetime**

1. Ian and Ruth Coffey, *Friends, Helpers, Lovers* (IVP, 1996), p. 177.
2. Tom Marshall, *Right Relationships* (Sovereign World, 1992), p. 24.
3. Mike Mason, *The Mystery of Marriage* (Triangle, 1997), p. 20.
4. Commencement address by Barbara Bush to the 1990 graduating class at Wellesley College (Wellesley College Library, Wellesley, Mass.), pp. 4–5.
5. Dietrich Bonhoeffer, *Letters and Papers from Prison* (S.C.M. Press, 1971), p. 42f.
6. Clio Turner, *Closer to God April–May–June 1999* (Scripture Union, 1999), p. 127.

**Appendix A – Ready for Marriage?**

1. These tests have been adapted from *I Married You* by Walter Trobisch (IVP, 1971), pp. 89–92.
2. John Gray, *Men are from Mars, Women are from Venus* (Thorsons, an Imprint of Harper Collins Publishers, 1993), p. 151.
3. Ed Wheat, *Love Life for Every Married Couple* (Marshall Pickering, 1980), p. 109.

**Appendix B – Engagement, Sex, and the Honeymoon**

1. Mike Mason, *The Mystery of Marriage* (Triangle, 1997), p. 100.
2. Paul Francis, *Teenagers: The Parents' One Hour Survival Guide* (Marshall Pickering, 1998), pp. 88–89.

**Appendix C – Working Out a Budget**

1. Rob Parsons, *Loving against the Odds* (Hodder and Stoughton, 1994), p. 190.

**Appendix D – Praying Together**

1. Nicky Gumbel, *30 Days* – A thirty day practical introduction to reading the Bible (HTB Publications, 1999).
2. *Daily Light—the Classic Scripture Selection* (Hodder and Stoughton, 1982).

# Recommended Reading


**MARRIAGE IN GENERAL**

Mike Mason, *The Mystery of Marriage* (Triangle, 1997)

Rob Parsons, *The Sixty Minute Marriage* (Hodder and Stoughton, 1997)

Gary Chapman, *The Five Love Languages* (Northfield Publishing, 1995)

Ed and Gay Wheat, *Love Life for Every Married Couple* (Marshall Pickering, 1984)

Bill and Lynne Hybels, *Love That Lasts* (Marshall Pickering, 1999)

Rob Parsons, *Loving against the Odds* (Hodder & Stoughton, 1994)

Judith Wallerstein, Sandra Blakeslee, *The Good Marriage: How and Why Love Lasts* (Houghton Mifflin Company, 1995)

**BUILDING THE SEXUAL RELATIONSHIP**

Ed and Gay Wheat, *Intended for Pleasure* (Scripture Union, 2000)

Richard and Lorraine Meier, Frank Minirth, and Paul Meier, *Sex in the Christian Marriage* (Fleming H. Revell Company/Baker Book House, 1997)

**HEALING THE EFFECTS OF CHILDHOOD PAIN**

Gary Chapman, *The Other Side of Love—Handling Anger in Godly Way* (Moody Press, 1999)

Mary Pytches, *Yesterday's Child* (Hodder and Stoughton, London, 1990)

Dr. David Ferguson and Dr. Don McMinn, *Top 10 Intimacy Needs* (Intimacy Press, 1994)

## FACING FINANCIAL ISSUES

Keith Tondeur and Larry Burkett, *Debt-Free Living* (Monarch Publications, 1997)

Keith Tondeur, *Financial Tips for the Family* (Hodder and Stoughton, 1997)

Ron and Judy Blue, *Money Talks and So Can We* (Zondervan Publishing House, 1999)

## FACING EATING DISORDERS

Helen Wilkinson, *Beyond Chaotic Eating* (Zondervan Publishing House, 1993)

Jo Ind, *Fat Is a Spiritual Issue* (Mowbray, 1993)

## REBUILDING A MARRIAGE

Gary Chapman, *Hope for the Separated* (Moody Press, 1996)

James Dobson, *Love Must Be Tough* (Kingsway, 1984)

## OTHER HELPFUL RESOURCES

Focus on the Family
Colorado Springs, CO 80995
www.family.org
(U.S.)1-800-A-FAMILY (Canada) 1-800-661-9800
Radio broadcast (Dr. James Dobson, Focus on the Family), resources, web site, referrals to local counselors

Smalley Relationship Center
1482 Lakeshore Drive, Branson, MO 65616
www.garysmalley.com
1-417-335-4321
To order resources: 1-800-84-TODAY
Conferences, resources, clinical services, on-line help

American Association of Christian Counselors
www.aacc.net
This organization will help you find counselors in your area who belong to the Coalition for Christians in Private Practice.

*The Marriage Course*, based on *The Marriage Book*, is designed to build healthy marriages that last a lifetime. If you are interested in information about *The Marriage Course* please contact one of the following:

**Alpha U.S.A.**
74 Trinity Place
New York, NY 10006
Tel: 888.949.2574
Fax: 212.406.7521
e-mail: info@alphausa.org
www.alphausa.org

**Alpha Canada**
Suite #230 – 11331 Coppersmith Way
Riverside Business Park
Richmond, BC V7A 5J9
Tel: 800.743.0899
Fax: 604.271.6124
e-mail: office@alphacanada.org
www.alphacanada.org

To purchase resources in Canada:

**Cook Communications Ministries**
P.O. Box 98, 55 Woodslee Avenue
Paris, ONT N3L 3E5
Tel: 800.263.2664
Fax: 800.461.8575
e-mail: custserv@cook.ca
www.cook.ca

Visit our website: www.themarriagecourse.org

**Resources currently available:**
- *The Marriage Course* DVD, eight talks
- *The Marriage Course Manual*
- *The Marriage Course Leaders' Guide*

If you are interested in finding out more about the Christian faith and would like to be put in touch with your nearest Alpha course, please contact one of the above offices.